THE
ROMAN LEGIONS

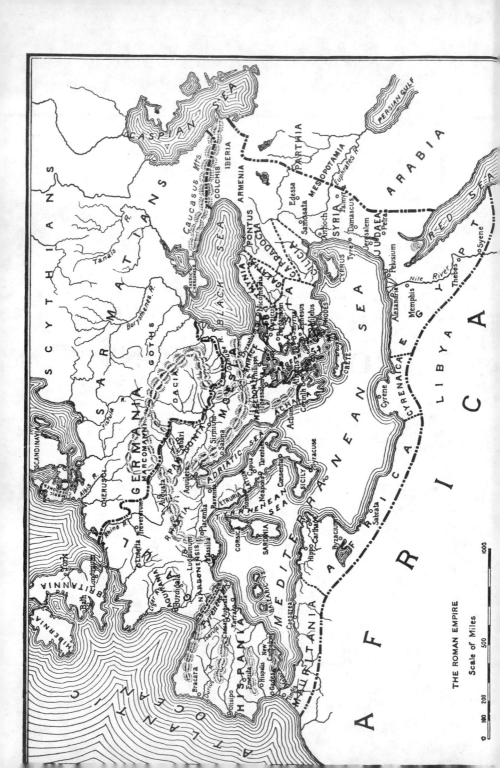

THE ROMAN EMPIRE

Scale of Miles

0   100   200   500   1000

THE
ROMAN LEGIONS

by

H.M.D. PARKER
Sometime Fellow and Tutor
of Magdalen College, Oxford

ARES PUBLISHERS INC.
CHICAGO   MCMLXXX

Exact Reprint of the Edition:
Oxford 1928
(with the Corrigenda of 1958)

ARES PUBLISHERS INC.
612 North Michigan Avenue
Chicago, Illinois 60611
Printed in the United States of America
International Standard Book Number
0-89005-356-1

PREFACE

THE history of the Roman legions seems to have attracted more attention on the Continent than in this country, and the absence of any comprehensive work in English on the subject may perhaps justify the appearance of this book. The period selected for study starts with the Marian army reforms and ends with the accession of Septimius Severus. My main purpose has been to examine the internal organization of the legions, the areas from which they drew their recruits, and the conditions under which their soldiers served and were discharged. An attempt has also been made to trace the movements of the legions in the first two centuries of the Principate, the circumstances in which new units were raised, and the normal orders of battle and march, while in the Introduction the stages by which the army developed in the pre-Marian Republic have been sketched in outline. On the other hand I have avoided a detailed account of particular campaigns, because, where the evidence permits, the material has been already collected and used by other English writers, while such subjects as camp-planning, siege operations, and field engineering seemed to me to lie outside the scope of the work.

In dealing with the different aspects of the subject I have thought it right to present in some detail the more important problems and to discuss their possible solution. Considerable portions of the book are in consequence technical and controversial ; but if these will only be of interest to students of the Roman Empire, it is permissible to hope that other sections may have a wider appeal.

My research in this subject has naturally been greatly assisted by the work of my predecessors in the same field. I hope that I have duly acknowledged my obligations in their proper places, but I wish here to mention the great debt which I owe to two German scholars—A. von Domaszewski and E. Ritterling. Even where I have thought fit to differ from their conclusions it is with a real sense of what I have learnt from them.

In preparing my work for publication I received much help from various friends in Oxford, and I gladly take this opportunity of thanking Dr. H. Stuart Jones, recently

Camden Professor of Ancient History, who read my MS.
and gave me valuable advice and criticism.   The final
proofs were revised and the index compiled by my former
pupil Mr. R. Meiggs, Assistant Master at Christ's Hospital,
to whom I offer my grateful thanks.   Lastly I should like to
express my appreciation of the help given me by the officials
of the Clarendon Press, and to thank the Delegates for
undertaking the publication of this book.

H. M. D. P.

OXFORD,
   February 1928

CONTENTS

APPENDIX

Four sketch maps are provided : German Frontier, p. 121; Danube Frontier, p. 124; Eastern Frontier, p. 127; Roman Britain, p. 130.

LIST OF ABBREVIATIONS

C. I. L. = Corpus Inscriptionum Latinarum.

E. E. = Ephemeris Epigraphica.

A. E. = L'Année Épigraphique.

I. G. R. R. = Inscriptiones Graecae ad res Romanas pertinentes.

Cl. Q. = Classical Quarterly.

Cl. Rev. = Classical Review.

J. R. S. = Journal of Roman Studies.

Dess. = Dessau, 'Inscriptiones Latinae Selectae'.

B. G. U. = Ägyptische Urkunden aus den Königlichen Museen zu Berlin.

Von Dom. 'Die Rang.' = A. von Domaszewski, 'Die Rangordnung des röm. Heeres'.

Von Dom. 'Die Fahn.' = A. von Domaszewski, 'Die Fahnen im röm. Heere'.

P–W. = Pauly–Wissowa, 'Real-Encyclopädie der Classischen Altertums-Wissenschaft'.

Br. = Brambach, 'Corpus Inscriptionum Rhenarum'.

Troms. 'Quaest. duo' = Tromsdorff, 'Quaestiones duo ad historiam leg. Rom. pertinentes'.

S–D. = Strachan–Davidson, 'Selections from Polybius'.

T. A. = Tacitus, Annals.

T. H. = Tacitus, Histories.

Cohen². = H. Cohen, 'Médailles Impériales', second edition.

INTRODUCTION

THE PRE-MARIAN ARMY

THE campaigning army of the Principate was divided into legions and *auxilia*, and the troops in either branch of the service were professional soldiers. This system of recruiting was not in itself a novelty. Just as the constitution of the Principate was in theory a continuation of the Republican form of government, so the army, the most important public service, was based on the principles laid down by Marius. An account, therefore, of the organization and employment of the legions under the Principate may conveniently start with a consideration of the nature of the Marian reforms, and to understand their significance it is necessary to outline the stages through which the army progressed in the earlier centuries of the Republic.

In the regal period the Roman army developed from a fighting force of nobles ranged around their chieftain to a citizen militia drawn from the richest men in the state. We are told that Romulus had an army of 3,000 *pedites* and 300 *celeres*, provided by the three primitive Roman tribes and their subdivisions of 30 *curiae*,[1] and this force in all probability represented the patricians or men of noble birth. Thus eligibility for service in the army depended originally at Rome, as in most primitive communities, upon γένος or ties of blood. As the pressure from tribes which lived in the

---

[1] Livy, i. 18. 8 ; Varro, de l.l. v. 89.

surrounding hills began to threaten the existence of
the small state, the nobles were not strong enough for
its defence, and the army was reinforced by recruits
from the plebeians. This change is ascribed by Livy
and Dionysius [1] to Servius Tullius, and his organization
of the Roman people in classes and centuries shows
that wealth and no longer birth was the qualification
for military service. Five classes were formed which
were distinguished from each other by the property
assessment necessary for their members, and from
either the first three or first four the heavy-armed
infantry was recruited. The remaining class or classes
furnished the *rorarii* or light-armed troops, while those
citizens whose wealth was above that of the highest
class composed the *equites*, who seem to have been
mounted infantry rather than cavalry. The soldiers
were obliged to find their own armour, and probably
the equipment varied with the means of the individual.
As a fighting force the heavy-armed infantry were
organized as a phalanx, inside which the soldiers were
distinguished by the names of *principes*, *hastati*, and
triarii.[2] The normal offensive weapons were the *hasta*
or thrusting-spear [3] and the Greek sword or dagger,
while for defence the richest soldiers had corselets,
clipei or round shields, and, in common with the
other ranks, helmets, and perhaps greaves. Such, in

[1] Livy, i. 43; Dion. Hal. iv. 16.   [2] Festus, p. 249.
[3] Festus, Epit. p. 101 M.

broad outline, was the army of the later regal period, and so far there is nothing distinctive in its organization. It is similar to the phalanges of the Greek States and is recruited from οἱ τὰ ὅπλα παρεχόμενοι (those who can provide themselves with suits of armour).

The next stage in the development of the army is associated traditionally with the name of Camillus. Rome was engaged in the long protracted siege of Veii, and had hardly recovered from this ten years' struggle when the Gauls swept down Italy, and after their victory at the Allia, captured Rome with the exception of the Capitol. On each occasion she was saved by the strategy of Camillus, and so it is not surprising that tradition has ascribed to him important reforms. These fall under three headings. 1. Pay was introduced for the soldiers.[1] 2. The defensive armour was improved by the adoption of the *scutum* or oval-shaped shield instead of the *clipeus*,[2] while a new offensive weapon, the *pilum*, was substituted for the *hasta*.[3] 3. The phalanx was abolished and the legion or levy of Roman citizens took its place, organized in maniples or small companies, at first, perhaps, consisting of 60 and later of 120 men each.[4]

That all these changes were effected at the same time and under the influence of one man is in itself improbable. Although the siege of Veii may well have necessitated the provision of pay for the troops, the adoption of new weapons and a new tactical formation is much more likely the result of a series of campaigns, in

[1] Livy, v. 7. 5; Plut. Cam. 2.   [2] Livy, viii. 8. 8.
[3] Plut. Cam. 40.   [4] Livy, viii. 8. 8.

which Rome was opposed to an enemy who successfully
employed them against her. In the fifth and fourth
centuries B.C. Etruria [1] and Samnium [2] were her chief
rivals, and in the literary evidence each is credited
with the invention of the *pilum*.[3] Further, the nature
of the new offensive weapon suggests that the maniple
was adopted to meet its special requirements. A
throwing-spear cannot be effectively used by soldiers
standing in the closed ranks of the phalanx, and therefore some sort of open-order formation was necessary
in which there was room to aim and hurl the spear.
If, then, the Romans learnt the advantages of the *pilum*
over the *hasta* from her enemies, it is probable that
the maniple began to be substituted for the phalanx
towards the end of the fifth century B.C. That it
was not a sudden or complete change is suggested by
Livy's account of the organization of the legion, which
despite its contradictory nature may be applied freely
to this period.[4] The *hastati* and *principes*, who by a
strange inversion now represented the first and second
lines respectively, are given by him the general name
of *antepilani* in order to afford a contrast with the third
line of *pilani* who, as their name implies, were still

[1] Livy, ii. 46 and xxviii. 45.
[2] Ined. Vat. iii; Drachmann, Kleine Texte, 97: "οὐκ ἦν ὁ
Σαυνιτικὸς ἡμῖν θυρεὸς πάτριος, οὐδ' ὑσσοὺς εἴχομεν . . . ἀλλὰ Σαυνίταις κατα-
στάντες εἰς πόλεμον καὶ τοῖς ἐκείνων θυρεοῖς καὶ ὑσσοῖς ὁπλισθέντες . . . ἀλλο-
τρίοις ὅπλοις καὶ ζηλώμασιν ἐδουλωσάμεθα τοὺς μέγ' ἐφ' ἑαυτοῖς πεφρονηκότας."
Sall. Cat. 51.
[3] Perhaps, however, the *pilum* is developed out of the native
Roman *verutum*, the weapon of the Servian light-armed troops
(Couissin, 'Les armes romaines', pp. 129-38 and 181-5).
[4] Livy, viii. 8.

drawn up in serried ranks.[1] Therefore, in all probability the first two lines alone were armed with the *pilum* and organized in maniples, and the third line continued as a phalanx armed with the *hasta*.

In the century and a half which started with the siege of Veii and culminated in the First Punic War two great developments had thus taken place in the Roman army. First the introduction of pay made winter campaigning possible, and secondly, by the adoption of a new offensive weapon and consequently of a new tactical formation, the Romans broke away from the tradition of Greek hoplite fighting, and started to practise a method of attack which in the next century saw the crushing defeat of the Macedonian phalanx.

The experience gained in the Punic wars played an important part in the further progress of the Roman legionary system, and this is reflected in Polybius' account of it.[2] In a normal year, apart from the *Socii*, or allies, who fought in separate units of their own, two armies, consisting of two legions apiece, were formed and placed under the command of the two consuls. Under the consuls were twenty-four military tribunes, six to each legion, who had previously served for five or ten years. To them was entrusted the duty of choosing soldiers for the annual armies from the tribes appointed by lot to provide them, and the method of selection resembled picking up sides for a game.

---

[1] Not so called because they were armed with the *pilum* (as Varro, o. c., v. 89, and Festus, p. 247, suppose), but derived from *pilus* = a closed rank (e. g. *primus pilus*, *agmen pilatum*, *legiones pilatae*).

[2] Pol. vi. 19 sq. (S–D., p. 243).

Groups of four men who appeared to be equal in age and physical fitness were selected by the presiding magistrate, and the tribunes of each potential legion were given first pick in rotation. The process continued till four legions of 4,200 men each had been formed. Each army was then organized separately. The youngest and poorest soldiers became *velites* or light-armed troops; those next to them in age composed the *hastati* or front-line troops; the soldiers in their prime made up the *principes* or second line; while the oldest men were assigned to the third line and called *triarii*. The normal method of division was such that the *velites, hastati,* and *principes* each numbered 1,200 men, while the *triarii* never exceeded 600, even if the legion was increased to 5,000 men. *Hastati, principes,* and *triarii* were then subdivided into maniples and centuries, so that there were ten maniples and twenty centuries in each line, making a total of thirty maniples and sixty centuries to the legion. Each maniple had two centurions chosen from the soldiers for their bravery and powers of endurance, two junior officers called *optiones*, and two *vexillarii* or standard-bearers. The senior centurion commanded the right and the junior the left century of the maniple, while the *velites* were not organized in separate maniples but were assigned in the proportion of twenty to each century of the three lines. In addition, there were 300 cavalry to each legion, organized into ten *turmae* or squadrons, and to each *turma* were allotted three *decuriones* corresponding to the three centurions of the infantry, three *optiones*, and one *vexillarius*.

The *velites* were distinguished from the other ranks by their armour. They were equipped with the *parma* or round buckler, which was considered sufficient to protect them, and had for their offensive weapon the *hasta velitaris*,[1] the handle of which measured three feet and the head about nine inches in length. The three other groups had a similar defensive armour consisting of the *scutum* or oval-shaped shield,[2] measuring about four feet in length and made of pieces of wood covered with hides and strengthened by an iron boss and iron rims, helmets distinguished by crests of different colours, greaves, and a breastplate of bronze, for which the richest soldiers substituted a species of chain armour. The offensive weapons of the *hastati* and *principes* were the *pilum* or throwing-spear,[3] which had a wooden handle of four and a half feet and an iron shank of the same length joined together by driving the shank up to half its length into the handle, and the *gladius*, or two-edged Spanish sword, carried on the right side. The *triarii*, on the other hand, still retained the *hasta* or thrusting-spear in place of the *pilum*.

On the field of battle the legion was drawn up in three lines. The front line consisted of the ten maniples of *hastati* with the two centuries in each

[1] This throwing-spear (=γρόσφος of Polybius) was lighter and had a shorter head than the old *verutum* (Couissin, o. c., pp. 218–19).

[2] The cylindrical shield, which is carried by the legionary of the first century A. D., does not seem to have been adopted till shortly before the time of Caesar. Perhaps it was the same as the shield of the Samnite gladiators (Couissin, o. c., pp. 247 and 820).

[3] Each soldier carried two *pila* differing from each other in the thickness of their handles (Couissin, o. c., p. 209).

maniple fighting side by side. Between the maniples a space was normally left equal to the frontage of a maniple. The *principes* were then drawn up in the same way as the *hastati*, so as to cover off the gaps between the front line maniples, while the *triarii* covered off the *hastati* units. That this was the normal tactical formation follows from Polybius' account of the Battle of Zama.[1] Scipio, he says, did not draw up the *principes*, as was customary, behind the intervals in the front line, but ordered them to cover off the maniples of *hastati*, in order that, if the Carthaginian elephants forced back the *velites* sent to oppose them, the latter might escape through the gaps to the rear of the legion without causing any disintegration in the second line maniples when the elephants followed in pursuit. In each century a soldier was allowed a square yard upon which to stand, and was separated from his neighbours by an additional three feet.[2] This gave ample room for the use of *pilum* and *gladius*. The battle then normally proceeded on the following lines. After some preliminary skirmishing by the light-armed troops and cavalry, the *hastati* advanced and on reaching striking distance hurled their *pila*. If the initial attack was successful, the whole legion moved forward, and when the *principes* came into effective range they hurled their spears over the heads of the *hastati*, or in different circumstances reinforced the front line by filling up the gaps between the maniples, while the *triarii* might be brought up on the flanks. When the soldiers reached close quarters they used

[1] Pol. xv. 9 (S–D., p. 375).   [2] Ibid. xviii. 18 (S–D., p. 431).

their swords to decide the issue. Similarly, if the *hastati* were forced to retire, they moved back under the covering fire of the *principes* into the intervals in the second line, and in a crisis the retreat was continued till the third line was reached.

Polybius' account is of course formal, and represents the paper organization of the army and the stereotyped method of attack and defence. In the crisis of the Second Punic War the legions were greatly increased both in number and size. For instance, in 211 B.C. there were twenty-three legions raised,[1] while in the Macedonian wars the strength of the units varied from 5,200 to 6,000 men.[2] Further, the peace-time system of recruiting was impossible in an emergency. When the need for troops was urgent there was nó time to pick out groups of men approximately equal in age and fitness, nor can recruiting have been confined to the propertied classes. A *dilectus* or levy was held, not only in Rome, but in other districts of Italy; for instance, in the year 212 B.C. Livy states that two boards of three men were specially appointed to recruit free-born citizens inside and outside the fiftieth milestone from Rome,[3] while after Cannae two legions were enlisted from slaves. Lastly, although it may have been the letter of the law that tribunes should have had at least five years' previous service, various examples suggest that not infrequently they were young men of aristocratic birth. For instance P. Cornelius Scipio was twenty when military tribune in 216 B.C.[4] and

[1] Livy, xxvi. 1. 13.
[2] Ibid. xlii. 31. 2.
[3] Ibid. xxv. 5. 6.
[4] Ibid. xxii. 53. 1, xxvi. 18. 7.

Titus Flamininus, who was consul at the early age of thirty in 198 B.C., was tribune in 210 B.C., and so can only have been eighteen.[1] This practice of appointing young men as military tribunes persisted during the remainder of the Republic, and .is largely responsible for the decline of the office and the rise of *legati*.

Since the period of the Samnite wars considerable improvements had thus been made in the Roman legion, in organization, armour, and tactics, which may be conveniently summarized.

1. The formation in maniples was now extended to the *triarii*, and the soldiers were subdivided into *hastati*, *principes*, and *triarii* on the basis of age and physical fitness instead of merely on the amount of property they possessed. The *velites* took the place of the old *rorarii*, and, while operating either independently or in conjunction with the *equites* in battle, were for administrative purposes attached to the centuries of heavy-armed infantry. Again, the growth of maniples and centuries brought the junior officers into greater prominence, and, while the tribunes started to decline in importance, the centurions began to figure as the mainstay of the legion.

2. The *pilum* was made more evenly balanced and given a greater driving power by decreasing the length of the spear-head. A similarity between the Polybian *pilum* and the Spanish *phalarica*[2] suggests that this change may have been a result of Rome's experience of fighting the Spanish tribes. Further, the substitution of the *pilum* for the *hasta* in the two front

---

[1] Plut. Flam. 1.   [2] Livy, xxi. 8. 10–11.

lines made it necessary that the legionary should have
also an effective weapon for close-range fighting. The
epithet 'Spanish' which Polybius applies to the *gladius*
argues the supersession of the old short-pointed
sword, and suggests that the 'cut and thrust' use of
the sword by the Spanish tribes so impressed the
Romans that they permanently employed the two-
edged sword in preference to the long unpointed
weapon of the Gauls.[1] Lastly, the retention of the
hasta as the offensive arm of the *triarii* even after their
organization in maniples shows that Rome was not
yet entirely convinced of the superiority of the *pilum*
in all circumstances, but preferred still to depend on
the thrusting-spear for the final reinforcements in the
attack, and conversely, in the event of *hastati* and
principes being driven back, for the last stand at the
third line.

3. The superiority of the open-order formation was
demonstrated in the Macedonian wars.[2] On a level
piece of ground the phalanx, by its compact weight, was
more or less invincible, but in uneven country its
unwieldiness placed it at a great disadvantage compared with the smaller units, whose soldiers could hurl
their spears from a distance, and then rush into close
quarters with their swords. Further, the fortune of
the day no longer depended upon keeping the phalanx
intact. The Roman formation in three lines showed
the possibilities of reinforcing and of mutual support.

[1] Pol. ii. 33. Suidas, s. v. Μάχαιρα (Couissin, o. c., pp. 220–32).
[2] See Pol. xviii. 12 (S-D., p. 431) for a comparison of the
phalanx and maniple.

If the *hastati* were driven back the battle was not ended; for an effective resistance might still be offered at the second or third line. Conversely, reinforcements could be sent either to the flanks or to fill the gaps caused by casualties in the firing line.

But despite these improvements the Roman legions still remained an annual levy, and as yet there was no professional army.[1] The property qualification, if reduced, and in a crisis even temporarily suspended, was not yet formally abolished, and the army continued in theory a citizen militia of peasant proprietors. The period of peace which followed a century of foreign wars was to show that further reforms were necessary.[2]

---

[1] The liability for service extended to twenty *stipendia* or campaigns.

[2] For further information see the following specialized works:

McCartney : ' The military indebtedness of early Rome to Etruria ' in Mem. of Amer. Acad. at Rome, 1917, p. 150.

Fell : ' Etruria and Rome.'

Randall-McIver : 'The Etruscans.'

Helbig : 'Sur les attributs des Saliens' and 'Contribution à l'histoire de l'Equitatus Romain', in Mém. de l'Acad. des Inscr. 1904, p. 206.

A. J. Reinach : ' L'origine du pilum' in Mém. de l'Acad. des Inscr. 1907, p. 226.

Schulten : ' Der Ursprung des Pilums' in Rhein. Mus. lxvi, 1911, p. 573.

E. Meyer : 'Kleine Schriften', vol. ii.

Delbrück : 'Geschichte der Kriegskunst', vol. i.

Couissin : 'Les armes romaines' (Paris, 1926).

I

THE MARIAN ARMY REFORMS

IN the latter half of the second century B.C. the maintenance of the army was complicated by the economic and political situation in Italy. From the Punic and Macedonian campaigns Rome and its legions had emergéd victorious, and the state as a whole acquired vast new tracts of territory and a steady increase in wealth. But, although the common soldiers profited individually, it was the political and military leaders, drawn from the senatorial order, that secured the greatest personal aggrandizement. The lion's share in the booty and loot of the wars fell into their hands and they returned home rich men, while later, as governors of the provinces, they found opportunities for acquiring further wealth. At the same time a large and influential body of business men was growing up in Rome and Italy. During the wars the members of this class had provided the army with its food, ammunition, and clothing, and in the years of peace that followed made fortunes from the farming of taxes in the provinces and the lending of money at extortionate rates of interest. As a result, the senatorial and equestrian orders became capitalist classes, and, wishing to find a safe investment for their money, looked to the land as the surest and best security for their wealth. Nor was there any lack of *ager publicus*. For even after a distribution of small holdings to the peasant-soldiers [1] there remained great

---

[1] E. g. Livy, xliv. 4.

tracts of land, both in and outside Italy, capable of improvement and development.   Such an exploitation was impossible without capital, and the Roman government, rather than let the land lie fallow, gladly leased the ground to the capitalist-buyer.   The peasant proprietor was thus placed in competition with the wealthy landlord with his cheap and plentiful slave labour and paid supervisors to superintend the work of the farm, while he himself continued to live in town and enjoy its pleasures and amusements.   The inevitable result ensued.   The small-holder, unable to find a profitable market for his goods, sold his land, and either became the tenant of the capitalist or migrated to Rome, attracted by the lure of cheap food.   The consequent unemployment and over-population in the Capital induced the Gracchi to attempt a re-establishment of small-holdings in Italy, but their efforts were largely unproductive.   The day of the peasant-proprietor was gone.[1]

This change in the ownership of the land in Italy had a serious effect upon legionary recruiting.   A certain property assessment was still the technical qualification for service in the legions, and at the same time the number of peasant-proprietors was rapidly diminishing.   The old areas of legionary recruiting were thus becoming barren, and yet the Senate, which had acquired sovereign control during the great wars, was as opposed to opening the ranks officially to the poorer Roman citizens as to extending the

[1] See further Rostovtzeff, 'A Social and Economic History of the Roman Empire', pp. 13-23.

franchise to the Italian allies, which would have auto-
matically increased the number of potential recruits
for the legions. The *Socii* were still organized in units
of their own, but under the supreme command of
Roman *praefecti*. In theory the proportion of troops
contributed by them was supposed to be no greater
than the contingents of Roman citizens, but gradually,
with the impoverishment of the legionary recruiting
areas and the unwillingness of the Roman middle-
classes to serve on campaigns which did not promise
to yield a lucrative return, the burden of military
service fell with increasing heaviness upon them. An
agitation arose for the extension of the franchise. The
cause of the allies was taken up by such democratic
statesmen as Fulvius Flaccus and Gaius Gracchus, but
their efforts merely served to stimulate the conservative
opposition of the Senate, and the discontented *Socii*
continued to provide their separate *alae* and *cohortes*.

Towards the end of the second century a crisis
arose. Rome was at war with the Numidian prince
Jugurtha, and after some initial failures had at length
selected the distinguished general Metellus to command the campaigning army. But still the war
dragged on and the expected Roman victory was not
forthcoming. Marius, a native of Arpinum, was serving on the staff,[1] and, partly perhaps from jealousy and
personal ambition, and partly from disapproval of his
strategy, had not given loyal support to Metellus. By
intrigue with his friends among the democrats at
home he was recalled, elected consul,[2] and given the

[1] Sall. Jug. 46.   [2] Ibid. 64.

province of Numidia,[1] with the command against Jugurtha in succession to Metellus. The Senate voted him a supplementary force for the legions, but, partly because he felt that the additional levy was insufficient, and partly on the suggestion of his democratic supporters, Marius started to raise troops on his own initiative and from unconstitutional sources. Thus he created a precedent which had the most important bearing on the subsequent political and military history of Rome.

Marius was not content to supplement his army by drawing upon 'the bravest men' in Latium[2] and recalling to the colours *evocati* or discharged veterans known to him by reputation. He employed another method of enlistment. 'Ipse interea milites scribere, non more maiorum neque ex classibus, sed uti cuiusque lubido erat, capite censos plerosque.'[3] Thus the proletariat of Rome, who had in the past been technically debarred from entering the legions and whose services had only been enlisted in times of crisis, were now legally qualified for enrolment. The political results of this high-handed innovation of Marius can be traced throughout the party politics of the last century : the military aspect is hardly less important. Recruits drawn largely from the proletariat of Rome now signed on for a definite period of service, and in all probability for twenty years. For in 67 B.C. a *lex Gabinia*[4] was passed, appointing Glabrio

---

[1] Sall. Jug. 82.   [2] Ibid. 84.   [3] Ibid. 86.
[4] Sallust, Hist. 5. 13, and see P–W. xiii, p. 403, s.v. ' Licinius Lucullus '.

to the province of Bithynia and ordering the discharge of the two legions in Lucullus' army which had originally been enlisted by Flaccus in 86 B.C. and had later espoused the cause of Fimbria. The soldiers had completed their *legitima stipendia*, and now refused to follow their unpopular new commander on any more campaigns. Hence, says Cicero, 'Lucullus partim militum qui iam stipendiis confectis erant dimisit, partim M'. Glabrioni tradidit'.[1] Thus in the last century of the Republic, as during the first century of the Principate, a Roman citizen was liable to serve in the legions for twenty years, even if successful generals not infrequently discharged their soldiers at the end of a campaign and before the *legitima stipendia* were completed. Further, in place of an annual *sacramentum* the soldiers took an oath that was binding during their whole military career, 'Se esse facturos pro republica, nec recessuros nisi praecepto consulis post completa stipendia'.[2] Two points merit attention. First, in place of an army drawn technically from the middle-classes and supplemented in a crisis from other sources by makeshift decrees of the Senate, the institution of a professional army was officially recognized.[3] Consequently training and discipline were raised to a much higher level of efficiency, and we shall see that it is through these professional soldiers that Rome not

---

[1] Cic. Pro Lege Man. ix. 26; cf. Plut. Lucullus 35. 8; Dio xxxvi. 14. 3; App. Mithr. 90, where the same situation is described.

[2] Servius ad Aen. viii. 1.

[3] See further Delbrück, 'Gesch. der Kriegskunst', i, especially pp. 450-5.

merely acquired the further additions to her territory
but administered them after their conquest. Secondly,
the policy inaugurated by Marius in the teeth of
Senatorial opposition of enlisting troops on his own
initiative set a dangerous precedent which was followed
by subsequent generals till the end of the Republic.
The result was that generals raised armies for their
own purposes, paid their soldiers from the booty which
they gained, and when their work was finished compelled the state to find land for their veterans.[1] Thus,
so far from there being a state army in the last century
of the Republic, there was rather a succession of armies
owing loyalty to their respective generals.[2] This
close relationship of the soldiers to their commanding officers, bound up, as it was, with the second part
of their *sacramentum*, 'we will only retire when our
service is completed with the permission of the consul',
and intensified by long campaigns outside Italy, was in
large measure the cause of the succession of civil wars
which marked the last century of the Republic: nor
was a solution found for the divorcement of the army
from the home government till Augustus became both
head of the state at home and commander-in-chief of
the forces in the field.

The next most important reform that may be
ascribed to Marius was of a tactical nature. The
battle of Pydna was the triumph of the maniple over

---

[1] E. g. Caesar's agrarian legislation for Pompey's veterans
(Suet. Caes. 20).
[2] E. g. Fimbria and Sulla in the Mithradatic War (see Th.
Reinach, 'Mithradate Eupator', pp. 190-211).

the phalanx, and this new disposition was adequate till
Rome came to meet an opponent who adopted a method
of attack different from the slow methodical advance
of the phalanx. No sooner was the Jugurthine campaign brought to a successful finish than Rome had
to meet an invasion from the north of Cimbri and
Teutones. The tactics of these German tribes were to
stake everything upon a vigorous onslaught at the start
of the battle, and to meet this method of attack the
formation in three lines of maniples was unsuited.
The units themselves were small, and the first line was
normally divided by gaps as wide as the maniples
themselves. Consequently an attack strongly pressed
home might easily overcome the resistance of the front
lines, and the enemy troops might advance through
the gaps and deliver an unimpeded assault upon the
second line of defence. In the war against the Insubres
the Romans had attempted to overcome this difficulty
by using their *pila* for thrusting instead of throwing,
so as to be able to resist in close formation the
onslaught of the enemy with their long unpointed
swords.[1] But the small size of the maniple was still
a weakness against such a type of fighting, and Marius
decided to strengthen his front line of defence by
increasing the size of the individual units and, if
necessary, reducing the gaps between them. Thus the
cohort took the place of the maniple as the tactical unit
of the Roman army, and the legion was organized into
ten cohorts, each of which was subdivided into six
centuries. The effect of this reform was to give much

[1] Pol. ii. 88.

greater cohesion and stability to the separate units that
composed the lines of attack and defence.   Further,
the division into three lines was no longer rigidly
adhered to.   It is true that Caesar's normal formation
was the *triplex acies*, with four cohorts in the front and
three in each of the other lines,[1] but on occasions two
or even one line might be adopted.   In the course of
a campaign in Aquitania in 56 B.C. Crassus employed
the *duplex acies*,[2] while a single line was adopted by
Caesar in Africa.[3]   It is not improbable that Marius
consolidated his front line of defence at the expense
of his reserve in first confronting the attack of the
Cimbri.

This tactical reform is usually assigned to Marius on
the ground that the last time we hear of maniples being
definitely employed in battle is by Metellus against
Jugurtha.[4] The justification of this view has, however,
been questioned, partly because of the inconsistencies
in Sallust's account, and partly because of an important assertion of Polybius which seems to contradict
the later historian. In describing P. Scipio's campaign
in Spain against Indibilis, Polybius mentions cohorts
and gives the impression that they had been adopted
at this time as new units in the Roman legion.[5]   Such
an authoritative statement suggests that the cohort was
substituted for the maniple in the Second Punic War,
and not as popularly supposed in the time of Marius.
But if this is so, it is strange that Polybius makes no

[1] B. G. i. 24. 2.   [2] Ibid. iii. 24. 1.
[3] Bell. Afric. 13. 2.   [4] Sall. Jug. 49.
[5] Pol. xi. 33 and cf. xi. 23.

mention of cohorts in his detailed examination of the
organization of the legion, although he recognizes their
existence in the contingents of *Socii*,[1] and that in his
comparison of Roman and Macedonian warfare it is
the maniple and not the cohort which he contrasts with
the phalanx.[2] Probably, then, Scipio's formation was
no more than an experiment. In the battle against
Indibilis he had to lead his troops into a valley where
the enemy were supported by their cavalry. The
maniple was too small a unit to operate by itself in
such circumstances ; hence Scipio joined together three
maniples into a composite unit, which Polybius calls
a cohort, and advanced with four of these 'cohorts'
into the valley. This disposition was therefore a temporary expedient, and Polybius shows that it was not
retained in the later fighting against Hannibal and in
the Macedonian campaigns. If then the maniple is
the tactical unit at Pydna, Sallust's statement that
Metellus fought in a similar formation against Jugurtha
may be accepted, because we know of no tactical
reforms in the intervening years. But in the campaigns against Sertorius the cohort seems already to
have taken the place of the maniple,[3] and Caesar consistently speaks of the cohort as his tactical unit. As
Marius is known to have introduced improvements in
armour and equipment, it is not improbable that its
permanent adoption in the legion was a further part of
his military reforms.

---

[1] Pol. vi. 24 (S–D., p. 249).   [2] Ibid. xviii. 12 (S–D., p. 429).
[3] Front. Strat. ii. 8. 5 and Schulten, 'Sertorius', especially
pp. 108–17.

The increase in the size of the tactical unit from 120 to 600 involved the necessity for a greater concentration upon the smaller contingents which composed the cohort. A hundred men can be handled fairly adequately as a compact body under the command of one man. Any additions to this number render advisable a delegation of duties to junior commanders. This principle was illustrated in the change made some years ago in the British army in the composition of the infantry battalion. Previously the companies numbered a hundred strong organized into four sections, and although this organization gave the section commanders an important post of responsibility, still the company was sufficiently small to be kept directly under the command of its company officer. The intention of the change was the creation of more composite units inside the company, and was in many respects parallel to the adoption of the cohort in place of the maniple. The new platoons that took the place of the old sections numbered originally about sixty-four men, and the company was 250 strong. The company thus became too large for the effective direct control of one man; consequently the platoon commanders develop in importance, and even have section commanders under them. In the same way the cohort which had a nominal strength of six hundred was subdivided into centuries, and it was largely on the skill and efficiency of the centurions that Rome depended for the effective execution of the tactical schemes of the legionary commander. At this period the centurions were soldiers who had gained experience in the ranks, and who were promoted as a reward for bravery in battle, or because they showed signs of being able to lead and discipline men.[1] They are the nearest approach to the sergeant-major of the British army except that they held commissioned rank, which they received from the military tribunes.

As a result of the change from the maniple to the cohort organization the old division of soldiers into *hastati*, *principes*, and *triarii* or *pilani* became obsolete. As soon as the tactical dispositions ceased to be limited rigidly to three lines, and an organization in one, two, or three lines became equally feasible, the differentiation of troops by reference to their projected position in the line of battle became pointless. In future the names *hastati*, *principes*, and *pilani* were retained simply for distinguishing the rank of the sixty centurions in a legion. By a strange inversion, similar to that which had previously reversed the position of the *principes* and *hastati*, the *pilani* (probably because they were originally the oldest soldiers) were now used to designate the senior centurions in each cohort, and the *hastati* denoted the junior.[2] The centurions, too, were distinguished by being called *prior* and *posterior* (i. e. front and rear rank), and no longer as right and left centurions, because the cohort had a frontage of three centuries with the remaining three centuries drawn up in rear of them.

The great ambition of all centurions was to become

[1] Pol. vi. 24 (S–D., p. 249).
[2] Thus the senior centurion is called *primus pilus*, and the junior *decimus hastatus posterior*.

primus pilus, or leading centurion, and from the evidence
of Polybius it is possible to trace a system of promotion, which may be best understood by the help of
a diagram.

The diagram shows that in each of the ten cohorts
of the legion there were two *pili*, two *principes*, and two
hastati centurions. On what system was seniority
reckoned? There are two possibilities : either all the
hastati centurions were junior in standing to all the
principes, and the *principes* to the *pili* centurions, or
seniority was by cohorts, the centurions of the first
cohort being the senior, and the centurions of the
tenth cohort the junior, officers in the legion. The best
evidence is to be found in considering the meaning of
the expression *primi ordines*. Centurions *primorum
ordinum* are coupled by Caesar [1] with the military
tribunes and may be regarded not merely as century
commanders but perhaps as forming a select staff that
the consul consulted. Again, Caesar talks of centurions
'qui primis ordinibus appropinquarent', referring to
the celebrated rivals Pullo and Vorenus,[2] who vied
with each other in showing bravery, no doubt with
a view to entering the coveted *primi ordines*. Now
this expression may bear three interpretations. Either
the *primi ordines* are the leading centurions (i. e. the
pili priores) in each of the ten cohorts, or they are the
six centurions of the first cohort, or they may be
a combination of the two. A passage from Caesar
gives a clue to the meaning of the term at least in the
last century of the Republic. '(Scaevam) Caesar . . . ab

[1] B. G. i. 41. 3.   [2] Ibid. v. 44. 1.

	Pilus prior.	Pilus posterior.	Princeps prior.	Princeps posterior.	Hastatus prior.	Hastatus posterior.
Cohort I						
Cohort II						
Cohort III						
Cohort IV						
Cohort V						
Cohort VI						
Cohort VII						
Cohort VIII						
Cohort IX						
Cohort X						

octavis ordinibus ad primipilum se traducere pronun-
tiavit.'[1] This is of course an exceptional promotion,
but the important point is that *octavi ordines* must
surely mean the centurions of cohort VIII.   If this is
right, then the *primi ordines* will be the centurions of
cohort I, and the remaining centurions will be similarly
distinguished as belonging to the *ordines* bearing the
number of the cohort in which they were serving.   It
follows then, that the senior centurions of the legion
are the centurions of the first cohort with the *primus
pilus* at their head, and the junior the centurions of the
tenth cohort.

How then were the centurions promoted ?   If a man
started as *decimus hastatus posterior*, must he have been
promoted fifty-nine times before becoming *primus pilus*,
or did each promotion involve a change of cohort, so
that after nine promotions the *decimus hastatus posterior*
might reach the first cohort ?   Under the Principate
both systems are found ; but whereas the former is
confined, as we shall see, to ex-rankers who never
climbed very far on the ladder of promotion, the latter
was the usual method of advance for centurions who
ultimately reached the highest rank.   The evidence
for the Republican period is much less decisive, but in
all probability the second method of promotion was the
normal, while military exigencies must have frequently
necessitated exceptional promotions like that of Scaeva.
The expression *octavi ordines* in the above-quoted
passage suggests that, with the exception of the leading cohort, there was not much difference in status

[1] B. C. iii. 53. 5.

between the six centurions of any one cohort (even if
for purposes of the roster a relative seniority was observed), because Caesar does not say that he promoted
Scaeva from a definite post in the eighth cohort, but
simply from the ranks of the eighth cohort.[1]   Therefore, although at times a centurion may have changed
rank inside a cohort (i. e. from *hastatus* to *princeps* or
from *princeps* to *pilus*), normally, when promoted, he
was transferred to the cohort next above that in which
he was serving.   Thus, suppose a man starts as *decimus
hastatus posterior*, in nine moves he might become
primus hastatus posterior, having kept the rank of a
hastatus centurion throughout.   He had now entered
the *primi ordines*, and if he were promoted again he
would be moved from rank to rank inside the first
cohort till ultimately he attained the post of *primus
pilus*.   Similarly, a centurion starting in the *pilus* or
princeps grade in the tenth cohort would be promoted
in the same rank from cohort to cohort till at least the
second cohort was reached.   Here he would wait till
a vacancy occurred in the *primi ordines*, and his next
promotion may well have involved a change of rank.
It is hardly likely that the *secundus pilus prior* would
be promoted directly to *primus pilus*, or for that matter
the *secundus princeps prior* to *primus princeps prior*;
more probably each in turn would start in the *hastatus*
grade of the *primi ordines* and gradually work his way
up to *primus pilus*.   Delays that must have occurred in
the promotion list were even in the Republic to some

[1] So Momms. in E. E. iv, p. 226, and von Dom. 'Die Rang.',
p. 94.

extent overcome by the transfer of centurions from legion to legion.[1]

Consistently with the establishment of a professional army Marius gave the individual legions an identity which they had not previously possessed. Each legion now had its *aquila* or eagle, which was regarded as the sacred emblem personifying its active existence. In time of peace it was kept in the *aerarium* at Rome ;[2] in time of war a little chapel was built for it and the other *signa* of the smaller units in each camp, and the *aquila* was honoured with a religious cult as the ' numen legionis '.[3] During the Republic the eagle was at first made of silver and later of gold ; it was placed at the top of a long pole, and decorated with various adornments. It was given into the care of the *primus pilus* or leading centurion, and while its safe custody was equivalent to the continuance of the legion as a fighting unit, however depleted in numbers, its loss brought the greatest ignominy on any survivors and might lead in some cases to the disbandment of the legion in disgrace.[4] With Marius the legion for the first time has one legionary standard. We must further inquire what *signa* had previously existed and if the newly organized cohort also received a standard of its own.

These questions may be most satisfactorily approached by considering the meaning of the term *antesignani*, which occurs frequently in Livy and Caesar, and it will be clearest to cite some passages from each

---

[1] B. G. vi. 40. 7.   [2] Livy, iii. 69. 8.
[3] T. A. ii. 17. 2.   [4] See below, ch. v, p. 145.

author to indicate the sense in which they respectively
use the word. In one of Rome's battles against the
Etruscans Livy describes the fighting in these words :
' Nihil ab ulla parte movetur fugae, cadunt antesignani
et ne nudentur propugnatoribus signa, fit ex secunda
prima acies.'[1]   Again, referring to the Latin War, he
says of one battle ' stragem et ante signa et post signa
factam : triarios postremo rem restituisse '.[2]   From
these two passages and from others that could be cited
it is clear that in Livy the *antesignani* are the first line
of troops or the *hastati*. What are these *signa* ; are
they the standards of the maniples, or were there, even
at this date, standards belonging to the legion as such,
i. e. *signa legionum* ?   Marquardt,[3] who takes the former
view, argues that on the march the *signa* preceded the
maniples (e. g. ' vadunt igitur in proelium urgentes
signiferos '),[4] and that, when the line of battle or *acies*
was formed, the *signa* were placed in the rear of the
first line, a conclusion which he regards as decisively
proved by the second passage quoted from Livy.
Against this theory von Domaszewski[5] holds that
prior to the reforms of Marius each legion had five
legionary standards.   This he argues from a statement
of Pliny : ' erat et antea prima cum quattuor aliis :
lupi, minotauri, equi, aprique singulos ordines ante-
ibant '.[6] These are identified as follows : Jupiter is the
eagle, Mars the wolf, and Quirinus the boar, and these

[1] Livy, ix. 39. 7.   [2] Ibid. viii. 11. 7.
[3] ' L'organisation militaire ', p. 48.
[4] Livy, ix. 13. 2.
[5] P-W. i. 2355-6, and von Dom. ' Die Fahn.', pp. 2-3 and 12.
[6] Plin. N. H. x. 4. 16.

are the three original *numina* of Rome. The minotaur
may represent Jupiter Feretrius or the god of the
offensive, the horse Jupiter Stator or the god of defence.
On this interpretation of *signa* the *antesignani* become
the troops which fight in front of the legionary
standards, which for safety on the field of battle may
be assumed to have been placed behind the *prima acies*
of *hastati*.. Two considerations suggest that this theory
is right. First, if the manipular standard was used as
a rallying point for its soldiers or to help to keep the
line intact during an advance, it would be of much
greater use in or near the front of its unit than in rear
of it. It is easier to look forward than backward for
one's ' dressing '. Secondly, if all the manipular *signa*
were placed behind the front line on the field of
battle, the *triarii* would lose touch with their standards
and have, in consequence, no rallying points. If, on
the other hand, the *signa* which the *hastati* protected
were legionary standards, then the manipular standards
were left in their natural position near the head of their
maniples both in the battle-field and on the line of
march. Further support for this opinion may perhaps
be obtained from considering the use of the word
antesignani in Caesar.

There are five passages, all of them in the ' Bellum
Civile ', in which Caesar uses the word, and the following are the three most important: (*a*) ' electos ex
omnibus legionibus fortissimos viros, antesignanos,
centuriones, Caesar ei classi attribuerat ';[1] (*b*) 'Huic suos
Caesar equites opposuit, expeditosque antesignanos ad-

[1] B. C. i. 57. 1.

miscuit CCCC ' ; [1] and (c) ' superius tamen institutum in equitibus servabat ut, quoniam numero multis partibus esset inferior, adulescentes atque expeditos ex ante-signanis electos mutatis ad pernicitatem armis inter equites proeliari iuberet '.[2] From these examples it is clear that the *antesignani* are no longer simply the first line of troops, but represent a picked body which, on certain occasions, operated in front of the line. For this purpose they were equipped as *expediti*, and, from the fact that not infrequently they seem to have operated with the cavalry, it is probable that they were taking the place of the *velites* who were abolished by Marius.[3] How this picked body was selected we do not know. Perhaps in each of Caesar's legions there was a special squad forming part of the front line, which was lightly equipped so as to be ready either to move rapidly and occupy some vantage point or to skirmish with the cavalry ; more probably the *ante-signani* were merely picked soldiers of the front line cohorts who were detailed to hold themselves in readi-ness for the command ' fall out the *antesignani* ', and who were transformed from heavy-armed infantry into *expediti* for the occasion.

What then is the meaning of *signa* in the Caesarian use of the word *antesignani*? An interesting passage in ' Bellum Africum ' describes an order given by Caesar to his troops, forbidding any man to advance more than four feet from the *signa*.[4] This looks as if there were

---

[1] Ibid. iii. 75. 5.
[2] Ibid. iii. 84. 3 (adopting Madvig's emendation).
[3] Sall. Jug. 46 and 105.   [4] Bell. Afric. 15. 1.

signa in the front ranks.   Von Domaszewski, however, later maintained [1] that *signa* in the passage in question means no more than 'body of troops', because an inscription [2] of the second century A.D. from Lambaesis distinguishes thirty *arma* belonging to *antesignani* from fourteen belonging to *postsignani*, from which he inferred that two-thirds of the legion stood in front of and one-third behind the standards.   Therefore the Caesarian *antesignani* are simply troops who operate in front of the remainder of the legion.   But surely the inference drawn from the Lambaesis inscription is dangerous. Why should the proportion of two to one in a small total of forty-four represent the ratio of *antesignani* to *postsignani* in a complete legion? [3]   Further, the distinction between *arma* of *antesignani* and *postsignani* clearly implies that the two groups were differently equipped. Now this is exactly what differentiates the Caesarian *antesignani* from the other legionary troops, and so the *antesignani* in the inscription may be similar to the Caesarian *expediti*.   If so, little importance can be attached to the figures thirty and fourteen for the *arma* of *antesignani* and *postsignani* respectively.   Again, although the interpretation of *signa* in the 'Bellum Africum' passage as 'body of troops' gives the required sense for *antesignani* in the other Caesarian passages, why should the title *antesignani* have been retained to designate this corps of *expediti*?   In Livy *antesignani*

---

[1] Sitzungsber. d. Heidelb. Acad. d. Wiss. Philos.-Hist. Kl. i. 1910, p. 9, n. 5.

[2] Mém. de l'Acad. des Inscr. xxxviii, 1909, p. 259.

[3] So too Rice Holmes, 'The Roman Republic', iii, p. 896, and for his discussion of the whole problem see, o. c., iii, pp. 391-7.

certainly means troops fighting in front of standards, and therefore some similar interpretation should explain the retention of the title by Caesar. The explanation may, I think, be on the following lines. When the five pre-Marian legionary standards were superseded by the single *aquila*, the word *signa* was applied to the manipular standards in opposition to the legionary *aquila*. For instance, Cerialis invites the soldiers of legion II *Adiutrix* to dedicate their ' nova signa novamque aquilam ' ;[1] Germanicus reminds the soldiers of legion I that they had received *nova signa* (i.e. new manipular standards) from Tiberius, who reconstructed this old Spanish legion in Germany,[2] while in Dio ἀετός is normally used to designate the *aquila* as opposed to the manipular σημεῖα.[3] Consequently, after the Marian reforms *antesignani* was no longer used to designate troops protecting the legionary standard (i. e. the *prima acies*), but might be applied to soldiers fighting in front of manipular standards. Now it is probable, as we have seen, that the manipular standards were retained for tactical reasons in the front ranks of their own units. Therefore Caesar called his special squad, which took the place of the *velites*, *antesignani*, because they skirmished in front of the manipular standards of the front line.

The answer to the second question, was there a standard belonging to the cohort?, has been already implicitly answered. The only passage which seems to suggest the existence of a special standard for the cohort

---

[1] T. H. v. 16.   [2] Id. A. i. 42. 6, and see ch. iii, p. 86.
[3] See Troms. ' Quaest. duo '.

is B. G. ii. 25, where Caesar says 'quartae cohortis omnibus centurionibus occisis signiferoque interfecto, signo amisso'. In itself this does not necessitate holding that there was only one *signum* in this cohort; more probably the lost *signum* belonged to the first maniple of the cohort, and was used as the standard of the whole cohort.[1] This view is strengthened by two other passages in Caesar, in one of which Caesar talks of 'continere ad signa manipulos'[2] and in the other of the Germans flinging themselves 'in signa manipulosque'.[3] This conjunction of *signa* and *manipuli* even after the adoption of the cohort as the tactical unit shows clearly that the men were still organized by maniples and rallied round the *signa* of the maniples. After Marius there was, therefore, one legionary standard called the *aquila* and thirty *signa* belonging to the maniples, which continued to be the units for administrative purposes between the cohorts and the centuries.[4]

With the adoption of a standard as the distinguishing mark of the individual legion, the custom was also started of giving the legions definite numbers in a series. Until the time of Caesar and Pompey how- ever—and then, as we shall see, the process is obscure —it is impossible to trace the identity of different

---

[1] See Rice Holmes, o. c., iii. p. 893.   [2] B. G. vi. 84. 6.
[3] Ibid. vi. 40. 1.
[4] So too Tacitus in Annals i. 18. 8 speaks of *signa cohortium*, but in A. i. 34. 4 Germanicus tells the soldiers 'discedere ad manipulos', i.e. to rally round their *signa*. The same explanation is applicable here as in B. G. ii. 25.

legions from year to year. The reason for this is that the legions were renumbered each year, and so the same legion might have different numbers in successive years. This confusion is doubtless the survival of the annual levy.

The remaining reforms of Marius are of more detailed and less general importance. We have noticed already the disappearance of the *velites*, and it is no great surprise to find that with them the Roman cavalry was gradually withdrawn from the legion. The inferiority of the Roman cavalry had been demonstrated by the Punic wars, and it was a wise expedient to substitute for it the more efficient services of foreign mercenaries. In the Gallic War Caesar made exclusive use of *equites* raised in Gaul, Spain, and Germany,[1] and the absence of Roman horsemen is sufficiently shown by the fact that, when Caesar goes to meet Ariovistus to arrange terms of a possible peace, he forms a mounted escort from the infantry of the tenth legion.[2] From the time of Marius onwards the policy of the Roman government was to draw such supernumerary troops as it required from the native peoples it conquered. In addition to the Gallic cavalry, there are other names familiar to the most casual reader of Caesar—Numidians, Cretan archers, and the Balearic slingers.[3]

The assimilation of *hastati*, *principes*, and *triarii* rendered any differentiation in armour meaningless. Consequently the *hasta*, which had been the offensive

---

[1] B. G. v. 5. 3 and v. 26. 3. [2] Ibid. i. 42. 6.
[3] Ibid. ii. 7. 1.

weapon of the *triarii*, is replaced by the *pilum*, so that the whole legion is now uniformly equipped. Further improvements were also made in the Roman armour and equipment. In the Polybian account the *pila* were said to have been made by driving the shank into the handle, which was so solidly fixed that, even if the blade were broken, it was not dislodged from the wood.[1] At some period between the Punic wars and the time of Marius this arrangement was modified by attaching the blade to the handle by two iron rivets or περόναι. Marius made a further improvement. For one of the iron rivets he substituted a wooden pin (ξύλινον ἧλον εὔθραυστον)[2] with the intention that, when the *pilum* struck the shield of the enemy, owing to the breaking of the wooden pin it would be bent in such a way that, while the blade by its sheer weight remained firmly embedded in the shield, the handle fell to the ground. The motive of course was to make it impossible for the enemy to hurl back the weapons originally aimed at him. A further improvement on the same lines, made by Caesar, may be conveniently noticed here. Beneath the head of the *pilum* the metal of the shank was left untempered, so that the impact with which the *pilum* met the *scutum* of the enemy bent the iron. It was thus impossible for the struck man to draw out the spear from his shield. That this final modification was successful may be judged from a passage in the 'Gallic War'. 'Many of the Gauls were struck by the first discharge of weapons, and, as the iron had become

[1] Pol. vi. 23 (S–D., p. 248).   [2] Plut. Marius 25.

bent, they were unable to draw them out, nor could
they fight conveniently with their left arm thus addi-
tionally encumbered.'[1] Lastly, an improvement was
made in the construction of the soldier's pack.[2] The
weight which the soldier carried on his back must
have been enormous, and almost incredible to those
who have not seen or felt the British soldier's pack
in the last war. In addition to his actual armour,
Josephus says that the Roman legionary carried a saw,
a basket, a spade, an axe, a leather thong, a sickle,
a chain, and three days' rations, not to mention some
kit.[3] Even granted that this was the 'model' pack,
the burden of the ordinary soldier, if he carried only
one-third of these accessories, must have been very
heavy. Marius is said to have devised a scheme by
which the soldier was able to remove his pack without
interfering with his armour. This would be parallel
to the way in which a British soldier can discard full
marching order, and remain dressed in light marching
order, without taking off his equipment.

The work of Marius may be conveniently summarized.
In place of the annual levy Rome started a professional
army. All citizens were liable for military service,
and, although conscription thus remained the rule, it
is probable, as we shall see when dealing with the
Principate, that the legions were normally maintained
by voluntary enlistment. The legions were now given
an identity, which later developed into a permanent

---

[1] B. G. i. 25. 3, and cf. corroborative archaeological evidence
in Couissin, o. c., pp. 281–5.

[2] Front. Strat. iv. 1. 7.   [3] Jos. B. J. iii. 5. 5.

system of enumeration, and the new tactical unit, the cohort, with its centuries composed of soldiers armed alike with the *pilum*, survived into the Principate as the basis of the future military organization. Lastly, by the enfranchising laws of 90–89 B.C. the recruiting area for legionary troops was extended to all Italy south of the Po. The *Socii* disappeared, and the Roman army was now composed of legions of citizen-soldiers and *auxilia* or detachments of foreign troops serving either as volunteers or as mercenaries.

II

THE ARMIES OF CAESAR AND POMPEY

THE forty years culminating in the murder of Julius Caesar were marked, somewhat paradoxically, by persistent threats to the internal stability of the state and by an unprecedented advance of Roman sovereignty outside Italy. A series of political feuds at home between two factions, calling themselves *optimates* and *populares*, extended even to the province of Spain, where Sertorius defied the generals of the Roman government for close on ten years. The slaves and gladiators were restless; the pirates were menacing the seaboard and corn routes of Italy. Conversely, the threatening advance of a possible rival to Rome in the person of Mithradates, King of Pontus, gave the opportunity for the reassertion of Roman military prestige in the East, and a settlement was secured at first temporarily by the victories of Sulla, and then finally by the later campaigns of Pompey. A further ten years saw the defeat of Ariovistus and the acquisition of Gaul by Julius Caesar. The bare citation of these familiar events is sufficient to arouse our admiration for the victories of the army and with it a certain curiosity. How had Rome achieved these successes? Had some new reform been introduced by one of her three greatest generals, which transformed the organization or the tactical dispositions of the legion and lent a fresh vitality to its soldiers? But no such change had taken place. It was the cohort as organized by Marius that conquered Greece and Gaul. Highly as this speaks for the administrative talents of that soldier, it is nevertheless to his immediate successors that the chief praise must be given for the victorious Roman campaigns. Under Marius the cohort was on its trial as a tactical unit. It had effectively resisted, it is true, the precipitate and undisciplined attacks of the Cimbri, but its worth had still to be established against a more experienced enemy. It is to Sulla, then, that a foremost place must be given in the annals of Roman military history, because Sulla was the first to make an effective use of the new formation against an opponent who was a serious rival to the growing Roman state. Mithradates was no novice in the art of war.[1] His large army comprised infantry, cavalry, and archers, and even included chariots armed with scythes—the ancient counterpart of the modern armoured car. No greater proof could be given of the success with which Sulla handled his troops than the determination of Mithradates to reform his own military organization on the model of his enemy's cohorts.[2]

If Sulla was the pioneer in the strategical handling of the cohort and effected its permanent adoption as the tactical unit of the legion, with Pompey and Caesar even greater progress was made in the art of cam-

---

[1] App. Mithr. 42, and see Th. Reinach, 'Mithradate Eupator', pp. 264–75.

[2] Ibid. 87, "τοὺς δ' ἐς ἴλας καὶ σπείρας ἀγχοτάτω τῆς Ἰταλικῆς συντάξεως καταλέγων".

paigning and disciplined leadership.[1] An impartial
survey of the work of the two men is hampered by the
absence of documents written by Pompey himself, so
that our knowledge of his strategy is derived from
the writings of his chief adversary, a biography of
Plutarch, and the unscientific comments of his friend
Cicero. We may perhaps, however, be justified in
claiming Pompey as the superior strategist and Caesar
as the greater leader and sterner disciplinarian.
The so-called abandonment of Italy by Pompey in
49 B. C. was based on what should have proved sound
calculation and foresight. His troops in Italy were
few compared with what Caesar both had and could
raise ; his military reputation was high in the East
and recruits would flock to his standards ; he held
command of the sea, and Italy might be starved out
and Caesar imprisoned and prevented from pursuit
across the Adriatic. That this strategical scheme was
frustrated was due partly to the inefficiency of Pompey's
subordinates entrusted with watching Brundisium and
the intervening channel, and partly to the good fortune
that so often attended Caesar's more hastily planned
actions. Again, Pompey's tactical position at Pharsalus on the slopes of Mount Dogandzis was well
chosen, because, if Caesar were obliged to offer battle
through the failure of his commissariat, he would have

---

[1] Both perhaps found their model in Sertorius, whose strategy
had defeated the generals of the Senate, including Pompey himself, and whose treatment of the Spanish tribes is in many respects
parallel to Caesar's administration in Gaul. (For an account of
Sertorius see Schulten, ' Sertorius ', especially pp. 140–65.)

to fight uphill on ground of Pompey's choosing. Here again Pompey was defeated by the impatient quarrelling and taunting reproaches of his subordinates, and even when driven into battle against his will, his plan of attack on Caesar's undefended right might well have succeeded, if his cavalry had shown any determination or power of resistance. Pompey's tactical schemes were ruined by his failure to command men and to inspire unquestioning discipline among his officers. With Caesar the case is different. At Gergovia[1] and Dyrrachium[2] defeat seemed almost inevitable; but in each instance he was able to turn the scales by the two great characteristics of his genius —rapidity of movement and the power of personality. Similarly the forced march to rescue Q. Cicero from the Nervii, or the dash into Spain between the departure of Pompey from Brundisium and his pursuit of him across the Adriatic, arouse a breathless admiration, just as the stern rebuke to the tenth legion contemptuously addressed as *Quirites*, or the marvellous control of the last line at Pharsalus, command an almost terror-struck appreciation. My purpose, however, is not to develop these attributes of Caesar and Pompey by a detailed examination of their different campaigns,[3] but rather to consider any modifications in command which the division of the Roman army under two generals produced, and to give some idea of the composition and distribution of their legions.

[1] B. G. vii. 50.   [2] B. C. iii. 71.
[3] For this see Rice Holmes, 'Roman Republic', vol. iii, *passim*.

The chief command still lay in theory with the consuls, who were supposed to have the first four legions of each year as their armies. But the actual raising of these legions had become a pure matter of form, and not infrequently they had no more than a paper existence; for after the time of Sulla it became the practice for the consuls to remain in Rome during their year of office. To command the legions in their place, men of military ability like Pompey and Caesar were appointed, and they were given a 'proconsular imperium' in that part of the Roman world where their campaigns were to be conducted. As an outward sign that their legions were not the consular armies, the custom arose of omitting the numbers 1-4 in the enumeration of their forces. Thus Caesar calls his first legion, in 58 B. C., VII,[1] and Pompey does not make use of the consular numbers till he himself is consul in 55 B. C.[2]

With the increase in the size of the armies under the supreme command of one man from a nominal two or four to a strength of anything from eight to twelve legions, the question of the command of the individual legions became of supreme importance. Next below the consuls in seniority were the military tribunes, but this office had now lost much of its former importance. The practice had grown of appointing young men of aristocratic birth, and in many cases they must have failed to show any great efficiency or power of command. For instance, Caesar himself says that the panic in the camp at Vesontio was due, in part at least,

[1] B. G. ii. 28. 4.   Ibid. vi. 1. 2.

to the military tribunes who had followed him from
Rome 'amicitiae causa'.[1] It is a mistake, however,
to suppose that the duties of the tribunes were quite
insignificant. They attended councils of war,[2] and on
the field of battle seem on occasions to have commanded
groups of cohorts,[3] while certain tribunes are specially
thanked by Caesar for their services in defence of
Q. Cicero's camp.[4] On the other hand, as the opportunities grew for legionary commanders to take the
initiative, so the necessity of filling these posts with
men of proved experience became clear. There is no
instance of a tribune commanding a legion in action
during the Gallic War. In their place Caesar started
to appoint *legati* both for the command of individual
legions and as the leaders of expeditionary forces
detached from the main body. This can be illustrated
from several passages in the 'Gallic War'. In the
campaign against Ariovistus, Caesar says 'singulis
legionibus singulos legatos praefecit',[5] and again, in the
winter of 55–54 B. C., he ordered the *legati* 'quos legionibus praefecerat' to build and repair as many ships as
possible for the projected invasion of Britain.[6] Similarly, when his army was distributed over Gaul because
of the difficulty of the food supply, the various areas
were entrusted to picked *legati*. For instance, in
54 B. C. C. Fabius is sent against the Morini, Q. Cicero
against the Nervii, and L. Roscius against the Esubii,

[1] B. G. i. 39. 2.   [2] Ibid. v. 28. 3.
[3] Ibid. ii. 26. 1 and Rice Holmes, 'Caesar's Conquest of Gaul',
ed. 2, p. 566.   [4] B. G. v. 52. 4.
[5] Ibid. i. 52. 1.   [6] Ibid. v. 1. 1.

each with one legion. Three legions are stationed among the Bellovaci under the command of Plancus and Trebonius, both of whom are called *legati*, while a legion and a half are sent against the Eburones under Sabinus and Cotta.[1] The organization of the more senior commands is a transitional stage between the old Republican custom of electing *tribuni militum* and the appointment of *legati* by Augustus as the permanent commanders of the legions. In the Caesarian army the appointment of *legati* to the command of legions appears to have been experimental, and their length of holding office limited by the requirements of the task in hand. It was a makeshift, the benefit of which was so apparent that it was adopted during the first two centuries of the Principate as a permanent solution.

Despite the appointment of *legati* to the command of legions and detachments, it is clear from the writings of Caesar that his chief confidence lay with the centurions. A number of examples from the 'Gallic War' will illustrate this point. When Q. Cicero was surprised at Aduatuca by an attack of the Germans, while his men were out foraging, P. Sextius Baculus, who held the post of *primus pilus* and had been left behind sick in camp, saved the situation by seizing any armour he could find and barring the entrance to Cicero's camp.[2] His example was followed by the other centurions of the cohort which had been left on guard, and such confidence was inspired in the inexperienced soldiers that they held on till relief reached them. After the unsuccessful attack on Gergovia Caesar makes particular.

---

[1] Ibid. v. 24. 2. 5.   [2] Ibid. vi. 38. 1.

mention of the loss of forty-six centurions,[1] and this same insistence on the value of the work of centurions in controlling and disciplining their men comes out in his reference to the losses sustained by the twelfth legion in 57 B. C. through an unexpected attack of the Nervii: 'quartae cohortis omnibus centurionibus occisis . . . reliquarum cohortium omnibus fere centurionibus aut vulneratis aut occisis '.[2] Lastly, in the mutiny already mentioned at Vesontio in 58 B. C., Caesar summoned all the centurions to a meeting and upbraided them with questioning his command, and not enforcing strict discipline among the common soldiers.[3]

The reason of course for the trust which Caesar had in his centurions was that they were men of military experience, who had in many cases served him for years, and willingly remained on after the completion of their *legitima stipendia*. After all, even the *legati* of his own choosing cannot have had much experience of war. Labienus was no doubt an exception, but it is difficult to believe that Q. Cicero was much of a soldier, while Cotta and Sabinus disagreed, and the worse strategist won the debate and brought disaster on his troops.[4] Under the Principate the chances of securing good *legati* were, as we shall see, no less precarious, and it is surprising that the Roman army reached such a degree of efficiency under comparatively inexperienced generals. Part of the explanation must surely lie in the influence and discipline of the centurions.

---

[1] B. G. vii. 51. 1.
[3] Ibid. i. 40. 1.
[2] Ibid. ii. 25. 1.
[4] Ibid. v. 81. 8.

The long duration of the campaigns of Caesar and Pompey in Gaul and the East involved the retention by each of them of the same legions for more than a year. It is consequently not surprising to discover that the legions begin to have permanent numbers, and that the system of annual renumbering, which we observed in the last chapter, becomes gradually obsolete. The basis upon which the numbering depended is not, however, easy to discover. Caesar's first legion in 58 B. C. was numbered VII, and subsequently, in addition to legion VI and the *Alaudae*,[1] he added a number of legions which continued the numerical series at least up to XLI. There is also an interesting inscription, which describes the career of a centurion of this date, who was successively centurion of the eighteenth legion in Lentulus Spinther's army and centurion of the second legion of Pompey. ' N. Granonius N. F. CΛΙ (i. e. his cognomen, perhaps Catulus) domo Luceria IIIIvir (i. e. a municipal magistrate) centurio Cornelei Spinteri legio. XIIX et Cn. Pompei Mag. legione secunda.'[2] L. Spinther was governor of the province of Cilicia from 56–53 B. C., and it seems as if Granonius' centurionship must fall within this period and that subsequently he served in Pompey's second legion, which only received this identity in 55 B. C., when Pompey was consul.[3] An attempt has been made to construct a West to East system of enumeration on this evidence,[4] but the most probable

---

[1] See p. 57.   [2] Dess. 2224.
[3] B. G. viii. 54. 2.
[4] Von Dom. ' Die Heere d. Bürgerkr.', in Neue Heidelb. Jahrb.

solution is that there was no permanent official numbering of the legions at this period. Pompey and Caesar,
because of the size of their armies, naturally gave their
legions permanent numbers, being careful, if they were
not consuls, to avoid the numbers I–IV, and, for convenience sake, each other's enumeration. The commanders of smaller forces, as the provincial governors
of Macedonia and Cilicia, did not have permanent
numbers for their legions, and the explanation of legion
XVIII in Spinther's army may be on the lines of
Mommsen's suggestion, namely, that Spinther calculated the number of legions in the Roman army of that
year and came to the conclusion, perhaps on the score
of his own seniority, that the legion in which Granonius
served was number XVIII.[1]

In the years 51 and 50 B. C. efforts were made to
effect a compromise between Caesar and Pompey.
These were fruitless in their results, and the Roman
Republic became divided into two camps. As the
army in consequence consisted entirely of legions
owing loyalty to either Caesar or Pompey, it may be
of interest to try and trace the number of legions
raised by each in the course of the Civil War, the titles
which they held, and, if possible, their distribution and
composition.

In 51 B. C. Caesar had eleven legions, which bore the
numbers I and VI–XV inclusive, but in the following
year, on the order of the Senate, he handed over I and
XV to Pompey for a contemplated expedition against

iv. 1894, p. 161, refuted by Kubitschek, s. v. 'Legio', in P–W.
xii, p. 1208.   [1] Dess. 2224, n. 4.

Parthia[1] which did not materialize. These legions were retained by Pompey and were subsequently numbered I and III in his army.[2] Caesar was thus left with nine legions. To fill the vacancy in his army he started to recruit fresh troops and certainly raised one legion from the Transalpine Gauls. This legion, which was distinguished by the Gallic name *Alaudae*,[3] was peculiar because it was not composed of Roman citizens, who, in theory, were alone eligible for legionary service. The legion itself, according to Suetonius, did not receive the franchise till some unspecified date after its enrolment, and the title *Alaudae*, as opposed to a definite number, is an indication of this fact. By 47 B.C., however, it is called *legio* V,[4] which implies that a *iusta legio* had by now been organized with an *aquila* and *signa*, and the enfranchisement of the soldiers may perhaps coincide with this event.[5] Whether Caesar raised a second legion in this year to take the place of the second dispatched to Pompey is not clear from the sources. Cicero, writing to Atticus, says 'nunc legiones XI',[6] which is supported by Florus, who compares the forces of the two sides, 'hinc XI legiones inde XVIII '.[7] On the other hand, Suetonius[8] and Plutarch[9] only credit Caesar with ten legions, and Florus' statement may well refer to the strength of the opposing armies at Pharsalus. Therefore the choice

---

[1] B. G. viii. 54. 2. 3.
[2] B. C. iii. 88–2.
[3] Suet. Caes. 24.
[4] Bell. Afric. 1. 5.
[5] So Ritterling, s.v. 'Legio', in P-W. xii, p. 1564.
[6] Ad Att. vii. 7. 6.
[7] Florus, iv. 2. 5.
[8] Suet. Caes. 29.
[9] Plut. Pompey 58.

lies between Cicero, whose figures are frequently inaccurate, and the joint testimony of Suetonius and Plutarch. Most probably Caesar started in 50 B. C. to recruit fresh troops to fill the gap in his army, but, not wishing to give the impression that he was preparing to fight against the authority of the Senate, refrained from organizing the new material into a *iusta legio* till the next year.[1]   When this legion was formed it probably bore the number XVI.

When Caesar learnt of the *Senatus consultum ultimum* passed on January 7th, 49 B. C., he immediately accepted the challenge and advanced with legion XIII to Ariminum,[2] where he was later joined by two more veteran legions, VIII and XII.[3]   An extensive *dilectus* was carried out in Italy and Transpadane Gaul, while desertions from the Pompeian troops, which were supposed to be holding up Caesar's advance at Corfinium, Sulmo, and neighbouring towns, greatly swelled his army.   Before proceeding to Brundisium, Caesar had obtained five new legions, which may be assumed to have borne the numbers XVI-XX.   Of these, two legions,[4] formed out of the *cohortes Domitianae* which surrendered at Corfinium, were dispatched to Sicily and subsequently fought under Curio in Africa. With the remaining six legions[5] at his disposal Caesar marched to Brundisium, where on his arrival he found that the two consuls had already crossed to Dyrrachium

---

[1] So Rice Holmes, 'Roman Republic', iii, p. 356.
[2] B. C. i. 8. 1.   [3] Ibid. i. 15. 8 and i. 18. 5.
[4] Ibid. i. 30. 2 (accepting Hoffmann's emendation), and see How, Cl. Q. 1924, p. 65.   [5] B. C. i. 25. 1.

with a large part of Pompey's army. Being compelled
to abandon for the present the project of pursuit
across the Adriatic, he decided to win over the two
Spains to his side. Meanwhile, the conscription of
fresh legions had been proceeding apace, and Caesar
dispatched one legion to Sardinia [1] and two more with
Curio to Sicily to secure the corn supply.[2] These
latter legions in all probability became the garrison
troops of Lilybaeum and Messana.[3]

For the campaign in Spain Caesar sent Fabius on in
advance with three legions which had been spending
the winter at Narbo,[4] and ordered three more 'quae
longius hiemabant', probably at Matisco, to follow.[5]
These legions were almost certainly veterans, but in
the actual fighting we only hear of the numbers IX and
XIV.[6] If, however, it is fair to assume that the three
veteran legions which had accompanied Caesar into
Italy were not called upon to make the long march into
Spain, but were ordered to rest in Italy, the remaining
four legions must have been numbered VI, VII, X,
and XI. Meanwhile, Marséilles was being besieged by
three legions under Trebonius. Their numbers are
not known, but they were, in all probability, newly
formed units.[7] If it is right to suppose that Caesar
numbered his legions in sequence in the order in which

---

[1] Ibid. i. 30. 2.   [2] Ibid. ii. 23. 1.
[3] Ibid. iii. 101. 8; Bell. Afric. 1. 1; and see Rice Holmes,
o. c., iii, p. 369, n. 5 (contra von Dom. 'Die Heere d. Bürgerkr.',
p. 165).
[4] B. C. i. 87. 1.   [5] Ibid. i. 87. 3 and i. 89. 2.
[6] Ibid. i. 45. 1 and i. 46. 4.
[7] Ibid. i. 86. 4 and Rice Holmes, o. c., iii, pp. 884–7.

they were recruited, it follows that by the end of the Ilerda campaign there were fifteen legions of recruits in his army ; for we hear of two legions numbered XXI and XXX arriving to form part of the garrison of the Spanish provinces.[1] Further, a legion numbered XXVII[2] accompanies the expeditionary force to Pharsalus. The presence of this single new legion in Caesar's army against Pompey is a little surprising, unless it had had some previous experience. Perhaps it was selected because it had taken part in the siege of Marseilles. If so, then the two remaining legions at Marseilles were, in all probability, numbered either XXV and XXVI or XXVIII and XXIX, all four of which subsequently went with Caesar to Africa in 47 B.C.[3] After the Ilerda campaign the Pompeian forces which had opposed Caesar in Spain were disbanded,[4] except two legions of Varro called II and *legio vernacula* which, as its title shows, had been enlisted from local sources in Spain.[5] These two legions along with XXI and XXX remain in Spain, and later another legion, raised locally with the title *legio* V,[6] is added. The remaining legions returned to Placentia.

It is now time to consider the forces on the side of Pompey, and here the numbers, both collectively and individually, are much harder to ascertain. In 51 B.C. Pompey has at Ariminum an unspecified number of troops,[7] but in the next year, as we have seen, he received two legions from Caesar and this brought his

---

[1] Bell. Alex. 53. 5.   [2] B.C. iii. 34. 2.
[3] Bell. Afric. 60. 1.   [4] B.C. i. 87. 5.   [5] Ibid. ii. 20. 4.
[6] Bell. Alex. 53. 5.   [7] How, Cicero, Select Letters, 30. 4.

total available in 50 B. C. up to ten.[1]   By desertion he
lost over four legions in Italy, but he recruited fresh
levies on his way to Brundisium, including eight
hundred slaves who were organized as cavalry.[2]   Caesar
says that Pompey transported five legions to Epirus,[3]
and that he had lost one hundred and thirty cohorts of
Roman citizens in Italy and Spain.[4]   As a round number this may be regarded as substantially correct; for
forty-two cohorts 'et non nullae . . . aliae' deserted to
Caesar in Italy,[5] and seven legions or seventy cohorts
were disbanded by Caesar after the Ilerda campaign.[6]
There were, besides, other Pompeian forces in the
provinces, notably two legions with Scipio in Syria [7]
and one in Africa.[8]   Pompey's force at Pharsalus consisted then of the five legions which he had transported
from Italy, one from Crete, one from Cilicia, two from
Asia newly recruited by Lentulus, and the two under
Scipio's command from Syria.[9]   The strength of these
eleven legions, according to Caesar's reckoning, was
45,000,[10] and in addition there were fifteen cohorts left
behind at Dyrrachium and seven cohorts detailed to
guard the camp at Pharsalus.   The figures seem high,
especially when compared with Caesar's eight legions,
which could only muster 22,000.[11]   Further, Pompey
had suffered losses, as, for instance, in the attempt of
Otacilius to oppose Antony's landing in Epirus,[12] and

[1] B. C. i. 6. 1.   [2] Ibid. iii. 4. 4.   [3] Ibid. iii. 4.1.
[4] Ibid. iii. 10. 5.
[5] Ibid. i. 12. 1, i. 15. 5-7, i. 18. 1, i. 24. 3-4.
[6] Ibid. i. 85. 6 and i. 87. 5.   [7] Ibid. i. 31. 2 and iii. 4. 3.
[8] Ibid. ii. 23. 4.   [9] Ibid. iii. 4. 1-3.   [10] Ibid. iii. 88. 5.
[11] Ibid. iii. 89. 2.   [12] Ibid. iii. 28. 6.

on the day of the six battles near Dyrrachium, where the total casualties were 2,000.[1]   On the other hand, Pompey's men had not, like Caesar's, suffered from malaria;[2] some cohorts had found their way under Afranius from Spain, and time-expired veterans (*evocati*) had volunteered their services.[3]   These additions might balance the casualties, and the figure 45,000 is not impossible.   On the opposite side the exact identity of the legions composing Caesar's force is not certain.   Twelve legions were ordered by Caesar to assemble at Brundisium for the campaign.[4]   Actually seven were transported with Caesar, and he was joined by four more under Antony.[5]   The following legions were certainly present : VI, VIII, IX, X, XI, XII of veteran legions, and XXVII from the recently recruited,[6] and the gaps may be filled with tolerable certainty.   In addition to VIII and XII, XIII had been resting in Italy and may be safely added to the list.   Secondly, on general grounds, it is natural that Caesar would use experienced troops against Pompey, and would not risk recruits or soldiers that had recently fought for the other side.   The veteran legions that had been engaged on the Ilerda campaign had returned to Placentia, and were consequently available.   Therefore the remaining three legions of the total force may well have been VII and XIV and the *Alaudae*, which was almost veteran when compared with the recently enlisted troops.

---

[1] B. C. iii. 53. 1.   [2] Ibid. iii. 87. 2.   [3] Ibid. iii. 88. 5.
[4] Ibid. iii. 6. 3 and iii. 29. 2.   [5] Ibid. iii. 2. 2.
[6] Ibid. iii. 34. 2–3, iii. 45. 2, iii. 89. 1 ; Bell. Alex. 33. 3.

After the battle of Pharsalus Caesar organized the defeated Pompeians into legions for his own use, two of which, XXXVI and XXXVII, are definitely mentioned in the 'Commentarii'.[1] Caesar himself set out for Egypt with two legions, VI and XXVII,[2] and ordered others 'quas ex Pompeianis militibus confecerat' to follow him.[3] Meanwhile, Domitius Calvinus, who had been entrusted with the administration of Asia and the neighbouring provinces, was drawn into a war against Pharnaces. His force was composed at first of three legions,[4] one of which, XXXVI, he keeps in his own army, and dispatches the other two to Caesar in Egypt. One of these, XXXVII, arrived at Alexandria, but the other was diverted on some expedition into Syria, and is rightly identified by von Domaszewski with the legion which subsequently served under the command of Sextus Caesar.[5] In view of the fact that this legion ought to have joined Caesar, and that the latter ordered 'the newly organized legions of Pompeians' to be sent to him, it follows that it was in all probability numbered either XXXV or XXXVIII. Domitius Calvinus replaced these two legions by a legion raised in the Pontic district 'ex tumultuariis militibus', which had the title *legio Pontica* but no number,[6] while King

---

[1] Bell. Alex. 34. 3 and 9. 3.

[2] Ibid. 33. 3. ; cf. B. C. iii. 106. 1. Perhaps he started with only legion VI (so Judeich on App. B. C. ii. 89 : see Rice Holmes, o. c., iii, p. 484).

[3] B. C. iii. 107. 1.   [4] Bell. Alex. 34. 3.

[5] Ibid. 34. 3 ; cf. 66. 1.

[6] Ibid. 34. 5. This shows that its soldiers were not Roman citizens.

Deiotarus sent two legions of his own to assist in the fighting against Pharnaces.[1]

The identification of XXXVI and XXXVII, and possibly of XXXV or XXXVIII, with the legions organized after Pharsalus, and the fact that XXX, which was now forming part of the garrison of Spain, is the next highest number which we have so far traced, suggests that, if Caesar preserved a definite sequence in his system of enumeration, at some time between the end of the Ilerda campaign and the battle of Pharsalus, legions, numbered certainly XXXI–XXXIV, must have been raised. Two legions were employed in the conquest of Illyricum under the command of Cornificius, who seems to have been there at the time of the battle of Pharsalus,[2] and is certainly in that district when Octavius arrives after Pharsalus is over. This, perhaps, will give a clue to the identification of the two legions. If the operations are in any way contemporary with Pharsalus, it is clear that there was no possibility of employing an ex-Pompeian legion from Pharsalus, and, further, that it was dangerous to make use of the eight cohorts which were garrisoning towns like Apollonia.[3] It follows that the two legions must have been composed of recruits and have come from Italy, and they may tentatively be given the numbers XXXI and XXXII. Further, when Caesar heard during

---

[1] Bell. Alex. 34. 4.   [2] Ibid. 42. 2–3.

[3] B. C. iii. 78. 4 and Rice Holmes, o. c., iii, pp. 476–7. Von Dom.'s theory that Caesar raised four legions after Pharsalus out of Pompey's troops, and that one of these was employed by Cornificius is chronologically unsound ('Die Heere d. Bürgerkr.', p. 171).

his pursuit of Pompey of the trouble in Illyricum,
he sent a dispatch to Gabinius, ordering him to go to
the assistance of Cornificius with the legions of recruits
' quae nuper erant conscriptae '.[1] This auxiliary force
met with a disaster, involving the loss of 2,000 men,
and Vatinius was sent to the rescue with a hurriedly
raised force composed of soldiers of the veteran legions
who had been left behind sick at Brundisium.[2] It is
probable that the force of Gabinius represents freshly
recruited legions numbered XXXIII, XXXIV, and
perhaps XXXV. This increase in the number of
legions may not be as formidable as it appears. The
need for men was pressing, but mere numbers without discipline and training would have been of little
service. Not improbably, therefore, the cohorts and
centuries were organized below their proper strength,
so that by greater individual attention from the instructors the recruits might more quickly become
efficient soldiers.

At the end of the Alexandrine War Caesar started
for Syria with legion VI and left the remainder of the
legions behind at Alexandria.[3] After assigning the
province of Syria and the command of the troops which
were stationed there to Sextus Caesar, Caesar came
into the Pontic district, where he found the legions
which had fought for Domitius against Pharnaces

[1] Bell. Alex. 42. 4.   [2] Ibid. 44. 4.
[3] Ibid. 33. 3. If Suetonius (Caesar 76) is right in saying that
the remaining legions numbered three, in addition to legions
XXVII and XXXVII we must suppose the recruiting of a new
legion (von Dom., o.c., p. 173, accepted by Rice Holmes, o.c.,
iii, p. 503).

greatly depleted.[1]   A short campaign, however, culmi-
nating in the battle of Zela was sufficient to settle the
fate of Pharnaces,[2] and Caesar sent on legion VI to
Italy, reduced, we are told, to 1,000 strong, while
XXXVI and *legio Pontica* remained in Pontus with
Caelius Vinicianus.[3]

On his arrival in Italy Caesar was met by the galling
necessity of quelling a mutiny among his veteran
legions, with his favourite tenth as ringleaders.[4]
Arrears of pay were their complaint, and the promise
of a settlement, after the projected campaign in Africa
was over, did little to allay the trouble.   It was not
till Caesar dismissed the tenth legion, and said that he
would give them what he promised, when he had
conquered with the help of others, that both the tenth
and the other recalcitrant legions begged to be rein-
stated and received an unmerited pardon.   Meanwhile
the Pompeians had rallied in Africa under Scipio and
Labienus.   The former's army is estimated at ten
legions,[5] and the latter states that he has a nondescript
force of 12,000 legionaries.[6]   To meet this opposition
Caesar started preparations in the autumn of 47.   The
veteran legions, perhaps because of their recent revolt,
seem to have collected slowly, and Caesar starts for
Africa with an army composed of five legions of recruits
and the V *Alaudae*.[7]   Later he is joined by four veteran
legions, and at the battle of Uzita the following legions

---

[1] Bell. Alex. 40. 4 (the legions are XXXVI and 'legio
Pontica').   [2] Ibid. 77. 1.
[3] Ibid. 77. 2.   [4] Suet. Caes. 70.
[5] Bell. Afric. 1. 4.   [6] Ibid. 19. 3.   [7] Ibid. 1. 1-5.

can be traced : V *Alaudae*, IX, X, XIII, XIV, XXV, XXVI, XXVIII, XXIX, and one other unnamed legion of recruits which may have been XXX, withdrawn for the occasion from Spain.[1] These legions were not at full strength, because later 3,000 absentees who had been sick or on furlough join their main body.[2] On the opposite side Caesar gives one piece of detail which is of interest. Among Scipio's legions were two numbered IV and VI.[3] This shows that the Pompeians had now a system of enumeration apparently running parallel to that of Caesar, while the nondescript character of Labienus' legions indicates that necessity had driven their leaders to depart from the rule that only Roman citizens might be legionary soldiers.[4]

The battle of Thapsus and the suicide of Scipio at Utica finished the opposition of the Pompeians in Africa, but Pompey's sons determined to make a renewed attempt in Spain to revive the fortune of their side. In this they were aided by the effects of the

[1] In Bell. Afric. 60. 2 three of the four mentioned legions of recruits are certain, i.e. XXVI, XXVIII, XXIX. The Oxford text reads XXV for the fourth in preference to XXX. This may be right, but not for the reason given by the emendator, Nipperdey. It is surely perverse to argue that legion XXX was raised before XXV and that, because it was formed in 49 B.C., it could not be called a legion of recruits. In all probability both XXV and XXX were raised in 49 B.C. and were legions of recruits as compared with the veteran Gallic legions. Not improbably legions XXV and XXVI were the two legions garrisoning Lilybaeum and Messana. (See Rice Holmes, o.c., iii, p. 523, for Nipperdey's and Schneider's theories.)

[2] Bell. Afric. 77. 3.   [3] Ibid. 35. 4.
[4] Ibid. 19. 3 ; cf. p. 63, n. 6.

maladministration of Q. Cassius, who had been left by
Caesar in Spain with a garrison of four legions composed of II, XXI, XXX, and *legio vernacula*, to which
he had added *legio* V.[1] A revolt had taken place
against his authority, and not even his death and the
dispatch of a successor in the person of Trebonius had
really settled the trouble, because, when news was
brought of the approach of Caesar, the two *vernaculae
legiones*, which must be the fifth and the *vernacula* of
Varro's army, deserted to the side of the Pompeians,
whose forces seem to have numbered fifteen legions.[2]
Unfortunately we cannot trace in detail the legions
that composed Caesar's army in Spain, estimated at
eighty cohorts, but mention is made of the following
at the battle of Munda: III, V (*Alaudae*), and X,[3] and
from another passage we may add VI [4] and infer the
loyalty of II, XXI, and XXX. The existence of a
legion numbered III is a little surprising, especially as
it does not appear in the sources before this date, but
the most probable explanation is that, after the death
of Pompey, Caesar, in virtue of his position as consul
and dictator, made use of the consular numbers for his
legions. If Cn. Pompey's taunt that Caesar's army in
Spain was composed of recruits is in any sense true,[5]
then III may be a new legion, and probably two more

---

[1] Bell. Alex. 53. 5.   [2] Bell. Hisp. 7. 4 and 34. 2.
[3] Ibid. 30. 7.
[4] Ibid. 12. 5.   Legions XXVIII and XXX are in Spain after
Caesar's death (Cic. ad Fam. x. 32. 4) and so may also have been
included in his army.
[5] Ibid. 26. 4.

legions were raised called I and IV, which, with the existing II, made up the consular quota.[1]

The defeat of his enemies in the Civil War left Caesar free for the burden of imperial government. With characteristic energy he carried through some necessary reforms at home, and then started to make preparations for a projected campaign against Parthia.[2] The veterans had now received their promised rewards, and were discharged with a donative and settled on the land in Italy.[3] A distant campaign would have been bound to stir up fresh grumbling, and Caesar wisely rewarded their loyal services in the past. But a great campaign, in addition to the garrisoning of the provinces, called for an increase in the army, and the order went out for the recruiting of fresh legions. The number raised is as obscure as the identity of individual legions is difficult. Two inscriptions found at Tuder speak of a legion numbered XLI, which apparently survived into the early Principate, because one of its centurions describes himself as belonging to 'leg. XXXXI Augusti Caesaris'.[4] Further, von Domaszewski[5] has calculated that on the death of Caesar there were thirty-seven legions in the Roman army, and by assuming the discharge of the nine veteran legions and the extinction of six more raised in Italy, he concludes that the legionary numbers actually went up to fifty-one, excluding the *legio Pontica* which never had a number.

[1] See Appendix A, pp. 264–5 (*contra* Ritterling, s.v. 'Legio', P–W. xii, p. 1518).
[2] Suet. Caes. 44.   [3] Ibid. 38.   [4] Dess. 2230, 2231.
[5] 'Die Heere d. Bürgerkr.'

This view necessitates holding that something like
twelve new legions were raised by Caesar after his
final Spanish campaign, and that the numerical series
continued, as though all legions bearing lower numbers
were still in existence. This is hardly credible; it is
more probable, not only that the numbers of legions
that were extinct were used for fresh legions, but that,
when legions had become greatly depleted, a fusion
took place, and while one of the old numbers was used
for the composite legion, the other was left available
for a legion of recruits.

The final period of the Republic, from 44 B.C. till the
battle of Actium, illustrates the same principles of
legionary recruiting. Each side raised the troops
necessary for its own purposes, and probably had its
own system of notation. The secondary sources from
which this period is known do not permit of such
a detailed investigation into the numbers of the legions
employed as the 'Commentarii' of Caesar. To illustrate
the extensive conscription it will, however, be sufficient
to cite the figures given for the opposing armies at
Philippi and Actium. Brutus and Cassius had nineteen,[1] while their opponents *possessed* more than forty
legions.[2] At Actium Antony had thirty-one legions,
nineteen forming the land army,[3] eight serving on the
fleet, and four stationed in Egypt;[4] Octavian had
between forty and forty-five.[5] This represents the
highest pitch of a system of conscription dictated by
the necessities of a civil war. After the battle Octavian

[1] Vell. ii. 65.   [2] Livy, Ep. cxxii.   [3] Plut. Ant. 68.
[4] Orosius, vi. 19.   [5] App. B. C. v. 127.

was left with an army numbering upwards of sixty legions. On him devolved the duty of deciding how many were necessary for the safe protection of the Empire, and of working out a scheme by which the soldiers would serve the state, and owe allegiance to their regimental officers merely as the servants of the government at home.

III

THE AUGUSTAN SYSTEM AND LEGIONS

AFTER the battle of Actium Augustus [1] started to put into effect his scheme of imperial defence. The army had grown to a strength that was far beyond the requirements of a peace establishment, and there was a further difficulty in the situation. Some of the extant legions had fought with Antony and Lepidus; others were Augustus' own soldiers, some of whom had served under Julius Caesar. Augustus' problem was, therefore, not merely the reduction of the strength of the army, but the much more difficult question how to constitute an adequate imperial force from the variety of troops that were to be found in the Roman Empire. The choice lay between three alternative policies. The legions of Antony and Lepidus might be disbanded and their soldiers settled in military colonies : or a selection of legions might be made from the remnants of the armies of the triumvirs : or the whole idea of a professional army might be given up and a system of national service substituted in its place. The first two solutions differed from each other only in detail, and the problem therefore resolved itself into a choice between national service and a professional army. Augustus determined to maintain the system of the Republic.

[1] For convenience I use Octavian's later title 'Augustus' throughout this chapter.

This decision has not passed uncriticized, and arguments can be advanced that might at first sight make it seem a strange, if not a mistaken, policy. The animosities aroused by a civil war die slowly, and peace may, perhaps, be most surely and quickly restored by giving as many citizens as possible an opportunity of working for the state. In an empire of wide territories and long frontiers the army is necessarily the most important public service. If, then, Augustus had substituted a citizen militia for a professional army, he might have succeeded in making men forget the past history of the individual legions and their leaders, with the jealousies and enmities that had caused the civil war. Secondly, national service was a possible remedy for unemployment, and the state would have less to fear from the discontented grumblings of veterans clamouring for farms and then refusing to live on them. The acquisition, too, of some military training by all citizens would be advantageous. The time might well be anticipated when Rome would have to face incursions of barbarians over her northern and eastern frontiers. If she could supplement the mobilized army by detachments of men who were not raw recruits but had served their time, the danger would be more efficiently and expeditiously averted. Lastly, through national service Rome and her provinces might have been drawn more closely together and the ground prepared for a uniformly constituted empire.

Whatever force these arguments may have in theory is overridden by a closer examination of the political situation after Actium. The time had come for some form of monarchy, but even if Augustus was at first welcomed as the saviour of society and no objection was raised to the fictitious combination of autocracy with the Republican constitution, without the army there could be no guarantee of the continuity of the Princeps' position. Nor were civil disturbances unknown in the first ten years of the Principate, and the conspiracies of Murena and Egnatius [1] might have fostered more serious revolts if the only state troops had been a short-service militia. Politically, therefore, it was imperative for the first Princeps to maintain his position through the support of an experienced army. From the financial and military standpoints, too, there were serious objections to the abolition of a professional army. If the existing legions were disbanded, their soldiers would have to be recompensed both for their past services and for the sudden and unexpected termination of their engagements. This would have involved large donatives and the still more difficult problem of finding employment for veterans. Some of them might have been retained as instructors for the new army, but this would hardly have affected the average common soldier. If, on the other hand, a system of military colonies had been attempted on a larger scale than was actually carried out, to provide the necessary money would have proved an insoluble problem. Financial administration had always been the weak spot in the Republican government, and there was little money to spare from the treasury in Rome.

[1] Suet. Aug. 19.

But the military aspect was the most vital. The outlying provinces had only recently been conquered. Gaul was as yet hardly organized as part of the Roman Empire, and the frontiers were not clearly demarcated. Revolts inside the provinces or invasions from beyond the frontiers could only be suppressed by a strong system of garrison defence, and for this only disciplined and experienced troops could be safely employed. The problem too was urgent ; for we hear of Augustus himself taking the field against the Cantabrians in 25 B.C., and unsettled conditions were reported from Pannonia, Rhaetia, and the Maritime Alps. In retaining an army which he could trust, Augustus showed himself a practical and far-sighted statesman, and the merits of his policy are recognized by Dio in his review of the Empire, when he puts into the mouth of Maecenas the following advice.[1] 'You will be wise to maintain a permanent force (στρατιώτας ἀθανάτους) raised from the citizens (i. e. legions), the subjects, and the allies (i. e. auxilia) distributed throughout the provinces as necessity requires. . . . We cannot rely on forces called out for the occasion owing to the distance which separates us from the borders of the Empire. If we allow all our subjects of military age to have arms and to undergo military training, there will be civil war ; but if we check all military activities, we shall run the risk of having nothing but raw and untrained troops when we need an army to help us.'

If expediency is the justification of Augustus' professional army, the same defence may be urged for the

[1] Dio, lii. 27.

way in which he carried out his scheme. An army selected entirely from his own legions would inevitably have given the impression of a desire to stress the victory of Actium as the triumph of Roman arms over foreigners. On the other hand, a judicious selection of legions from the armies of Antony and Lepidus was an admission that these legions were Roman, even if they had fought in the cause of unsuccessful aspirants to monarchy. Further, the legions of Antony were probably largely recruited from the East, and were in consequence composed of soldiers speaking Greek and accustomed to the climatic conditions of Syria and Egypt. They might, therefore, be profitably retained in the areas from which they were recruited, and we shall see in a later chapter that this was the policy adopted under the Principate with regard to the army of the Eastern provinces ; doubtless it had a precedent in the example set by Augustus himself.

There is, then, in a sense, nothing new about the Augustan military organization. The professional army was preferred to a citizen militia ; the legions left over from the armies of the triumvirs were retained, as far as it was feasible ; the actual internal machinery of the legion itself was unchanged. But there were two serious defects in the Republican system which Augustus tried to remedy. All through the Republic the military finances had been chaotic. No attempt seems to have been made to budget for the requirements of the army in any year, nor to create a fund from which the discharge donatives might be paid to the time-expired soldiers. Long service and no donative were the complaints which stirred even Caesar's veteran legions to the verge of open mutiny, and Caesar could only reconcile them by promising to pay what was due out of the booty of his next campaign. This hand-to-mouth existence was perhaps inevitable during a period of civil war, but was impossible in peace time. Augustus found at least a partial remedy for the evil in the creation of a military treasury (*aerarium militare*), which was fed by a five per cent. tax on inheritances and a one per cent. tax on auction sales in Rome.[1] It is clear that this new treasury, even if supplemented by free-will offerings from the Princeps, would take years before it could meet all the demands made on it, and it is not surprising to find the soldiers in Pannonia and Germany in 14 A. D. making use of the accession of a new Princeps to urge their old complaints of poor pay and long service.[2] However, the establishment of the *aerarium militare* was the first real attempt to treat the question of discharge donatives as a business proposition, and that it was regarded by Augustus' successors as a sound principle may be gathered from Tiberius' refusal to reduce permanently the duration of legionary service from twenty to sixteen years, because the military treasury would not be able to meet the increased demands upon it.[3] The second evil which characterized the last century of the Republic was the enormous increase in the actual number of the legions, which individual generals raised as they

[1] Mon. Anc. 17 ; Suet. Aug. 49 ; T. A. i. 78. 2.
[2] T. A. i. 17. 6.   [3] Ibid. i. 78. 2.

required them. After Actium Augustus was left with something approaching sixty legions. This force was obviously greatly in excess of the requirements of imperial defence, and Augustus reduced his army to a strength which has been variously represented by different scholars, and which will now be discussed.

Mommsen [1] was of the opinion that Augustus reduced his legions to eighteen in number, of which twelve belonged to his own original army and six to those of Antony and Lepidus, and that these legions were numbered I–XII with duplicates. This total remained unchanged till the Pannonian rising of 6 A.D., when Augustus added eight new legions numbered XIII–XX. Three years later three legions, numbered XVII–XIX, were destroyed in the Varian disaster at *Saltus Teutoburgensis*, and to replace these Augustus recruited two fresh legions numbered XXI and XXII, so that the total was twenty-five, which agrees with Tacitus' statistics for the year 23 A.D. [2]

In support of this opinion Mommsen put forward the following arguments. 1. All the legions known to us before 6 A.D. are included in the series I–XII. 2. The legions which have duplicate numbers are all below XII in numerical order, and so may come from the triumvirs' armies. 3. The legions consecutively numbered above XII are all found on the Rhine or the Danube frontier, and so were recruited especially for the campaigns of 6 A.D. and the following years, whereas the legions below the number XII are found indiscriminately in the other provinces. 4. Augustus

[1] Res Gestae divi Augusti, p. 70.　　　[2] T. A. iv. 5.

established a number of colonies composed of veteran soldiers, particularly in the provinces of Spain and Gallia Narbonensis, and the legions to which they belonged are recorded on coins. All the legions thus described in numismatic evidence belong to a series included in the numbers I–XII.

These arguments as presented by Mommsen, which have been accepted by many scholars, have at first sight a cumulative force which amounts to probability. A fresh examination of the evidence, however, by Hardy, in his article on 'The Legions in the Pannonian Rising ',[1] has exposed the weakness of the theory, and the latter scholar has suggested a modified view of his own, which must next be examined.

In reply to Mommsen, Hardy puts forward the following arguments, which are intended to answer the four points that have been cited above. 1. Although it is true that we do not hear of any legions numbered above XII before 6 A. D., we do not possess definite evidence for the existence of each of the eighteen legions inclusive of I-XII. For instance, III *Cyrenaica* can only be inferred as existing from its *cognomen*, which is supposed to prove that it belonged to Lepidus' army, while there is no evidence for the existence of III *Augusta*, IV *Scythica*, VI *Ferrata*, and IX *Hispana*. In view, therefore, of our incomplete knowledge of legions numbered I–XII, it is unsafe to argue for the non-existence before 6 A. D. of XIII–XX. 2. With the exception of legion X, all other duplicates occur between I–VI; therefore the argument that XIII–XX are later in date than I–XII

[1] Roman Studies (Series 1), p. 162.

applies more or less to the series VII–XII. 3. Legions
XIII–XVI are not found on the Rhine or Danube
frontier till 14 A.D., but, if Suetonius is right in saying
that Tiberius had fifteen legions in his army in 6 A.D.,
it is probable that there must have been a redistribution of the legions before then, and there is nothing
to show that XIII–XVI had not been moved from
the Eastern provinces to Pannonia for this concentration. 4. The argument from coins is not conclusive.
Only eleven of the eighteen legions can be proved
from this source to have existed in the early years of
Augustus, and consequently the same objection applies
here as in point one, namely, that the existence of
the remaining seven is as doubtful as the eight which
Mommsen holds did not come into being till after
6 A.D.

Hardy then goes on to give his own theory. Augustus
retained twenty-two of the original legions (or possibly
twenty-three, if it is assumed that a legion, numbered
V, was destroyed in the disaster of Lollius in 16 B.C.
in Germany), which were numbered I–XVI with duplicates. In 6 A.D. XVII–XIX were recruited in Rome,
and Tiberius added XX, which was raised in Pannonia ;
then, after the Varian disaster XXI and XXII were
enlisted. In support of this opinion Hardy puts forward
the following arguments. 1. Legions XIII and XIV
are called *gemina*, and Caesar tells us that this means
a legion made out of two.[1] Mommsen in order to
support his theory has to maintain that *gemina* means
' simultaneously raised ' ; but, apart from the fact that

[1] B. C. iii. 4. 1.

this contradicts the authority of Caesar, it is strange
that this title should have been confined to XIII and
XIV, and not have been given to all legions numbered
XIII–XX, which, on Mommsen's hypothesis, were
simultaneously recruited.   Further, XIII has the lion
for the emblem on its standard and XIV the capricorn ;
if they were twin legions they would naturally have
the same sign, and if they were raised by Augustus we
should expect this to be the capricorn.[1]   2. Tacitus
makes Maroboduus say that in 6 A.D. he was opposed
by twelve legions.[2]   If this is so, and still more if
Suetonius' figures of fifteen legions are accepted, how
could the rest of the Empire have been garrisoned by
either six or three legions ?   3. Mommsen's third
argument about legions consecutively numbered being
found together in the same province applies with
peculiar force to XVII–XIX, which are grouped
together in Lower Germany immediately after the
Pannonian rebellion.   We know of no other instance
of three consecutively numbered legions serving together in the same province, and it follows that
Augustus sent them there to take the place of three
legions which were dispatched to help Tiberius in
Pannonia.   The absence of legion XX, so far from
destroying this contention, really confirms it, because,
whereas XVII–XIX were recruited in Rome, Tiberius
raised XX for his own requirements in Pannonia, and
this, Hardy thinks, is reflected in Germanicus' address
to legions I and XX in Annals i. 42, where he accepts
von Domaszewski's interpretation of the passage.

[1] See Appendix A (b), p. 262.   [2] T. A. ii. 46. 2.

Hardy's thesis, which apparently he still adhered to in his recent edition of the *Monumentum Ancyranum*,[1] cannot, however, be accepted. As far as it corrects the opinion of Mommsen it is satisfactory, but on its more positive side it seems to distort certain statements of Tacitus and Velleius, and to disregard the important evidence of Egyptian papyri.

Hardy maintains that XVII–XIX were raised 'with all possible haste'[2] by Augustus in Rome to take the place of three legions sent from Germany to assist Tiberius in Illyricum in 6 A.D. He argues that it was 'the obvious course' for Tiberius to take some of the German legions because of their close proximity; but to support this contention he is obliged to hold that two statements of Velleius[3] are chronologically in the wrong order, and he seems further to misunderstand another statement of the same author.[4] The situation was as follows. A great joint attack was planned for the year 6 A.D. against Maroboduus, with a view to the conquest of the land between the Rhine and the Elbe. Tiberius was to command the force from Illyricum and Sentius Saturninus the army from Germany. Great preparations were made to bring the legions up to full strength, and even cohorts of freedmen called *cohortes voluntariorum* were formed.[5] But during the first campaign Pannonia broke into rebellion. The number of Tiberius' legions can be gathered from two passages in Velleius which are clearly, despite Hardy, dependent

---

[1] O. c., p. 35, n. 1.   [2] O. c., p. 177.
[3] Vell. ii. 112. 4 and ii. 113. 1.
[4] I. e. 'ex transmarinis provinciis'.   [5] Dio, lv. 31.

upon each other. Velleius says that A. Caecina and
Plautius Silvanus brought five legions ' ex transmarinis
provinciis', which narrowly missed suffering a defeat
at the hands of the Pannonians, who had now broken
into revolt.[1] However, they reached Tiberius' head-
quarters, and then Velleius says 'iunctis exercitibus
quique sub Caesare fuerant, quique ad eum venerant,
contractisque in una castra decem legionibus'.[2] Clearly,
then, Tiberius at the start of 6 A. D. had five legions
('exercitus qui in Illyrico merebat'),[3] and, feeling
that this was insufficient, he had sent orders before
the outbreak of the revolt for reinforcements to come
to him 'ex transmarinis provinciis'. Now in 44 B.C.
Antony had ordered his army 'ex transmarinis provinciis' to assemble at Brundisium,[4] and there is no
doubt that this means the Macedonian legions. In
the present passage it is noteworthy that there are
two consular commanders, Caecina and Silvanus. This
implies that all the legions did not come from the
same province, and, further, five legions is too large
a force for the province of Macedonia. The conclusion
is clear. Caecina, probably anachronistically styled by
Dio 'τῆς πλησιοχώρου Μυσίας ἄρχων',[5] brought the three
Macedonian legions to help Tiberius, and he was joined
by Silvanus with either two legions from Syria or one
from Syria and one from Egypt. This force had not
arrived when Tiberius set out against Maroboduus,
because it was nearly overwhelmed by the rebels, who

[1] Vell. ii. 112. 4.   [2] Ibid. ii. 113. 1.   [3] Ibid. ii. 109. 5.
[4] Ibid. ii. 61. 2.   Here I follow Ritterling, s.v. 'Legio', P–W.
xii, p. 1235.   [5] Dio, lv. 29. 3.

had not yet broken into revolt when Tiberius crossed
the Danube, but it was concentrated by Tiberius in
the winter of 6–7 A.D. with the Illyrican army, and
this brought the total of Tiberius' army to Velleius'
figure of ten legions. If this is the right interpretation of Velleius, then there is no need to accuse him
of chronological blunderings, and the total of ten
legions is arrived at without any assumption of the
withdrawal of three legions from Germany. But what
of Tacitus' statement. that Maroboduus says that in
6 A. D. he was opposed by twelve Roman legions?[1]
We have seen that the Illyrican army numbered five
legions, and the evidence of Velleius points to the fact
that in Germany on the Rhine there were five, or
possibly even six, legions ; for after the loss of three
legions in 9 A. D. L. Asprenas has still two left,[2] and
a garrison at Aliso may account for a sixth. In
addition, archaeological discoveries at Oberhausen,[3]
strengthened by a mutilated inscription which appears
to mention a 'legatus pro praetore in Vindolicis',[4]
show that at this time there was a standing force in
Vindelicia and Rhaetia. This implies that the district
was not, as subsequently, organized into a province
under a *procurator*, but was controlled by a Roman
force of one or two legions, and this arrangement probably lasted till 9 A. D. or at least till the revolt of
6 A. D. Tacitus' total of twelve legions is therefore

[1] T. A. ii. 46. 2.   [2] Vell. ii. 120. 3.

[3] Ritt. Zeits. d. Hist. Vereins f. Schwaben und Neuburg, xl.
1914, p. 173.

[4] Dess. 847 (adopting Ritterling's reading legato pro [pr. in]
Vindol(iciis) in P–W. xii, p. 1226).

derived from the five Illyrican legions, the five or six Rhine legions, and the two or one legions in Vindelicia. Lastly, if Suetonius' figure of fifteen legions [1] is to be accepted, it is safest to assume that he included in the combined armies of Tiberius and Saturninus the three Macedonian legions, which in fact did not operate north of the Save and Drave.

Hardy's first argument, therefore, for the recruiting of three legions in Rome in 6 A. D. fails because there is no evidence that there were three legions withdrawn from Germany to Illyricum in that year, whose place the hypothetical three new legions are supposed to have taken. And there is further evidence against Hardy affecting not only legions XVII–XIX but also legion XX. Referring to the disaster of 9 A.D., Velleius describes XVII–XIX as 'exercitus omnium fortissimus, disciplina, manu, experientiaque bellorum inter Romanos milites princeps'.[2] How can such a panegyric, even allowing for exaggeration, be applied to three newly raised legions? Even if von Domaszewski's suggestion that the recruits were strengthened by some veterans be accepted, the appellation 'princeps inter Romanos milites' is absurd for what at the best must have been very raw material. Further, it is most improbable that three newly raised legions would be brigaded together, especially on such an important frontier as Germany. If there had been such an extensive recruiting of new legions as Hardy supposes, it is much more probable that some of them would have been sent to Spain, and the Spanish legions moved to

[1] Suet. Tib. 16.   [2] Vell. ii. 119. 2.

Germany to form the nucleus of the defence on the Rhine.

The recruiting of legion XX by Tiberius is made to depend upon a passage in the Annals. Germanicus is addressing the mutinous troops, and he says ' primane et vicensima legiones, illa signis a Tiberio acceptis, tu tot proeliorum socia, tot praemiis aucta, egregiam duci vestro gratiam refertis ? ' [1] Supporters of the view that legion XX did not exist before 6 A. D. eagerly accept von Domaszewski's interpretation of this passage. The scene, we are told, is in the camp of the first legion. The first legion is drawn up in front, the twentieth remains in the background. Consequently ' *tu* ' in the passage quoted means legion I and ' *illa* ' is ' that legion standing over there ', the twentieth—a most ingenious interpretation, but obviously only invented to support a preconceived theory of the origin of XX. [2] If, on the other hand, we take the passage in a normal grammatical way, Germanicus is reminding legion I that it received its *signa* from Tiberius, and legion XX of its long, distinguished career. [3] But how is this statement that legion I received its standards from Tiberius to be explained ? Two possible and similar solutions suggest themselves. There is evidence from coins belonging to the military colonies in Spain that legion I may have taken part in the fighting connected with the Cantabrian War of 25 B. C. [4] It is also stated in the literary sources that

[1] T. A. i. 42. 6.   [2] See Furneaux's note on T. A. i. 42. 6.
[3] Dess. 2270, 2651, and Appendix A, p. 271.
[4] Cohen 1², p. 152, nos. 632–4.

the Romans suffered severe defeats, and one legion in particular seems to have disgraced itself.[1]   There is no further trace of this old legion I, and the legion of that number in Germany has on one stone the *cognomen* *Germanica*.[2]   It is not improbable, therefore, that the old legion I was reformed in Germany by Tiberius at some period during his command of the armies of the Rhine and perhaps after the Varian disaster, and so Germanicus can remind the soldiers that they had received their standards from Tiberius.[3]   An alternative solution with similar results may be found in stressing the strict meaning of *signa*, which are the standards of the maniples as opposed to the *aquila* or legionary standard. If Germanicus had wanted to state that legion I had been formed by Tiberius, would he not have made mention of the receiving of its *aquila* from him, in the same way as, in the war against Civilis, Cerialis encourages the soldiers of legion II *Adiutrix* to dedicate their 'nova signa novamque aquilam'?[4]   Perhaps, then, legion I had received some new manipular standards from Tiberius for their services to him in Germany, or more probably, when it was reorganized, the old *aquila* still survived, but new manipular standards were given by Tiberius to take the place of those lost in Spain.

Legions XXI and XXII are, according to Hardy's theory, recruited after the loss of XVII–XIX in 9 A. D.

[1] Orosius, vi. 21. 10 ; Florus, iv. 12. 56 ; Dio, liv. 11. 5.
[2] C. I. L. xii. 2234.
[3] So Ritterling, s. v. ' Legio ', P-W. xii, p. 1222.
[4] T. H. v. 16.

Before giving the final and decisive argument against
this view, it is worth observing that the passage in
Tacitus referring to the revolt of the German legions
in 14 A. D., which ascribes part of the cause to the
'vernacula multitudo, nuper acto in urbe dilectu',[1]
does not prove anything about the origin of legion
XXI. Tacitus has stated that the revolt broke out
among the fifth and the twenty-first legions and spread
to the first and the twentieth, and then comments
upon the ill effects of the 'vernacula multitudo'.
There is nothing to show that this city rabble was
confined to legion XXI, and even if there were, it
would not prove that XXI was a new legion, but
merely that fresh drafts had been dispatched to an
already existing legion. It is fundamentally unsound
to conclude that when the word *dilectus* is found in
a literary source the recruiting of a new legion is
implied. But the question of the recruiting not merely
of two new legions, but of any new legions by Augustus
after 6 A. D., is finally settled by two papyri discovered
in Egypt. In the first, of date 8 B. C.,[2] mention is made
of two men called Ti. Aufidius and Ignatius Festus,
who are described as soldiers of legion XXII; in
the second there is a record of a contract made at
Alexandria in 5 B. C. which contains these words :
'Μάρκος Σεμπρώνιος Μ. υἱός, φυλῆς Αἰμιλίας, στρατιώτης τῶν
ἐκ τῆς κβ' λεγέωνος σπείρης'.[3] These papyri prove that

----

[1] Id. A. i. 31. 4.   [2] B. G. U. iv. 1104.

[3] Ibid. iv. 1108. In Dess. 2274 Sex. Munatius is called 'meiles
leg. XXII'. The spelling of 'meiles' and the absence of a
cognomen confirms an early date for the origin of the legion.
(Dess. 'Gesch. d. röm. Kaiserz.' i, p. 220, n. 2.)

legion XXII existed as part of the Augustan army at least as early as 8 B.C. Therefore all legions bearing numbers below XXII also existed in 8 B.C., and consequently there was no recruiting of new legions by Augustus either in 6 or 9 A.D. If a date were to be attempted for the origin of XXI and XXII, there is a *terminus a quo* in the year 25 B.C., when Galatia was left by King Amyntas, Deiotarus' successor, to Rome and was formed into a province.[1] In the last chapter we saw that Deiotarus provided two legions of his own for the war against Pharnaces, which were trained in accordance with Roman discipline.[2] The fact that XXII subsequently has an unofficial *cognomen Deiotariana* suggests that in origin this legion was part of Deiotarus' own native troops. It cannot, therefore, have been incorporated as a Roman legion before 25 B.C. Perhaps we can go even farther. It is probable that a legion numbered five (not the *Alaudae*) was lost in the Lollian disaster of 16 B.C.[3] The German army would not be left thus diminished, and it may be that legion XXI has its origin in this year.[4] If so, then XXII, which from 25 B.C. had existed as a remnant of Amyntas' army bequeathed with his kingdom to Rome, may have been transformed definitely at this date into a legion of the Roman army.

In 16 B.C., therefore, Augustus had twenty-eight legions; this number was not subsequently increased during his Principate, and the total was reduced by

[1] Dio, liii. 26.   [2] Bell. Alex. 84. 4.
[3] Vell. ii. 97.
[4] Ritterling, o.c., P–W. xii, p. 1225.

the loss of three legions in the Varian disaster to twenty-five, which agrees with Tacitus' record for the year 23 A. D.

The distribution of the legions during the Principate of Augustus cannot be traced in detail, because the literary sources, while mentioning particular campaigns, rarely indicate either the number or identity of the legions engaged. The concentration of a large army under Tiberius in Pannonia in 6–7 A. D., however, suggests that troops were freely moved from province to province to meet the military requirements of the occasion. In the period of the Cantabrian Wars (25 B. C.) Florus [1] indicates the presence of at least three legions in Spain, which were probably VI *Victrix*, X *Gemina*, and V *Alaudae*, whose place was subsequently taken by IV *Macedonica*. But if the evidence of coins from military colonies in Spain stamped with the names of legions can be taken as proof that these legions had actually operated in the same province, then legions I and II can be added to the list,[2] while IX, by its *cognomen*, must have been in Spain for some years. Legions II and V were probably not moved to Germany till after 6 A. D., and a similar date may represent the re-constitution of legion I by Tiberius in Germany. In the same years expeditions were made from Egypt against the Arabians and Ethiopians,[3] and the force consisted of three legions, which formed at this period the garrison of the new province, and of auxiliary troops from client kings, perhaps including

[1] Florus, iv. 12. 48.   [2] Cohen, 1², p. 152, 682–4.
[3] Dio, liv. 5. 4.

the future XXII *Deiotariana*.[1] In 20 B. C. Tiberius
was sent with an army ' ad visendas ordinandasque
quae sub Oriente sunt provincias '.[2] The strength of
his force is unknown, but it is probable that it consisted of the Illyrican and Macedonian legions with
possible detachments (*vexillationes*) from Syria.   In the
following year Cornelius Balbus celebrated a triumph
for a victory over the Gaetuli ; [3] the main body of his
army must have been the African legion, but we do
not know whether further help was sent from Spain
or Egypt.   From 16 B.C. onwards the centre of military
activity is to be found on the Rhine, and to a lesser
degree on the Danube fronts, and the culmination of
the strategical plans of Drusus and his successors was
the projected joint attack of Tiberius and Sentius
Saturninus in 6 A. D. on the district lying between the
rivers Rhine and Elbe.

From this necessarily bare summary of campaigns
in Spain, Egypt, and the East, and from the detailed
evidence that has already been given of the army of
Tiberius in 6-7 A. D., it is possible to indicate what was
the normal distribution of the legions in the early
years of the Principate of Augustus, with the qualification that considerable movements of troops in the
period is rendered probable by the dangers that
threatened different parts of the Empire.   Without
attempting to identify individual units, which could
only be guesswork based on the analogy of later
distributions, the normal allocation of the legions in

---

[1] Strabo, xviii. 1, 12, p. 797.   [2] Vell. ii. 94. 4.
[3] Cagnat, ' L'Armée r. d'Afrique ' (1913), p. 6 sq.

the period of Augustus' Principate, included in the years 16 B. C. and 6 A. D., was probably as follows :

Spain	.	. 5 legions
Germany	.	5 or 6 legions
Vindelicia	.	2 or 1 legions
Illyricum	.	. 5 legions
Macedonia		4 or 3 legions
Syria [1]	.	3 or 4 legions
Egypt	.	. 3 legions
Africa	.	. 1 legion

$= 28$ legions.

After the disaster of Varus the Rhine defences had to be strengthened, and the garrison was not merely brought up to its original numbers but increased to an army of eight legions. This end was probably attained by moving two legions from Spain (II and V), XIII and XX from Illyricum, and XXI from Vindelicia, which ceased to be garrisoned by any troops. About the same time the Illyrican and Macedonian legions were distributed over the newly organized provinces of Dalmatia, Pannonia, and Moesia, while in all proba- bility the army of Egypt was reduced to two legions. Such was the distribution of the legions at the death of Augustus, at which point Tacitus starts his history, and our information becomes more certain.

[1] Possibly an increase in the size of the Syrian army dates from G. Caesar's Armenian expedition in 1 B. C.

IV

THE POST-AUGUSTAN LEGIONS

NO fresh legions were added by Tiberius to the Augustan total of twenty-five, and it has been commonly supposed that Claudius was the first Princeps to increase the size of the army. Two new legions are known to have been in existence in the year 43 A. D., and it has been thought that the motive for their enlistment was the contemplated invasion of Britain. These legions were numbered XV and XXII and had the *cognomen Primigenia*. This has been explained as meaning that the new legions received the *aquilae* of the old legions bearing the same numbers (i. e. XV *Apollinaris* and XXII *Deiotariana*), while the latter retained their old *cognomina*. Thus in a sense the new creations could be called 'first born'. But such an interpretation is artificial and unsatisfactory. Consequently Ritterling, in search of a more convincing explanation, has put forward the theory that XV and XXII were raised, not by Claudius, but by his predecessor Caligula in 39 A. D., and argues for his position on the following grounds.[1]

1. All the literary sources agree that Caligula concentrated immense forces on the Rhine for a projected invasion of Germany followed by an attack upon Britain. The evidence of Suetonius is the most important: 'legionibus et auxiliis undique excitis,

[1] S. v. 'Legio', P–W. xii, p. 1246.

dilectibus ubique acerbissime actis ; contracto et omnis generis commeatu, quanto nunquam antea '.[1]   To this may be added the significant phrases of Tacitus in the Agricola and Germania, 'ingentes adversus Germaniam conatus '[2] and 'ingentes Gaii Caesaris minae'.[3]   2. The character of Caligula is marked by filial affection for his father Germanicus.   A suitable way of showing this would be the revival of his projected schemes in Germany, which had been stopped, gossip said, by the malignity of Tiberius.   3. An inscription suggests that legion XV *Pg.* is older than 42 A. D.   It reads : 'Ti. Iulio Ti. f. Falerna Italico centurioni leg. VII Macedonicae, cent. leg. XV Primigeniae, cent. leg. XIII Geminae primo pilo.'[4]   Now legion VII received the honorary titles *Claudia pia fidelis* for its loyalty in the mutiny of Scribonianus in Dalmatia in 42 A. D.[5] Once this title had been received it would almost inevitably be found in all subsequent inscriptions referring to legion VII.   Therefore XV *Pg.* must have existed before 42 A. D., as Italicus left legion VII before the revolt of Scribonianus.   4. The two new legions have the *cognomen Primigenia.*   The true explanation of this title is to be found by connecting it closely with *Fortuna publica   Primigenia.*   In this way it will be parallel to such other legionary *cognomina* as *Minervia* and *Apollinaris.*   Now Caligula had a special object in calling his legions not merely *Fortunia* but *Primigenia.*   He wanted to link the household of Germanicus in the closest possible bonds with the

[1] Suet. Cal. 43.   [2] Ag. 13.   [3] Ger. 37.
[4] C. I. L. x. 4723.   [5] Suet. Cl. 13 ; Dio, lv. 23. 4.

goddess *Fortuna Primigenia* : for Germanicus himself seems to have regarded her as his personal protecting deity. It is noticeable that the oldest temple of *Fortuna Primigenia* at Rome was dedicated on 25 May,[1] while Germanicus was born on 24 May [2] and celebrated his triumph for his German campaigns on 26 May 17 A. D.[3] How could Caligula commemorate his father more fittingly than by calling his two new legions after his protecting deity? 5. There is further significance in the choice of the numbers XV and XXII. The new legions were sent to Germany to join the legions there which had fought with Germanicus. Therefore, as a mark of honour, one legion was selected from each of the double camps at Vetera and Moguntiacum, and the new legions were given numbers following theirs. Thus XV *Pg.* comes next to XIV *Gemina* at Moguntiacum, and XXII *Pg.* follows legion XXI at Vetera. 6. Finally, to bind the legions to his person and to thwart the schemes of Lentulus, the rebellious governor of Upper Germany, Caligula outstripped all precedent by a special gift of 100 *denarii* to each soldier, and perhaps in this way stopped the spread of a dangerous mutiny.[4]

Such are the attractive and ingenious arguments advanced for hailing Caligula and not Claudius as the founder of two new legions. A closer examination, however, may perhaps show that the theory depends almost exclusively on the proposed explanation of the

[1] Fasti Venus. C. I. L. ix. 421.
[2] Acta Arval. C. I. L. vi. 2028, for 38 A. D.   [3] T. A. ii. 41. 2.
[4] Suet. Cal. 46.

cognomen Primigenia, and to a lesser degree on the
motive for the choice of the numbers XV and XXII.
1. The literary evidence itself does not definitely state
that fresh legions were raised, but merely that large
forces were collected in Germany.   The language of
Suetonius is strikingly parallel to that employed by
Velleius in his account of the Pannonian rising of
6 A. D., and it was shown in the last chapter, and
Ritterling himself agrees, that *dilectus* in the latter
case meant fresh levies for old legions, and not new
legions.   2. The inscription of the centurion Italicus
does not necessarily preclude a Claudian origin for
legion XV *Pg*.   Claudius must have planned his expedition to Britain at least as early as 42 A. D.   To take
the place of the German legions which he detailed
for the campaign of 43 A. D., he must have started to
recruit new legions and to drill them in the spring of
the previous year.   Instructors were necessary, and
consequently centurions, of whom Italicus may have
been one, would be withdrawn from their old units in
time to assist in the preparation of the new legions.
Consequently Italicus may have left legion VII before
the revolt of Scribonianus.   But supposing that he was
still with legion VII after the Scribonianus episode, is
it impossible that the dedication put up to him should
omit the new official titles of the legion and choose
instead the old unofficial *cognomen*, which has only been
found in three other inscriptions?   The memorial was
not set up by the legion itself but by some unnamed
person, and, as Italicus in all probability joined the
legion before 42 A. D., the old unofficial title might

naturally be found on his epitaph instead of the new *cognomen*.[1]   3. Ritterling's view that throughout the Principate new legions were numbered so as to reflect honour on those immediately preceding them in numerical order is very far fetched. To call two new legions XV and XXII seems a very indirect way of reflecting honour on XIV and XXI. It is doubtful if the soldiers of the older units would have appreciated the point when informed of the Princeps' decision by their legionary commanders. If Caligula wanted to honour his father's legions, surely he would have given them some such honorary title as *Germanica* or *Victrix*. Clearly the numbers XV and XXII were chosen to suit the numerical series in the two provinces of Germany. If legion XV was at first in the Upper Province, as is probable from four inscriptions from Moguntiacum recording the deaths of soldiers in their first year of service,[2] and XXII in the Lower Province, the legions before the expedition to Britain started would be as follows: in Lower Germany I, V, XX, XXI, XXII, in Upper Germany II, XIII, XIV, XV, XVI. This explanation leaves the question open whether it was Caligula who assembled this large force in Germany in 39 or Claudius who brought his new legions to take over duties from the legions detailed for Britain at a convenient time before the departure of the expedition.

If these criticisms have any weight, then neither the statement of Suetonius, nor the inscription of the

[1] Cf. Dess. ' Gesch. d. röm. Kaiserz.' ii, p. 146, n. 3.
[2] C. I. L. xiii. 11853-6.

centurion Italicus, nor the theory of the choice of
numbers for the new legions, can be used as definite
evidence to prove that Caligula recruited legions XV
and XXII : for none of the three precludes a Claudian
origin. There remains the proposed interpretation of
Primigenia and the supposed filial affection of Caligula.
The latter is as questionable as it is unimportant for
deciding the issue. The former is plausibly attractive,
and indeed it would be pleasant to think that Caligula
did do something that had a permanent value. On
the other hand, the great invasion of Britain is on
general grounds a satisfactory reason for an increase
in the size of the Roman army, and may not Claudius
with his strange antiquarian tastes have had an interest
in *Fortuna Primigenia*, and as an omen of good luck
have called his new legions after that goddess ?

Early in Claudius' Principate there were, therefore,
twenty-seven legions in the Roman army, and this
total remained unchanged till 67 or possibly 66 A. D.
At this time Nero was planning a great expedition
against the Al ani, who lived ' ad Caspias portas ', and
for this purpose raised a new legion which he called
I *Italica*,[1] recruited, according to Suetonius, and as its
cognomen would in part imply, from Italian recruits
who were six feet in height. The so-called *dies
natalis* of the legion, on which it received its *aquila* and
signa, was 20 September.[2] Was this in the autumn of
67 or 66 A. D. ? An inscription [3] describing the career
of Antonius Naso shows that at the time of Nero's

---

[1] Suet. Nero 19.   [2] C. I. L. iii. 7591.
[3] Dess. 9199. Cf. T. H. i. 20.

death he was *trib. coh.* XV *urb.*, and then before the end of 68 A. D. successively *trib. coh.* XI *urb.* and *trib. coh.* IX *praet.* Before becoming *trib. coh.* XV *urb.* he held the post of *trib. coh.* IV *Vigilum*, and before that was *trib. leg.* I *Italicae.* If the legion was only formed on 20 September 67, was there time for Naso to be *trib. coh.* IV *Vigilum* before becoming *trib. coh.* XV *urb.*, which office he was holding at Nero's death? The advancement would be unusually rapid, but, in view of his quick promotions under Galba, not impossible. Further, Nero's Eastern expedition was cancelled because of the revolt of Vindex in Gaul, and it seems as if legion I *Italica* had not yet left Italy, or had only proceeded a short way on its journey, when the news arrived; for it was diverted to Lugdunum in March or April 68.[1] This suggests that the legion had only been formed in September 67; for if its *dies natalis* had been in 66 it would hardly still be found in Italy early in 68. It is more or less certain, therefore, that Nero formed his new legion I *Italica* in September 67 A. D.

After Galba had been proclaimed *Imperator* by legion VI *Victrix* in Spain,[2] he proceeded to raise a new legion locally before starting on his journey to Rome to make good his claim to the Principate.[3] This legion was numbered VII and had the unofficial *cognomen Galbiana*, and later, perhaps after the depletion of its numbers at Cremona, the official title *Gemina.*[4] The *dies natalis* of the legion was 10 June 68 A. D.[5] Con-

---

[1] Dio, lxiii. 27. 1.   [2] T. H. v. 16.
[3] Ibid. ii. 11.   [4] Ibid. iii. 22.   [5] Dess. 9125.

sistently with his theory for the numbering of new legions, Ritterling holds that Galba called his new legion VII to reflect honour on VI *Victrix*, which had been the first to hail him as *imperator*. This is plausible but unnecessary. More probably Galba selected the number VII simply for the sake of convenience. The only other legion in Spain at this date was VI *Victrix*; therefore it was natural to continue the series for any other legions raised in that province.

Meanwhile, Nero had started to form another legion, which was subsequently known as I *Adiutrix*, and embodied in a composite force a number of marines, who were not Roman citizens, from the fleets at Misenum and Ravenna. This unit was stationed at Rome at the date of Galba's arrival, 'remanente ea, quam e classe Nero conscripserat ',[1] but there is little doubt that it had not yet been formed into a *iusta legio* by the bestowal of an *aquila* and *signa*. Dio definitely states that it was Galba who created I *Adiutrix*,[2] and Suetonius, in his life of the same Princeps, gives a similar impression—'classiarios quos Nero ex remigibus iustos milites fecerat . . . aquilam et signa pertinacius flagitantes'.[3] It is perhaps further significant that Tacitus at first calls the unit *legio classiariorum*, and only gives it its official title I *Adiutrix* when it becomes part of Otho's expeditionary force against Vitellius at Bedriacum.[4]

In the next year a second legion was recruited from the marines which was subsequently known as II

---

[1] T. H. i. 6.
[2] Dio, lv. 24. 2.
[3] Suet. Galb. 12.
[4] E.g. T. H. i. 36; cf. ii. 11 and ii. 43.

Adiutrix. On the strength of a passage of Tacitus, which ascribes to Vitellius an *e classicis legio*,[1] which subsequently deserted to the Flavians at Narnia in December 69, it has been thought by some historians, including Mommsen, that this was the composite force which later became legion II *Adiutrix.* But the kernel of the new legion is rather to be found in the marines, who earlier in 69 deserted to the side of Vespasian from the fleet at Ravenna under the instigation of Lucilius Bassus,[2] and who were used by Mucianus in his advance on Rome. For on a *diploma* of the legion, dated 7 March 70, the unit is already described as *legio* II *Adiutrix pia fidelis*;[3] and, as this particular combination of *cognomina* seems regularly to have been a recognition of loyalty in the face of civil disturbances, it is probable that it was Mucianus who recruited the legion while on his way to Rome, and that the marines' voluntary abandonment of Vitellius for Vespasian was remembered and collectively rewarded when they became regular legionary soldiers during the winter of 69–70 A. D.

But the interest of the *adiutrices* legions does not rest so much on the exact occasions of their enlistment as on the status of their soldiers after the *iustae legiones* had been formed. In the light of the extant discharge

---

[1] Ibid. iii. 55.

[2] Ibid. iii. 40 and Ritterling in P–W. xii, p. 1438.

[3] Dess. 1989. The word *diploma* has been popularly employed to describe the discharge certificate which a veteran received, because the document was in the shape of a diptych. I have, therefore, adopted the popular term, although it is not found in any ancient authority.

diplomata for the legions it has usually been thought
that the soldiers continued without the rights and
privileges of Roman citizens till the time of their dis-
charge, for the *diplomata* state : $\begin{cases} \text{`Galba} \\ \text{Vespasianus dedit} \end{cases}$
veteranis qui militaverunt in legione $\left. \begin{matrix} \text{I} \\ \text{II} \end{matrix} \right\}$ adiutrice
civitatem ipsis liberis posterisque eorum et conubium
cum uxoribus.'[1]   Ritterling,[2] however, holds that the
dates of these *diplomata* represent the actual days on
which the two *legiones adiutrices* were made into *iustae
legiones*, and that on 22 December 68 and 7 March 70
Galba and Vespasian respectively did four things.
The legions were given numbers and standards ; the
serving soldiers were enfranchised ; the veterans who
were time-expired were discharged, and these veterans received the *civitas* and *conubium*.   This theory
implies that the formation of a *iusta legio* out of a composite unit involved not merely the grant of an official
number and standards, but also the bestowal of citizen-
rights upon such of its soldiers as had not yet been
enfranchised.   This the author thinks is confirmed by
the history of the *Alaudae* legion, which did not receive the official number five till 47 B.C., when in all
probability its soldiers were made Roman citizens.[3]
Lastly, it is noteworthy that the emblem on the
standard of I *Adiutrix* is the capricorn, the Zodiac
sign for the month from 17 December to 15 January,
and on the standard of II *Adiutrix* Pegasus, which, if

[1] Dess. 1988, 1989.   [2] O.c., P–W. xii, pp. 1882 and 1439.
[3] See ch. ii, p. 57.

identified with *equus Gorgoneus*, is the constellation which rises in the heavens on 7 March.[1] Thus the emblems on both the legionary standards refer to the *dies natales* of the two legions on 22 December 68 and 7 March 70 respectively.

For the moment let us leave on one side the possible significance of the emblems on the standards and see how far the theory satisfies the actual evidence of the *diplomata*. Four points merit attention. 1. The inscriptions in question are concerned exclusively with veterans who are being discharged, and there is no mention of serving soldiers. 2. The veterans are described as having served in *legio* I or II *Adiutrix*, and not in a *legio classiariorum*. Therefore the units in question must surely have been *iustae legiones* for some time before the days on which the veterans were discharged. 3. If, then, the transformation of a composite unit into a *iusta legio* involved not merely the bestowal of *aquila* and *signa*, but also the grant of *civitas*, to its serving soldiers, why is it necessary to give the citizenship to veterans on their discharge who *ex hypothesi* must have been serving soldiers when the *iusta legio* was formed? 4. The analogy from the *Alaudae* legion does not carry much weight; for it is but one example of Caesar's liberal tendencies in the extension of the franchise to the Gauls whether Transpadane or Transalpine.[2] Of greater significance is a

---

[1] ' Iamque, ubi caeruleum variabunt sidera coelum,
    Suspice ; Gorgonei colla videbis equi.'

(Ovid, Fast. iii. 449–50.)

[2] Suet. Caes. 24.

diploma of Domitian's Principate referring to certain soldiers of legion X *Fretensis*.[1] From this inscription it is clear that an extraordinary *dilectus* had taken place for this legion in 68 and 69 A. D., and that the enlisted recruits, like the marines of I and II *Adiutrices*, were non-citizens. On the *diploma* dated 93 A. D. these soldiers receive the *civitas* when their service of twenty-five years is completed. The inference is clear. A *iusta legio*, in an emergency at any rate, did not necessarily imply that all its soldiers were Roman citizens. If, then, soldiers belonging to an old legion were allowed to remain without the citizenship till their service was completed, it is not improbable that the same conditions applied to the two *adiutrices* legions whose *cognomina* indicate their inferiority. Whether this is so, or whether some imperial *constitutio* was passed later in the reign of Vespasian enfranchising the two legions of marines, the *diplomata* which we have been considering cannot be used with reference to the status of their serving soldiers. They are concerned solely with veterans who, because of their previous service on the fleet, became time-expired at a very early stage in the history of the two new legions.

Similarly the dates on the *diplomata* are the days on which the discharges took place, and no inference can be drawn from them as to the *dies natales* of the two legions. The *iustae legiones*, it is true, cannot have been very long in existence before these first batches of veterans were discharged, but neither from the *diplomata*

[1] Dess. 9059.

themselves nor, in this case, from the emblems on the standards can any certain conclusions be drawn as to the actual day of their creation. By no means all the emblems have reference to the *dies natales* of the different legions : [1] for instance, the bull indicates that a legion was originally formed by Caesar, because it is the Zodiac sign for the month from 17 April to 18 May, which was sacred to Venus, the goddess-mother of the Julian *gens*, while the capricorn on the standards of other legions than I *Adiutrix* suggests Augustus as their founder on the same principle as Lady-day is celebrated on 25 March. On the standard of I *Adiutrix* the capricorn may well have reference to 24 December, the birthday of Galba, the founder of the legion : [2] Pegasus is a puzzle. Ritterling's identification of him as a constellation is attractive, but on any ordinary reading of the *diploma* of legion II *Adiutrix* 7 March, the day on which the constellation rises, should be later in the year than the legion's *dies natalis*. Now Pegasus is also found on the standards of II *Augusta* side by side with the capricorn, [3] and as the former does not figure alone on this legion's *aquila*, while the latter does, clearly the capricorn is the older emblem and will as such have reference to Augustus as the founder of the legion. The addition of Pegasus to the legion's standard cannot, then, reasonably be taken as referring to its *dies natalis*. But II *Augusta* was the legion which Vespasian commanded in Claudius'

[1] See App. A, pp. 261-3, and von Dom. ' Die Fahn.' *passim*.
[2] Suet. Galb. 4.
[3] C. I. L. vii. 517, 519, &c. ; Ritt., o. c., P–W. xii, p. 1457.

invasion of Britain.[1] Therefore if II *Adiutrix*, which was certainly raised by Vespasian, has Pegasus as its emblem, and the only other legion which also has Pegasus is II *Augusta*, which Vespasian commanded earlier in his career, it is tempting to suggest that the latter must have received this additional emblem from its former commander after he became Princeps. Now Vespasian was first hailed as *Imperator* at Alexandria in July 69 A. D.,[2] and according to one tradition Pegasus is the horse of the East. Perhaps, then, Vespasian, whom the prophets and oracles of the East foretold as the divine ruler of the world,[3] had a superstitious reverence for the winged horse and gave him as an emblem to two of his legions, one of which (II *Augusta*) had been his first command, the other (II *Adiutrix*) the first creation of his Principate.

Early in the year 70 A. D. there were, therefore, thirty-one legions in the Roman army, and passing mention must be made of yet another, which had a very temporary existence. Clodius Macer, the governor of Africa, had at the end of Nero's reign set himself up as a candidate for the Principate, and for that purpose raised an extra legion to supplement legion III *Augusta*. This he called *legio* I *Macriana*, and, although it was disbanded by Galba, it was again pressed into service by Vitellius and only finally disappeared on his death. Some doubt has been felt whether this legion was ever a *iusta legio*, but the collective force of two passages in the 'Histories' ('Africa

[1] Suet. Vesp. 4 ; Tac. Agr. 13. 5.   [2] T. H. ii. 79.
[3] Ibid. ii. 78.

ac legiones in ea'[1] and 'In Africa legio cohortesque delectae a Clodio Macro'[2]), and of coins stamped with the inscription *legio I Macriana* [3] makes it certain that a second legion existed temporarily in Africa.

After the revolt of Civilis the four German legions which had either surrendered or lost their *aquilae* were cashiered, and consequently I *Germanica*, IV *Macedonica*, XV *Primigenia*, and XVI disappeared. In their place Vespasian, during the summer of 70, recruited two fresh legions called IV *Flavia felix* and XVI *Flavia firma*.[4] The *cognomina* show the dynasty by which they were founded, and the Zodiac sign of the lion on their standards may imply that they were recruited between 20 July and 29 August. Why the numbers IV and XVI should have been selected rather than I and XV presents some difficulty. Ritterling,[5] as might be expected, holds that the choice had nothing to do with the fact that two legions numbered IV and XVI had been cashiered, but was meant to reflect honour on III *Gallica* and XV *Apollinaris*, which had been the first to declare for Vespasian and to bring other legions to his side. But the explanation is much simpler. After the cashiering of I *Germanica* there were still two legions numbered I in existence, namely, I *Italica* and I *Adiutrix*. Vespasian, being a practical man, did not want to complicate further the confused enumeration of the legions, and so refrained from starting a new imperial series with a legion called

---

[1] T. H. i. 11.   [2] Ibid. ii. 97.
[3] Mattingly, 'Roman Imperial Coinage', i, p. 194.
[4] Dio, lv. 24. 8.   [5] O.c., P–W. xii, p. 1268.

I *Flavia*. Again, with the disappearance of XVI (*Gallica*) there was no unit left bearing that number, and so it was natural to fill this gap in a series which was continuous from I to XXII with the exception of XVII–XIX, which for sentimental reasons were never replaced. XVI then was an obvious number for one of the two new legions, and IV was preferred to XV because it was the lower number in the series and, unlike I, not already duplicated. The two new Flavian legions were thus intended to take the place of the four cashiered, and, as two were thought sufficient in view of the existence of I and II *Adiutrices*, the numbers were selected so as to cause the least possible confusion.

The occasion of the next addition to the Roman legions was in all probability Domitian's campaign against the Chatti in 83 A.D. in continuation of Vespasian's work in the Neckar district. At all events a new legion was raised in Domitian's Principate bearing the number I and the *cognomen Minervia*.[1] This title was given as an honour to Domitian's protecting deity Minerva,[2] and the ram, which was sacred to her, was chosen as the Zodiac sign for the legion's standard. That the year 83 A.D. was the date of the legion's formation is rendered probable by the fact that in the same year XXI *Rapax* vacated its camp at Bonna and

[1] Dio, lv. 24. 8. At first it was called I *Flavia* (C. I. L. xiii. 8062ª) and then I *Flavia Minervia* (Bonn. Jahrb. xlix. 191). For its loyalty in the revolt of Saturninus it received the additional titles *pia fidelis Domitiana*, the last epithet being erased when Domitian suffered *damnatio memoriae* (Dess. 2279).

[2] Suet. Dom. 15.

moved into the Upper Province,[1] and the earliest traces of the new legion have been found at this site. Further, the fact that the new legion was sent to Germany implies the necessity of reinforcements for some extensive campaign, and this can only be the war against the Chatti. Therefore 83 is a more probable year for the *dies natalis* of the new legion than 87 A. D.,[2] when the Romans suffered a severe defeat, with the possible loss of a legion, on the Danube front.

Trajan raised two new legions called *legio* XXX *Ulpia* and *legio* II *Traiana*. Now in the year 83 A. D. there were thirty legions in the Roman army, and the problem, which has aroused much controversy, is how many legions were lost in the latter half of Domitian's Principate, and, alternatively, in what order were Trajan's new legions recruited. For one thing is clear, that when legion XXX was mobilized, twenty-nine other legions must have been in existence. Let us look first at the literary evidence for Domitian's wars on the Danube.

The most important evidence is that of Suetonius. Referring to Domitian, he says : 'Expeditiones partim sponte suscepit, partim necessario . . . necessario unam in Sarmatas, legione cum legato caesa, in Dacos duas, primam Oppio Sabino consulari oppresso, secundam Cornelio Fusco, praefecto cohortium praetorianarum, cui belli summam commiserat.'[3] From this statement

[1] Dess. 2285.

[2] Ritterling, o.c., P-W. xii, p. 1420 ; *contra* Schilling, 'De Leg. I Min. et XXX Ulp.', pp. 4–25.   [3] Suet. Dom. 6.

it is clear that in two campaigns against the Dacians, probably between 85 and 88 A.D., the Romans met with two severe defeats in which the leaders of the expeditions were killed, and that in a war against the Sarmatians in 92 A.D. a legion with its general was cut to pieces. This latter statement is confirmed by Eutropius—'in Sarmatia legio cum duce interfecta est',[1] while in addition Dio tells us that in the Dacian War of 101 A.D. Trajan recovered τὸ σημεῖον, which had been lost in the defeat of Cornelius Fuscus.[2]

The literary evidence is decisive for the loss of a legion—V *Alaudae*—in 92 A.D.; does it also imply the disappearance of a second legion in 87 A.D.? Now the *aquila* was regarded as the 'numen legionis',[3] and its loss was normally followed by the disbandment of its legion in disgrace. This, for instance, was the fate of the four German legions in the Civilis revolt. But although this was the normal it was not the universal practice; for Suetonius says that XII *Fulminata* lost its *aquila* under Cestius Gallus in 66 A.D.,[4] and it certainly continued to exist. It looks as if the fate of a legion which had abandoned its *aquila* was determined by expediency. In the Jewish and Dacian wars the need for men was urgent, and therefore it was impolitic to cashier even a remnant of a legion; after the Civilis revolt, on the other hand, which savoured

---

[1] Eutrop. vii. 23. 4.

[2] Dio, lxviii. 9. 7. Troms. 'Quaest. duo', thinks that σημεῖον = *signum*, as ἀετός elsewhere in Dio = *aquila*. But the article τὸ is against this; and cf. Arrian ἐκτ. κατ᾿ 'Αλ. (Filow, 'Die Leg. d. Prov. Moes.', p. 88).

[3] T. A. ii. 17. 12.   [4] Suet. Vesp. 4.

of civil war, it was undesirable to retain disaffected
and untrustworthy troops in the service of Rome, and
so the legions which had lost their *aquilae* were
cashiered and new ones recruited in their place.   The
literary evidence, then, for Domitian's wars on the
Danube, while not precluding the possibility of the
loss of two legions—V *Alaudae* and XXI *Rapax*—does
not necessarily imply it.   An attempt to solve the
problem whether there were twenty-eight or twenty-
nine legions extant in 98 A. D. must therefore turn on
the probable dates of the formation of Trajan's new
units.

If there were only twenty-eight legions in the
Roman army on the death of Domitian it is clear
that legion II *Traiana* must have been raised before
legion XXX *Ulpia*, because the number of the latter
legion certainly means that thirty legions was the
total strength at the time of its formation.   The additional cognomen *Victrix*,[1] which is found on grave-
stones of the Trajanic period belonging to soldiers of
legion XXX, implies that that legion took part in
Trajan's Dacian wars, although we do not know what
camp it occupied in Moesia.   If, then, legion XXX was
recruited either before the first Dacian War of Trajan
or between the two campaigns, II *Traiana* must also
have been enlisted early in his Principate, if the statement that there were only twenty-eight legions in the
Roman army in 98 A. D. is to hold good.   Now it used
to be thought that the earliest traces of II *Traiana*
were to be found in Egypt, and consequently the

[1] C. I. L. xiii. 1884.

theory was advanced that when Arabia was made
into a province in 106 A. D., III *Cyrenaica* was sent to
garrison it and II *Traiana* was formed in Egypt to
take its place. The inscription, however, referring to a
vexillatio of II *Traiana* at Memphis, which was formerly
dated February 5, 109 A. D., is now rightly assigned
to the year 128 A. D.,[1] while Wilcken's restoration of
an Egyptian papyrus shows that III *Cyrenaica* and
XXII *Deiotariana* were still encamped together at
Nicopolis in 119 A. D.[2] It is most improbable that a
third legion was stationed in Egypt at this period,
and so the theory that II *Traiana* was raised to take
the place of III *Cyrenaica* must be abandoned. The
earliest record of the legion is most probably to be
found in an inscription describing the career of
Numisius Sabinus, which also has reference to XXI
Rapax. It reads as follows : '. . . Numisio Sabino leg.
Aug. pro praetore Galatiae, Pisidiae, Paphlagoniae . . .
procos. prov. Sardiniae, leg. legionum I Italicae et II
Traianae Fortis . . . curatori viarum Clodiae Cassiae
Anniae Ciminiae Traianae novae, praetori, trib. pl.,
quaestori, IIIviro capitali, trib. mil. leg. XXI Ra-
pacis.'[3] When Numisius is in command of II *Traiana*
he has the title of *legatus*; therefore the legion was
not in Egypt at that time, because in that case he
would have been called *praefectus*. Further, the combination of two legions under the command of one
legatus suggests that the legions were brigaded together

[1] C. I. L. iii. 14147⁶.
[2] B. G. U. i. 140 ; Bruns, 'Fontes Iuris Romani', i, p. 421.
[3] Dess. 1038.   Riccobono. *Leges*, no. 78.

for some important campaign, and the choice lies between the second Dacian War and Trajan's Parthian War. In support of the former it might be urged that I *Italica* was on the Danube, and just possibly the inscription may imply that Numisius was governor of the province of Moesia. On the other hand, if the posts held by Numisius are recorded in exact chronological order, then, before becoming *legatus* of II *Traiana* he was *curator* of *Via Traiana nova*, which was only constructed in 109 A. D. Therefore his command of the legion must have been in the Parthian War of 114–117 A. D., and, if so, he can hardly have been tribune of XXI *Rapax* as early as 91 A. D., which is the latest date possible if that legion was destroyed in 92 A. D. Therefore if Numisius was *legatus* of II *Traiana* in Trajan's Parthian War, the theory that two legions were destroyed under Domitian must be abandoned, and with it the view that II *Traiana* was raised before XXX.

But let us suppose that Numisius was in command of II *Traiana* in the second Dacian War, and see if the theory that legion II *Traiana* was recruited before legion XXX can be maintained. The question turns on the choice of numbers for the new legions. Ritterling[1] holds that II *Traiana* was not Trajan's second legion, but was so called to reflect honour on some one of the legions numbered I, and suggests either I *Adiutrix* or I *Minervia*. But the former had done nothing to merit such a remarkable honour, nor would Trajan single out a legion of Domitian and

[1] O. c., P–W. xii, p. 1484.

make it the first of his new imperial series. Further,
if any such intention had been in the mind of the
Princeps, it is surely not unreasonable to ask why
XXX *Ulpia* was so called, when there was no legion
XXIX to honour. The choice seems strangely in-
consistent. But surely the selection of the number
XXX for one of the legions really decides the issue.
Trajan wanted to show the actual strength of the
Roman legionary army; therefore, if there had only
been twenty-eight legions in 98 A. D., he would have
called his first legion XXIX. Instead, a legion was
formed called XXX, and there is little doubt that his
next creation would have been called XXXI, had not
a legion—the XXI *Rapax*—in the meanwhile disappeared. The army was thus again reduced to
twenty-nine legions, and as Trajan had already given
the first of his legions the number XXX, he decided
to call the next his own second legion, with Hercules,
his protecting deity, as its emblem. Lastly, if an
attempt were made to date the formation of II
Traiana, the possibilities lie between the first and the
second Dacian War or between the Dacian wars and
the Parthian War, according to the interpretation of
the Numisius inscription. Unfortunately the circumstances in which the *Rapax* disappeared are unknown.
It might be inferred from two grave-stones at Vindonissa with the number of the legion erased that
it had suffered *damnatio memoriae*,[1] and perhaps the
history of I *Adiutrix* may suggest the occasion. At

[1] C. I. L. xiii. 5201, 11514; Cheesman, Cl. Rev. 1910, xxiii,
p. 155 ; *contra* Ritterling, o. c., P–W. xii, p. 1789.

some time between the years 98 and 114 A. D. this
legion received the *cognomina pia fidelis*.[1] Now this
honour always implied loyalty to the reigning Princeps
in face of civil disturbances. May the XXI *Rapax*
have taken up the cause of some rebellious *legatus*
(perhaps Calpurnius Crassus [2]) and been cashiered in
disgrace, while I *Adiutrix* was rewarded for its
fidelity ?

There was thus only one legion lost during
Domitian's wars, namely, V *Alaudae* against the
Sarmatians in 92, and in consequence twenty-nine
legions survived in 98 A. D. Trajan raised legion
XXX for the Dacian wars and II *Traiana*, after the
disappearance of the *Rapax* possibly in a civil dis-
turbance, either for the second Dacian War or for his
projected Eastern campaign.

An inscription engraved on two columns, giving a
list of the legions in geographical order, was discovered at Rome.[3] On it are twenty-eight legions
distributed through the provinces in a west to east
enumeration, and at the end, out of geographical order,
are added two legions raised by Marcus Aurelius
and three by Septimius Severus. Legions IX *Hispana* and XXII *Deiotariana* are not mentioned, and,
as it is probable that these were destroyed during the
British and Jewish rebellions of Hadrian's Principate
respectively, the list can be satisfactorily dated to the

---

[1] It is not found on Dess. 2720, dated 98 A. D. at the earliest,
but is found on C. I. L. iii. 1004, dated probably 114 A. D. (cf. Dess.
2476).

[2] Dio, lxviii. 16. 2.   [3] Dess. 2288.

reign of Antoninus Pius. An army of twenty-eight
legions proved adequate for the defence of the Empire till the outbreak of the Marcomannic War. The
Parthian War was not yet finished and the legions
which had been sent to the East from the Danube
front could not be immediately recalled. Consequently M. Aurelius proceeded to raise two new
legions, which were later called II *Italica* and III
Italica, and there is good evidence to show that this
was in 165. 1. The two legions had at first the
honorary titles of *Pia*[1] and *Concors*[2] respectively, and
so must have existed before the death of L. Verus in
169 A. D.   2. Vettius Sabinianus was, if not actually
the first, one of the first commanders of III *Italica*,
and the inscription which describes his career makes
it certain that he cannot have held this post later
than 166 A. D.[3] 3. A second inscription says that
M. Claudius Fronto, when of praetorian rank, was
' missus ad iuventutem per Italiam legendam '.[4]
Taken in conjunction with the *cognomen Italica*, which
is the later official title of both legions, it seems
certain that he must have been acting as recruiting
officer for the two new legions, which continued the

[1] C. I. L. iii. 1980.   The emblem is the she-wolf with twins
(Cohen, v², p. 388, nos. 472-6) (perhaps symbolical of the *divi
fratres* ?).

[2] A. E. 1920, no. 45.   The emblem is the stork, the symbol of
concord (Cohen, v². p. 389, nos. 487-98).

[3] A. E. 1920, no. 45, and Ritterling, o. c., P-W. xii, p. 1300.

[4] Dess. 1097.   Fronto receives four *hastae purae* and four *vexilla*
at the triumph, and so must then have been *consularis* (see
ch. viii, p. 281).

series started by Nero's I *Italica*. As Fronto is of consular rank at the time of the triumph for the Parthian War, held in the summer of 166, he must have carried out his recruiting duties in 165 A. D.

With the addition of Marcus' two legions the strength of the Roman army reached once again a total of thirty legions, and this figure remained unchanged till the Principate of Septimius Severus.

V

THE MOVEMENTS OF THE LEGIONS BETWEEN
14 AND 180 A. D.

A STUDY of the distribution of the legions under the Principate, apart from its intrinsic interest, throws light on the Roman system of frontier defence and illustrates the changing importance of the different parts of the Empire. The combination of literary and epigraphical evidence makes it possible not merely to state the size of a provincial garrison at any particular date, but also to trace the identity of most of the individual units and the camps which they occupied. In this chapter, therefore, I shall try to follow the chief movements of troops that occurred in these years, and from a consideration of their grouping to indicate the developments in frontier defence, the relative importance of different frontiers, and the areas from which the most persistent opposition threatened. The choice of the period selected is not altogether arbitrary; for, while Tacitus gives a statistical record of the distribution of the army in the early part of the Principate of Tiberius,[1] the inscription found at Rome engraved on two columns with a geographical list of the legions from west to east cannot be much earlier than 138 nor later than 161 A. D.[2] There is therefore a suitable starting

---

[1] T. A. iv. 5.   [2] Dess. 2288.

and finishing point corresponding roughly with the accessions of Tiberius and Marcus Aurelius, and epigraphical evidence makes it feasible to extend the inquiry to the death of the latter Princeps.

Tiberius.

Between the death of Augustus and the year 23 A. D., to which Tacitus assigns his statistical record, no changes of any great importance took place in the positions of the legions. The garrison of Egypt was reduced from three to two legions, if this had not already taken place in the lifetime of Augustus, and the only other event of note is the transfer in 20 A. D. of IX *Hispana* to Africa under L. Cornelius Scipio to strengthen the garrison of that province in the guerilla warfare with Tacfarinas,[1] whence, after a stay of four years, it returned to its old head-quarters in Pannonia.[2] Our inquiry may therefore start with a consideration of Tacitus' list for the year 23 A. D. (in which, for convenience sake, I am showing IX *Hispana* in Pannonia and not in Africa). The distribution of the legions was as follows :

Germania Inferior		I *Germanica*, V *Alaudae*, XX *Valeria*, XXI.
„	Superior	II *Augusta*. XIII *Gemina*, XIV *Gemina*, XVI.
Dalmatia	. .	VII, XI.
Moesia .	. .	IV *Scythica*, V *Macedonica*.
Pannonia	. .	VIII *Augusta*, IX *Hispana*, XV *Apollinaris*.
Syria .	. .	III *Gallica*, VI *Ferrata*, X *Fretensis*, XII *Fulminata*.
Egypt .	. .	III *Cyrenaica*, XXII *Deiotariana*.
Africa .	. .	III *Augusta*.
Spain .	. .	IV *Macedonica*, VI *Victrix*, X *Gemina*.

[1] T. A. iii. 9. 1.   [2] Ibid. iv. 23. 2.

The most striking thing about this distribution is the great importance attached to the Rhine frontier. This was due to several reasons. First, the disaster to Varus and the comparative failures of Germanicus had shown that, even if the Rhine and not the Elbe was to be the permanent Roman frontier, the possibility of incursions from the German tribes living on the right bank of the Rhine could not be profitably neglected. Roman troops must be ready to undertake punitive expeditions into the heart of Germany, even if the line of demarcation between Rome and Germany was to be left at the Rhine. Secondly, there were no legionary troops in Gaul.[1] The policy of the Roman government was one of extreme tolerance, and the Gallic tribes were to be given the opportunity of assimilating without compulsion Roman institutions and Roman manners. But at the same time the rising of Vercingetorix was sufficiently recent to encourage native leaders like Florus and Sacrovir to raise the standard of rebellion,[2] and the only hope of maintaining Roman sovereignty was to have troops near the scene of possible insurrections which, without giving the impression of holding down Gaul by force, would be ready to quell the slightest sign of insubordination. The positions, too, of the legions at this date throw an interesting light on the quarter from which German unrest might be expected. In

---

[1] T. H. i. 64. There was only an extra urban cohort stationed at Lugdunum to guard the imperial mint, bearing the number XIII (T. A. iii. 41. 1, and Mattingly, 'R. Imperial Coinage', i, p. 4). [2] T. A. iii. 44.

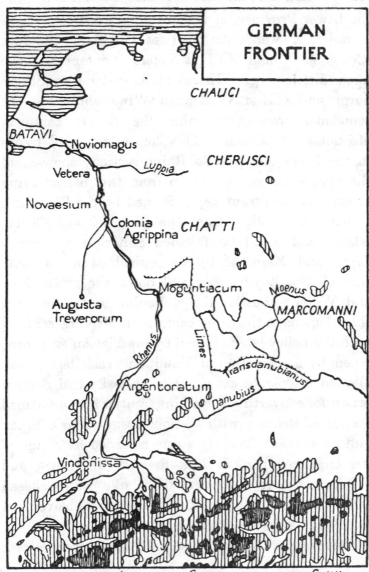

GERMAN FRONTIER

CHAUCI

BATAVI

Noviomagus

CHERUSCI

Luppia

Vetera

Novaesium

Colonia
Agrippina

CHATTI

Moguntiacum

Moenus

MARCOMANNI

Augusta
Treverorum

Rhenus

Limes

Transdanubianus

Argentoratum

Danubius

Vindonissa

Mountains above 9000 ft. ▓▓▓ 3000-9000 ft. ||||||

1″ = 96 miles

the Lower Province, or rather military district, legions I and XX were stationed at Oppidum Ubiorum (Cologne),[1] V and XXI at Vetera (Xanten);[2] in the upper district, legion II was at Argentoratum (Strassburg)[3] and XIII at Vindonissa (Windisch),[4] while the remainder were garrisoning the double camp at Moguntiacum (Mainz).[5] This concentration of troops in the lower and middle Rhine sections shows that the opposition was no longer from the district lying around the re-entrant angle formed by the Rhine and Danube, but rather from the Cherusci and Chatti, whose land could be invaded either up the rivers Lippe and Main, or by the circuitous naval route through the Zuyder Zee and down the rivers Ems and Weser.[6] Lastly, the stationing of two or even three legions in the same camp is in striking contrast with the policy later adopted by the Flavian emperors, when, by a regulation of Domitian,[7] each legion was allotted a separate camp. The necessity had not yet arisen for converting the Rhine frontier into a fortified system of defence with sections assigned to a legion and its *auxilia*. The river was regarded as a line of demarcation setting a limit to Rome's advance, and the legions were concentrated in large camps chosen rather as starting-points for taking the offensive than as links in a system of fortifications.

Compared with the Rhine the Danube frontier was

---

[1] T. A. i. 31. 3 and i. 39. 1.
[2] Ibid. i. 45. 1.   [3] Dess. 2246.   [4] C. I. L. xiii. 5206.
[5] Dess. 2262 and 2265.
[6] E.g. the campaigns of Germanicus.   [7] Suet. Dom. 7.

only of secondary importance, and between the years
14 and 62 A. D. the number of legions garrisoning the
provinces of Dalmatia, Pannonia, and Moesia could
be temporarily weakened with impunity, when the
need for troops was urgent in other parts of the
Empire. In Illyricum, which up to 6 A. D. had united
under one military command the subsequent provinces
of Dalmatia and Pannonia, the chief opposition to
Rome had been from the native tribes, which had
broken into open revolt under Bato. Their complete
suppression by Tiberius in the war of 6–9 A. D. left
the Romans undisputed masters, and as yet there was
no immediate danger from tribes like the Iazyges and
Sarmatae, who were still living in South Russia and
Bessarabia, and did not migrate to Hungary till the
reign of Nero. Consequently the Romans were left
free to organize the new provinces by the construction
of roads and the settlement of military garrisons, and
for this purpose, in 14 A. D., a force of two legions
in Dalmatia and three in Pannonia was considered
sufficient. The exact position of these legions is not
easy to determine. In Dalmatia, epigraphical evidence
shows that legion VII was at Delminium [1] and XI at
Burnum,[2] but the camps in Pannonia cannot be so
certainly identified. Augustus, in the Monumentum,
boasted that he had extended the boundaries of Rome
'ad ripas fluminis Danuvii',[3] but this statement seems
an exaggeration. Forts garrisoned by *auxilia* were
probably to be found along the Danube at such places
as Teutoburgium and Aquincum, but these were in

[1] Dess. 2252, 2253.   [2] Ibid. 2257, 2259.   [3] Mon. Anc. 30.

DANUBE
FRONTIER
Land above 3000 feet

1" ≅ 130 miles

Tyras
Pyretus
Hierasus
Troesmis
Danubius
Durostorum
Novae
Oescus
Almus
Utus
Ratiaria
Margus
Viminacium
Apulum
Potaissa
Marisus
Tibiscus
Tisia
Singidunum
Sirmium
Dravus
Aquincum
Mursella
Brigetio
Danubius
Carnuntum
Vindobona
Poetovio
Siscia
Burnum
Delminium

the nature of outposts. The Roman legionary forces up to 50 A. D. [1] were almost certainly on the line of the river Drave. Tacitus suggests that each legion here had its own *hiberna*,[2] and as Poetovio is the head-quarters of legion XIII in 69 A. D.[3] it may well have been garrisoned throughout the period, and was in all probability at this date the camp of VIII *Aug.*[4] Perhaps the other two sites are Siscia and Sirmium. In the district known later as the province of Moesia, Rome had had to contend, especially in the years 13–11 B. C., with tribal raids from across the Balkans, which threatened the Roman province of Macedonia and Rome's allies the kings of Thrace. This danger was averted by L. Calpurnius Piso,[5] who defeated the invading Bessi and established Rhoemetalces as King of Thrace. In 6 A. D. the latter and A. Caecina, the military governor of the district, lent help to Tiberius in the Pannonian revolt, and it is probably after this that a great expedition, boasted of by Augustus in the Monumentum, was carried out across the Danube, which resulted in the settlement of 50,000 Dacians on the right bank of the river.[6] The Romans thus for the time averted the danger along the lower Danube of further hostile raids, and the district was organized into a province. The exact limits of this new province are hard to ascertain. The country near the mouth of the river was certainly included in the

[1] T. A. xii. 29. 1: the Vannius episode.

[2] Ibid. i. 30. 4.   [3] Id. H. iii. 1.

[4] C. I. L. iii. 4060.   [5] Dio, liv. 34. 6.

[6] Mon. Anc. 30; Dio, lv. 30; Strabo, p. 303; Hardy, 'Mon. Anc.', p. 142.

kingdom of Thrace,[1] and this makes it probable that the actual province was confined to what was subsequently Moesia Superior, i. e. the region immediately north of Macedonia. The garrison was limited to two legions, which are mentioned in an inscription of the time of Tiberius. Their camps may have been at Ratiaria and Viminacium.[2]

The choice of a line of demarcation between Rome and Parthia was rendered extraordinarily difficult by the geographical features of the country. The river Euphrates in its upper and lower reaches was a possibility, but the difficulty of holding such a length of front was increased by the huge barrier of mountains that separated Mesopotamia from Armenia and Cappadocia. A large number of legions would have been required to hold even the vulnerable points on this line, and, doubtless from financial reasons as well as military and political inexpediency, Augustus decided against such a course and concentrated his army in Syria, while making use of the client kings of Armenia, Commagene, and Adiabene to act as buffer states between Rome and Parthia. How far the Parthian menace was real, and how far it was exaggerated by the surviving horror caused by the loss of standards at Carrhae in 53 B.C. cannot be discussed here, but it is at least reasonable to argue, from the presence of four legions in Syria and two in Egypt, that the real fear of the Roman statesmen was for the safety of Egypt and the corn-supply of Rome. The Oriental monarchies of the past had confined

---

[1] T. A. ii. 65. 1.   [2] Dess. 2281.

EASTERN FRONTIER

Halys
Scylax
Lycus
Satala
Euphrates
Halys
Arsamosata
Melitene
Arabissos
Samosata
Sarmalus
Sarus
Zeugma
Carrhae
Pyramus
Cyrrhus
Antioch
Euphrates
Orontes
Laodiceia
Apamea
Raphaneae
Berytus
Sidon
Tyre

Mountains above 9000 ft.

5000 ft. – 9000 ft.

3000 ft. – 5000 ft.

1" = 96 miles

their activities largely to Syria and Palestine as the approach to Egypt ; may not the same project have enticed the kings of Parthia when they were not being hampered by civil distractions ? In the reign of Tiberius three of the legions of the Syrian garrison can be located. VI *Ferrata* was stationed at Apamea near the maritime Laodicea,[1] and X *Fretensis* at Cyrrhus,[2] which lay on the road from Antioch to Zeugma, one of the chief places for crossing the Euphrates, while XII *Fulminata* was at Raphaneae.[3] The camp of III *Gallica* cannot be identified. The position of these legions shows that, though the Euphrates itself was not actually held at the start of this period, important towns on the main lines of possible Parthian invasions were strongly garrisoned. This distribution remained unchanged till the reign of Nero.

The strength of the garrisons of the provinces of Africa and Spain calls for no particular comment. The long duration and fluctuating successes of the Cantabrian War are sufficient to account for the retention of three legions in Spain,[4] but epigraphical evidence suggests that there was a further object. Detachments could be easily transhipped to help III *Aug.* in Africa against the attacks of the Gaetuli and the Moorish tribes, and that a part of X *Gemina* served in Mauretania in 40 A. D. may be gathered

---

[1] T. A. ii. 79. 3.   [2] Ibid. ii. 57. 2.

[3] Jos. B. J. vii. 1. 3.

[4] Legions VI and X probably occupied one camp near Bracaraugusta (Dess. 2644).   Legion IV was in Cantabria (Dess. 2454, 2455).

from an inscription referring to a soldier of that unit.[1] It is perhaps justifiable to infer that the subsequent reduction of the army in Spain from three legions to one legion was made feasible not merely by the growing civilization of Spain itself, but also by the peaceful conditions produced in Africa by the uninterrupted occupation of legion III *Aug.*, whose roads and buildings still survive to-day.

Caligula–Claudius.

The number and distribution of the legions ascribed by Tacitus to the year 23 A.D. remained unaltered during the rest of the Principate of Tiberius, except for some temporary movements of troops to meet local disturbances. The first change took place either in 39, when Caligula may have raised the two legions called *Primigeniae* for his projected German campaign, or, more probably, in 42–43 A.D., when Claudius was planning an invasion of Britain. At all events, early in the reign of the latter Princeps there were twenty-seven legions, and the garrison of the Rhine had been increased from eight to ten legions. After the revolt of Scribonianus and the consequent bestowal of honorary titles on VII and XI,[2] preparations proceeded for the expedition to Britain. The force was composed of four legions, of which three (II *Aug.*, XIV *Gem.*, and XX *Valeria*) were taken from the German army, and the fourth (IX *Hispana*) was withdrawn from the garrison of Pannonia.[3] Probably

---

[1] C: I. L. viii. 21669, and see Cagnat, 'L'Armée r. d'Afrique (1913), p. 28 sq.

[2] Suet. Cl. 13.   [3] T. A. xiv. 82. 6.

BRITAIN

there were also detachments from other legions; for
an inscription speaks of a *vexillatio* from VIII *Aug.*,
while an unnamed tribune of V *Alaudae* received
decorations from Claudius,[1] although it is not clear
whether this was for service in Britain or in Germany. The dispatch of this army called for a redistribution of the legions, and the changes made show the
determination of the Roman government to keep the
garrison of the Rhine, if possible, up to its former
strength of eight legions. IV *Macedonica* was transferred from Spain to Upper Germany,[2] and some mutual changes took place in the composition of the two
armies of the Rhine. There is abundant epigraphical
evidence to show that XXII *Pg.* was stationed at
Moguntiacum[3] and XV *Pg.* at Bonna,[4] which must
imply that they changed provinces after the departure of the army for Britain. Secondly, at some unspecified date between 43 and 69 A. D., legion XVI
moved from Moguntiacum to Novaesium,[5] while XXI
is found from *tegulae* to have been stationed at
Vindonissa.[6] Perhaps the former move may be connected with a war against the Chauci and Frisii in
47 A. D.,[7] perhaps it was simply due to the departure
of legion XX to Britain. For the latter an explanation can be found in the events taking place in

---

[1] Dess. 2701 and 974.   [2] Ibid. 2248.
[3] E. g. Dess. 2276; at first it was in the Upper Province.

[4] E.g. Dess. 2275; C. I. L. xiii. 11853-6.
[5] A grave-stone of an *eques* (C. I. L. xiii. 8552) and *tegulae* (Br.
262, 276).
[6] Inscr. Helvet. 344. 1-5.   [7] T.A. xi. 18. 1.

Pannonia and Moesia between 46 and 50 A. D. VIII *Augusta* was transferred from Pannonia to Moesia some time before 58, and very probably in connexion with, and perhaps two years before, the formation of the new province of Thrace in 46 A. D.[1] As IX *Hispana* had already departed for Britain, this reduced the garrison of Pannonia to one legion. The insecurity of this position was brought home to the Roman government by the expulsion of Vannius from his kingdom by the Suebi in 50 A. D.[2] The governor of Pannonia was ordered to move forward to the Danube with a picked force, and he occupied Carnuntum. This greatly reduced the number of troops on the Drave, and it must have been at this date that legion XIII was moved from Upper Germany to Poetovio,[3] and its place taken by XXI at Vindonissa. The army on the Rhine, therefore, at the death of Claudius numbered seven legions, of which I, V, XV, and XVI were in the Lower, and IV, XXI, and XXII in the Upper, Province.

Nero.

The chief military events of importance in the Principate of Nero took place in Britain and the East. To the former province, however, despite the disaster to the ninth legion near Camulodunum (Colchester), in the

[1] T. A. xii. 15. C. I. L. ii. 3272 shows a certain Valerianus in charge of *vexillationes* from legions V *Maced.*, VIII *Aug.*, and perhaps IV *Scyth.* (so Ritterling, s. v. Legio, P–W. xii, p. 1648) operating in Thrace. These detachments must come from the Moesian legions, and the probable date is 46 A. D. (see further Filow, ' Die Leg. d. Prov. Moes.', p. 10).

[2] T. A. xii. 29. 1.   [3] Dess. 2880.

rising of Boudicca, no new legions were dispatched, but the gaps were filled by *vexillationes* numbering 2,000 men from the German legions.[1] It will be sufficient, therefore, for present purposes to indicate the positions of the four legions forming the British garrison in 62 A. D. The Roman Conquest had advanced as far north as a line drawn from Chester to Lincoln, while in the west the Silures were held back, but imperfectly subdued, by two Roman garrisons at Glevum (Gloucester) and Viroconium (Wroxeter). The ninth legion was stationed at Lindum (Lincoln),[2] the second at Gloucester,[3] while the fourteenth and twentieth shared a double camp at Wroxeter,[4] till the former left the province and the latter moved to Deva (Chester), perhaps early in Vespasian's Principate. In return for their distinguished services in Britain, legions XIV and XX received the honorary titles of *Martia victrix* and *Victrix* respectively.[5]

The policy hitherto followed by Rome of maintaining non-Parthian vassal princes on the throne of Armenia had not proved successful, and in 55 A. D. the situation became critical. The reigning King of Parthia, Vologeses, had driven out the Roman protégé Radamistus from Armenia, and entrusted the government to his brother Tiridates.[6] With commendable vigour,

[1] T. A. xiv. 38. 1.
[2] Dess. 2255. Under the Flavians it moved to Eburacum (York) (C. I. L. vii. 243).
[3] Haverfield, in E. E. ix, p. 526. The legion most probably did not move to Caerleon till A.D. 75.
[4] C. I. L. vii. 154 and 156.   [5] Id. xi. 395, dated 66 A. D.
[6] T. A. xii. 50. 1. See on the Parthian question Schur, in

Nero and his advisers took up the challenge and chose an able general in Corbulo, who was entrusted with the duty of driving Tiridates out of Armenia. His early successes more than justified his appointment, and if the Roman government had not been so short-sighted in its selection of a new king for Armenia, the Parthians, hampered as they were by civil disturbances, would have been forced to acknowledge the supremacy of Rome in Armenia and to give up, temporarily at least, a policy of western expansion.

The Parthian campaigns may be most conveniently divided into two halves corresponding to the military positions of Corbulo. In 55 he was sent out as a *legatus* of the province of Cappadocia,[1] and technically this was his official position till 60 A. D. In itself this was an exceptional command, because, although Cappadocia had been made into a province by Tiberius, it had previously been governed by a *procurator* with no other military support than *auxilia*; the title of *legatus pro praetore* implies a legionary army. In 60 Corbulo became governor of Syria,[2] and, after the disgrace of Paetus, was made commander-in-chief of the East with powers similar to those given to Pompey against the Pirates.[3]

After Corbulo had been appointed *legatus* of Cappadocia, in 55, two legions, III *Gallica* and VI *Ferrata*, were withdrawn from Syria to form the nucleus of his army.[4] X *Fretensis* and XII *Fulminata*

remained in Syria under Quadratus. Tacitus says
that in addition to these legions and auxiliary troops
'adiecta ex Germania legio'.[1] The identity of this
legion has caused much controversy. It is significant
that it did not form part of Corbulo's subsequent
expeditionary force, but was sent on to Syria, from
which at least a large detachment, if not the whole,
of X *Fretensis* was withdrawn and added to Corbulo's
army.[2] The most probable solution is that the additional legion, to which Tacitus refers, is IV *Scythica*,
which was taken from Moesia and not from Germany,[3]
and that Tacitus has confused the identity of the two
legions numbered IV. For IV *Scythica* is definitely
stated by Tacitus to have formed part of the Syrian
army in 62 A. D.[4] Therefore it must have been
moved at some date between 55 and 62 from Moesia
to Syria. Secondly, the inconsistency in Tacitus'
narrative can be explained on the ground that Corbulo's need for reinforcements before advancing on
Artaxata in 58 A. D. was urgent, and it was quicker to
take a legion from Syria than from Moesia. In the
place of IV *Scythica* it is probable that VII *Claudia*
was summoned from Dalmatia. It is hardly likely
that Moesia would be left depleted of troops, in view
of the movements of tribes across the Danube, and
the occasion of the transference of the Dalmatian
legion may well be 58,[5] rather than 62 A. D., when

[1] Ibid. xiii. 35. 4.   [2] Ibid. xiii. 40. 8.
[3] No traces of legion IV *Scyth.* have been found in Germany.
[4] T. A. xv. 6. 5.
[5] Dess. 986, inscr. of Plautius Silvanus, governor of Moesia, in
which the words occur 'quamvis partem magnam ad expeditionem

V *Macedonica* was moved into Cappadocia to strengthen the army of Paetus.[1]   In 59 Tigranocerta capitulated, and Corbulo seems to have regarded his campaign as finished when the home government in the following year sent out a client prince called Tigranes to become King of Armenia.   Corbulo was ordered to support him, but gave him only a moderate force of 1,000 men,[2] while he himself with his remaining legions retired into Syria, which had been given to him as his province after the departure of Ummidius Quadratus.

The appointment of Tigranes as King of Armenia was a failure.   A plundering raid into Adiabene stirred Vologeses to a counter-invasion of Armenia in support of Tiridates.   Corbulo sent two legions, IV and XII, to help Tigranes,[3] and asked the Princeps to send out a governor for Cappadocia.   About the same time an embassy arrived from Vologeses, and the Roman government, incensed at the terms which he suggested, now contemplated the annexation of Armenia as a Roman province.   Paetus was sent out as governor of Cappadocia, and the Eastern command was divided between him and Corbulo in Syria.   A redistribution of legions took place.   V *Macedonica* was sent to join IV and XII in Cappadocia, while III, VI, and X remained with Corbulo in Syria.[4]   The armies seemed adequate for the expulsion of the Parthians from Armenia, but a disastrous campaign

in Armeniam misisset ', rightly interpreted by Ritt., o.c., P–W. xii, p. 1256, as referring to 62, and not 58 A. D. as Filow, o. c., p. 20.

[1] T. A. xv. 6. 5.   [2] Ibid. xiv. 26. 3.
[3] Ibid. xv. 8. 1.   [4] Ibid. xv. 6. 5.

by Paetus, which was intensified by the slowness of
Corbulo in coming to his rescue, led to a pact being
made with Parthia, by which Paetus agreed to give
up Armenia and retire west of the Euphrates. The
insulting character, however, of the embassy sent
by Vologeses to confirm the treaty at Rome aroused
the government to make a further effort against the
Parthians, and Corbulo was appointed commander-in-
chief. He had seven legions now at his disposal, for
XV *Apollinaris*, which in 50 A. D. had been sent. to
Carnuntum, was summoned to Syria.[1] Its place was
probably taken by X *Gemina* from Spain, which has
left records at Carnuntum that can be dated to this
period.[2] Of this combined force Corbulo sent back
IV and XII, which had disgraced themselves, to
Syria, and with the remainder moved into Cappadocia.[3] No military successes of any note were
achieved, and the only difference between the treaty
now formed and the pact of Paetus was that Tiridates
should go to Rome in person and receive his crown
from Nero's hand. Thus a long campaign, which had
involved many changes in the armies of the Danube
and Eastern provinces, and which at one time boded
well for the acquisition of Armenia as a Roman
province, ended in a compromise that was not a final
solution of the Armenian question. The grouping of
the troops, however, is interesting, because it shows
that, while Dalmatia and Pannonia could be safely

[1] T. A. xv. 25. 5.
[2] C. I. L. iii. 14358 13ᵃ, 18ᵃ, and 23, with Rhein. Mus. lix,
pp. 55–63.   [3] T. A. xv. 26. 2.

retained by a smaller force than before, Moesia was never left without at least two legions. The explanation of the latter danger is suggested by the defeat of the Sarmatae by Plautius Silvanus [1] and by a projected invasion of the Caucasus by Nero.

The rest of Nero's Principate is marked by the great Jewish rebellion which broke out in 66 A. D. as a result of unrest dating from Caligula's attempt to set up a statue of himself in the temple at Jerusalem. Cestius Gallus, the governor of Syria, advanced into Judaea with XII *Fulm.* and detachments of IV *Scyth.* and VI *Ferrata.*[2]   But meeting with a serious reverse, in which XII *Fulm.* lost its *aquila,*[3] he was forced to make an ignominious retreat, and Vespasian was appointed imperial governor of Judaea.   In the winter of 67 his army was concentrated at Ptolemais, and consisted of XV *Apoll.* with V *Maced.* and X *Fret.* brought from Alexandria by Titus.[4]   Meanwhile, Mucianus, who had succeeded Cestius Gallus, had with him in Syria III *Gall.,* IV *Scyth.,* VI *Ferr.,* and XII *Fulm.* In the next two years Vespasian gradually reduced the insurrection in Samaria and Galilee, and in 68 A. D. established a garrison at Emmaus, which was occupied by V *Maced.*[5]   In 69 A. D. he was succeeded in command by his son Titus, who in the siege of Jerusalem had in his army the three legions which had fought under his father and XII *Fulm.,* which was taken from Syria.[6]   However, the latter did not stay

[1] Dess. 986.
[2] Jos. B. J. ii. 18. 9 and ii. 19. 7.   [3] Suet. Vesp. 4.
[4] Jos. B. J. iii. 4. 2.   [5] Ibid. iv. 8. 1.   [6] T. H. v. 1.

long, for Titus mistrusted the soldiers after their defeat under Cestius Gallus and dispatched the legion to Melitene.[1]

In 66 A. D. Nero was planning two expeditions, one to the Caucasus against the Al ani, and one against the Ethiopians. For the former project he formed a new legion called I *Italica*,[2] and summoned XIV *Gem.* from Britain with detachments from some of the German legions.[3] At the same time Egypt was strengthened by a detachment from the African army,[4] and in 66 A. D. V *Maced.* and X *Fret.* were temporarily stationed at Alexandria, perhaps for the purpose of this campaign. But the Jewish rebellion necessitated their employment in Judaea and the African scheme was abandoned. In 68 A. D. III *Gall.* was transferred from Syria to Moesia,[5] and the garrison of that province was brought back to its normal three legions. Meanwhile, Nero's expedition to the Caucasus was also given up because of the revolt of Vindex in Gaul, and I *Italica* was sent to garrison Lugdunum,[6] while XIV *Gem.*, which had probably reached Dalmatia on its way from Britain, was ordered to proceed into Italy. Foreign wars were now for a time rendered unimportant by a variety of attempts in different parts of the Empire to set up candidates for the Principate. Before examining the part played by the legions in these civil wars, it will be

[1] Jos. B. J. vii. 1. 8.   [2] Suet. Nero 19.
[3] T. H. i. 6.
[4] Ibid. i. 70.   [5] Ibid. ii. 74.
[6] Ibid. i. 6.

convenient to set out in tabular form the positions of the different units on the death of Nero.[1]

Germany Inferior		I, V *Alaudae*, XV *Primigenia*, XVI.
„	Superior	IV *Macedonica*. XXI, XXII *Primigenia*.
Dalmatia	. .	XI *Claudia p. f.*
Pannonia	. .	X *Gemina* and XIII *Gemina*.
Moesia .	. .	III *Gallica*, VII *Claudia p. f*, VIII *Augusta*.
Syria .	. .	IV *Scythica*, VI *Ferrata*, XII *Fulminata*.
Judaea .	. .	V *Macedonica*, X *Fretensis*, XV *Apollinaris*.
Egypt .	. .	III *Cyrenaica*, XXII *Deiotariana*.
Africa .	. .	III *Augusta*.
Spain .	. .	VI *Victrix*.
Lugdunum .	.	I *Italica*.
Britain	. .	II *Augusta*, IX *Hispana*, XX *Valeria victrix*.
Italy .	. .	XIV *Gemina Martia victrix*.

Galba.

Before leaving Spain Galba recruited a new legion called VII *Gemina*,[2] which he brought with him to Rome and then dispatched to Pannonia. During his short Principate he effected the following changes. X *Gemina* was sent back to Spain,[3] and XIV *Gemina* was ordered to Dalmatia, while the organization of a legion recruited by Nero from marines was completed and given the title of I *Adiutrix*.[4]

Otho.

Otho's accession was secured by the praetorian

---

[1] Josephus' distribution of the legions which he assigns to 66 A.D. is in all probability anachronistic and represents rather the fresh allocation made by Vespasian (B. J. ii. 16. 4).

[2] T. H. i. 6 ; Dess. 9125 for the *dies natalis* of the legion.

[3] Ibid. ii. 58.   [4] Ibid. i. 6.

guards, but, on hearing of Vitellius' adoption by the German legions as prospective Princeps, he summoned to Italy legions VII *Gemina* and XIII *Gemina* from Pannonia, XI *Claudia* from Dalmatia, and a detachment from the Moesian legions and from XIV *Gemina*, while I *Adiutrix* was at his disposal in Rome.[1] On the other side, Vitellius had at Bedriacum three German legions (V *Alaudae*, XXI *Rapax*, and XXII *Pg.*) and I *Ital.* from Lugdunum with their eagles, and detachments from the remaining four German legions and from the three legions in Britain.[2] It is important to emphasize the difference between legions and detachments of legions in Vitellius' army, in view of the treatment meted out to the remnants of those German legions which took the side of Civilis. The *aquila* was the 'numen legionis': its abandonment or loss was normally equivalent to the destruction of the legion itself.

Vitellius.

After the first battle of Bedriacum Vitellius sent I *Adiutrix* to Spain, XIII *Gemina* to build an amphitheatre at Cremona, after which it retired into winter quarters in Pannonia, and VII *Gemina* and XI *Claudia* to their respective head-quarters in Pannonia and Dalmatia,[3] while XIV *Gemina* returned to Britain.[4] His own victorious army was retained in Italy. Meanwhile, Vespasian had been acclaimed *Imperator* by the legions at Alexandria,[5] and, while remaining himself

---

[1] Ibid. ii. 11.   [2] Ibid. ii. 100.   [3] Ibid. ii. 67.
[4] Ibid. ii. 66.   [5] Ibid. ii. 79.

with Titus to complete the subjugation of Judaea, he sent forward Mucianus and Antonius Primus, the *legatus* of legion VII *Gemina*, to deal with the situation in Italy.   Mucianus had with him legion VI *Ferrata* and detachments amounting to 13,000 from the Syrian and Judaean armies,[1] while the army of Primus [2] consisted of the legions on the Danube front, some of which were still harbouring resentment against Vitellius for the defeat of their old commander Otho.   The details of this force were III *Gallica*, VII *Claudia*, and VIII *Augusta* (from Moesia), VII *Gemina* and XIII *Gemina* (from Pannonia), to which was added later XI *Claudia* (from Dalmatia).[3]   On the death of Valens, Spain, at the instigation of legion I *Adiutrix*, declared for Vespasian,[4] and Britain and Gaul were both friendly disposed towards him.   The result, therefore, of the defeat of Vitellius at Bedriacum was the consolidation of all the Roman Empire, except Germany, in loyalty to Vespasian.   The conquered legions of Vitellius were dispersed through Illyricum and Moesia,[5] and the organization of a second legion of marines, who had deserted Vitellius for Vespasian at the instigation of Lucilius Bassus, was completed, and the legion itself was retained in Italy and called II *Adiutrix*.[6]   At this point an insurrection broke out in Germany at the instigation of Civilis, a Batavian

---

[1] T. H. ii. 83 ; it remained in Moesia for a time (iii. 46) and then proceeded to Italy.

[2] Ibid. ii. 85, 86.

[3] Ibid. iii. 50.

[4] Ibid. iii. 44.

[5] Ibid. iii. 35.

[6] Ibid. iii. 12, 36, 40, 55.

chief, who was later joined by two Gauls, called Tutor and Sabinus, who had dreams of a *regnum Galliarum* independent of the rule of Rome.

The history of the revolt of Civilis is marked by the incompetent command of Flaccus and Vocula over the remnants of the legions that Vitellius had left behind, and by a lack of discipline and obedience on the part of the Roman soldiers which is in dismal contrast to the normal attitude of Roman legionary troops. A narrative of events is unnecessary; it is sufficient to say that XV *Pg.*,[1] with what remained of V *Alaudae*, was massacred at Vetera,[2] while the remaining legions actually took the oath of loyalty to 'the kingdom of the Gauls'! Upon their submission legions I and XVI were sent to garrison the city of the Treveri,[3] while IV *Maced.* with the remnants of XXII *Pg.* were probably retained by Civilis in Lower Germany. Meanwhile, preparations were being made by Mucianus, who had entered Rome, to restore peace and security to the provinces of the Roman Empire. Partly for military reasons, and partly perhaps from jealousy of Primus, III *Gallica* and VII *Gemina*, which had formed the nucleus of the latter's army, were

---

[1] Whether a coin struck in Gaul with Mars as 'Deliverer' on the obverse and Victory on the reverse making a trophy of the spoils of legio XV *Primigenia*, is rightly referred to the Fall of Vetera, and as such belongs to the coinage of the 'regnum Galliarum', is questionable (Mattingly, 'R. Imperial Coinage', i, p. 180). Perhaps the coin has reference to Verginius Rufus, 'adsertor libertatis' in 68 A. D. (Dess. Gesch. d. röm. Kaiserz. ii, p. 387, n. 1).

[2] T. H. iv. 60.   [3] Ibid. iv. 62.

sent back to their respective provinces of Syria and
Pannonia.[1] About the same time VII *Cl.* and I *Ital.*
were moved to Moesia,[2] and it is probable that VI
Ferrata returned to Syria.[3] The expedition against
Civilis was then entrusted to Cerialis, and the following legions were put under his command : II *Adiutrix*, VIII *Augusta*, XI *Claudia*, XIII *Gemina*, all belonging to the victorious army, XXI *Rapax*, which
had previously belonged to Vitellius, XIV *Gemina*,
summoned from Britain, and I *Adiutrix* and VI
Victrix from Spain.[4] The arrival of this large army
in Germany caused the Treveri to return to their
loyalty to Rome, and legions I *Germanica* and XVI,
which had been stationed in their chief city, took the
oath of allegiance to Vespasian.[5] Before the final
conquest of Civilis, however, Cerialis further strengthened his army by withdrawing from its province X
Gemina, the last of the three Spanish legions,[6] so that
his total force in Germany consisted of nine legions,
with two legions which had come over from the rebels.
It is clear that such a disintegration of the army
could not be allowed to continue, and many important
changes were made by Vespasian in 70–71 A. D. These
will perhaps be most easily understood if the position
of the legions at the end of the revolt of Civilis is set
out in tabular form.

[1] T. H. iv. 39.

[2] They are not in Cerialis' army (ibid. iv. 68), and a defeat
sustained by Font. Agrippa may perhaps account for their dispatch
to Moesia (Jos. B. J. vii. 4. 3).

[3] Filow, o. c., p. 28.

[4] T. H. iv. 68.

[5] Ibid. iv. 70.

[6] Ibid. v. 19.

Germany under Cerialis	I *Adi.*, II *Adi.*, VI *Vic.*, VIII *Aug.*, X *Gem.*, XI *Cl.*, XIII *Gem.*, XIV *Gem.*, XXI *Rapax* with I *Germ.*, and XVI.
Surrendered or destroyed	IV *Mac.*, XV *Pg.*, and parts of V *Alaud.* and XXII *Pg.*
Pannonia	VII *Gem.*
Illyricum	Remnants of XXII *Pg.*
Moesia	I *Ital.*, VII *Cl.*, part of V *Alaud.*
Syria	III *Gall.*, IV *Scyth.*, VI *Ferr.*, XII *Fulm.*
Judaea	V *Maced.*, X *Fret.*, XV *Apoll.*
Egypt	III *Cyren.* and XXII *Deiot.*
Africa	III *Aug.*
Britain	II *Aug.*, IX *Hisp.*, and XX *V.v.*

Vespasian.

At the start of his Principate Vespasian disbanded four legions and created two new ones in addition to legion II *Adiutrix.* The units singled out for this disgrace were the four German legions which had either surrendered to Civilis or lost their eagles, and consequently I *Germ.*, IV *Maced.*, XV *Pg.*, and XVI disappear. Their place was taken by two legions having the same numbers as two of the disbanded units, and *cognomina* showing the dynasty under which they were formed. They were called IV *Flavia felix* and XVI *Flavia firma.*[1]

After this reconstruction Vespasian undertook a fresh distribution of the legions. The Rhine garrison was brought back to its old strength of eight legions, and although the Lower Province has at first the larger force because of the unrest of the Batavians, the operations of Clemens in 72–73 A. D. on the right

[1] Dio, lv. 24. 3.

bank of the Rhine in the Upper Province suggest that with Vespasian a new policy of frontier defence was inaugurated. The scheme was to make one frontier of the Rhine and Danube and to remove the re-entrant angle formed by the sources of these two rivers, and this was ultimately achieved by the construction of the famous *limes* in the reigns of Domitian, Hadrian, and Antoninus Pius. Thus the old natural frontier of the Rhine as delimiting the advance of Roman conquest gives way to an artificial line of fortified defence. In 70 the legions were divided as follows : in the Lower Province Cerialis had II *Adi.*, VI *Vic.*, XIII *Gem.*, XXI *Rapax*, and X *Gem.*, while in the Upper Province I *Adi.*, VIII *Aug.*, XI *Cl.*, and XIV *Gem.* were under the command of Annius Gallus.[1] When the danger from the revolt was over, legion XIII returned to its old camp Poetovio in Pannonia, and Cerialis departed to govern Britain with II *Adi.* At about the same time XXII *Pg.* was brought from Pannonia to Germania Inferior,[2] and the legions were then stationed in the following camps : in the Lower Province VI was at Novaesium,[3] X at Arenacum[4] and then at Noviomagus,[5] which may also have been the head-quarters of XXII unless it was at Colonia Agrippinensis, while XXI was stationed at Bonna.[6] In the Upper Province I and XIV garrisoned Moguntiacum,[7]

---

[1] T. H. iv. 68 and v. 19.

[2] *Tegulae* from Vetera collected by Steiner, 'Katalog d. Mus. zu Xanten ', 1911, pp. 59–61, and cf. C. I. L. xiii. 8175.

[3] Br. 264 a.   [4] T. H. v. 20.   [5] C. I. L. xiii. 8732-6.

[6] Inscriptions with *cognomen Rapax*, e. g. C. I. L. xiii. 8849.

[7] Dess. 2277 and C. I. L. xiii. 6896, 6920.

XI Vindonissa,[1] and VIII Argentoratum.[2] The operations of Clemens may have necessitated an increase in
the army of Upper Germany to five legions; if so,
perhaps legion VII *Gemina* took part in his campaigns,
while proceeding from Pannonia to its old home in
Spain, which had temporarily been denuded of all
legionary troops; for an inscription describing the
career of Ti: Staberius Secundus, who in 78 A. D. was
'praefectus alae Moesicae',[3] calls him 'trib. mil. leg.
VII Gem. felicis in Germania'.[4] This latter post was
held before the former, and it is probable that Secundus
was tribune of the legion when it received the *cognomen Felix* for its share in the campaign of Clemens.

An alteration in the garrison of the Danube was
made. The legions numbered seven, and they were
distributed in the proportion of four legions to Moesia,
two to Pannonia, and one to Dalmatia. This strength-
ening of the army of Moesia is easily understood
by the following considerations. In 68–69 A. D. the
Rhoxolani had invaded the province and had been
defeated by legion III *Gallica*.[5] In 69 an incursion of
Dacians had compelled legion VI *Ferrata* to be withdrawn temporarily from the Flavian expeditionary
force into Italy,[6] and in 70 Fonteius Agrippa, the
governor of the province, had met with a serious
defeat.[7] A concentration of troops, especially on the
lower Danube, thus became necessary, if the river was

[1] C. I. L. xiii. 5207–17.
[2] Ibid. 9082, 'iter derectum ab Argentorate in ripam Danuvii'.
[3] Dess. 9052.   [4] Ibid. 2729.
[5] T. H. i. 79.   [6] Ibid. iii. 46.
[7] Jos. B. J. vii. 4. 3.

to be held as a frontier. The legions were allotted as follows : IV *F.f.* took the place of XI *Cl.* in Dalmatia ;[1] XIII returned to Pannonia from Germany and, after a temporary garrisoning of Poetovio, was posted to Vindobona;[2] while XV *Apoll.* was recalled from the East and sent to Carnuntum.[3] In Moesia the four legions were I *Italica* and V *Alaudae*, which formerly belonged to Vitellius' army, VII *Claudia* sent back from Rome in 69, and V *Macedonica* recalled from the East.[4]

In the East Vespasian made one important innovation, which was instrumental in maintaining peace between Rome and Parthia till the last years of Trajan's Principate. He changed Cappadocia into an imperial province of the first rank, and posted a consular legate to it in place of a *procurator.*[5] The garrison of the province should have, in consequence, consisted of two legions, of which one was certainly XII *Fulminata*, withdrawn from Syria ;[6] the other was probably the new legion XVI *F. f.*, although there is no positive evidence for its presence at such an early date in the province. XII *Fulminata* was encamped at Melitene, while XVI *F.f.* was probably stationed in the north of the province ; for the danger to Cappadocia was not only from the Parthian side, but also from the Scythians and Sarmatians. This is confirmed by Philo, writing in 40 A. D., who points out that the Euphrates is a frontier both against Parthia and Sar-

[1] Dio, lv. 24. 8.
[2] C. I. L. 11855-9—*tegulae* of the same style (see Ritterling, s. v. legio, P-W. xii, p. 1715).
[3] Ibid. iii. 4483.   [4] Jos. B. J. vii. 5. 3.
[5] Suet. Vesp. 8 ; cf. T. A. ii. 42. 6.   [6] Dio, lv. 23. 5.

matia,[1] and perhaps by some lines of Statius addressed
to Victorius Marcellus, who is expecting the command
of a legion towards the end of Domitian's reign :

> Forsitan ibis
> Aut Histrum servare latus metuendaque portae
> Limina Caspiacae.[2]

As XV *Apoll.*, which succeeded XVI *F. f.* in Cappadocia in the reign of Trajan, was stationed at Satala,[3]
this may well have been the camp of the second legion
of the province from the beginning.

When the Jewish revolt had been quelled, the
remaining legions of the East were divided between
the provinces of Syria and Judaea. The former was
given three legions, the latter one. IV *Scythica* was
posted to Cyrrhus in place of X *Fretensis*, which was
used by Titus in Judaea and subsequently garrisoned
the latter province at Jerusalem.[4] In 72 A. D. Commagene was transformed from a client kingdom into
a Roman province [5] with the help of legion VI *Ferrata*,
which had been sent back from Italy, and probably
it helped to garrison the new province [6] till proceeding into Galilee at the end of Trajan's Principate.
The third Syrian legion (III *Gallica*) seems to have
been at Raphaneae ; for a tribune of this legion
becomes a quaestor of Titus,[7] who probably reviewed
the troops at Raphaneae in 70 A. D., while the soldiers
are recruited almost exclusively from Syria.

---

[1] Philo ad Gaium, p. 547; see Knox-McElderry, in Cl. Q. 1909, p. 46.
[2] Stat. Silvae, iv. 4. 61.   [3] C. I. L. iii. 806 and Dess. 8795.
[4] Jos. B. J. vii. 1. 2. ; Dess. 9059.   [5] Suet. Vesp. 8.
[6] Samosata was perhaps not a permanent camp till after Trajan's
Parthian War (Dio, lxviii. 19. 2).   [7] Dess. 1008.

Domitian.

The absence of trustworthy literary sources makes it impossible to follow the movements of the legions in the reigns of Domitian, Trajan, and Hadrian with the same detail as in the preceding period, but from the evidence of epigraphy it is usually possible to discover what were the most important campaigns and the number of the legions employed in them. The Principates of Domitian and Trajan are marked by a new offensive on the Rhine, and by campaigns on the Danube in which serious defeats were at first sustained at the hands of the Suebi and Dacians under their king Decebalus, but which led to the annexation of Dacia on the left bank of the river as a Roman province. In 83 A. D. Domitian inaugurated a great campaign against the Chatti, who lived in the middle-Rhine section, and the grouping of the legions in this war indicates that this was not simply a minor punitive expedition but an attempt to establish a permanent frontier in the Taunus region, which, if extended south, might link up with the line already marked out by Vespasian in the Neckar district, by his annexation of the *agri decumates*.[1] For this war Domitian raised a new legion called I *Minervia*, which was posted to Lower Germany;[2] at the same period XXI *Rapax* was moved into the Upper Province. This is indicated by the Mirebeau tiles discovered near Dijon, which have inscribed on them the names of the four legions of Upper Germany and

[1] See further Henderson, 'Five Roman Emperors', pp. 117-54.
[2] Dio, lv. 24. 8; Dess. 2279.

legion XXI,[1] and also to a lesser extent by an inscription
recording the military tribunate of one Sosius Senecio,[2]
who was probably the consul of 99 A. D. and so may
have held his earlier appointment some fifteen years
previously. The legions in 83 A. D. were therefore
distributed as follows in Germany: in the Lower
Province, I *Min.*, VI *Vic.*, X *Gem.*, XXII *Pg.*; in the
Upper Province, I *Adi.*, VIII *Aug.*, XI *Cl.*, XIV *Gem.*,
XXI *Rapax.* In addition, there was a detachment
from IX *Hispana*, which Tacitus says was weakened
at this time,[3] and from the remaining British legions,
which were under the command of C. Velius Rufus,
a *primus pilus* centurion.[4] The exact results of this
campaign are difficult to discover, but a statement of
Frontinus makes it almost certain that forts were definitely established in the *limes* section, and that the
frontier was correspondingly advanced from the Rhine.[5]

The centre of interest now changed to the Danube,
where Suetonius says that two severe defeats were
sustained at the hands of the Dacians by Oppius
Sabinus and Cornelius Fuscus, who, although prefect
of the praetorian cohorts, had been entrusted with
the office of commander-in-chief.[6] These reverses probably occurred in 86–88 A. D. The seriousness of the
situation drove the Princeps to reinforce the army of
the Danube, and it is probable that I *Adiutrix* was
taken from Germany and II *Adiutrix* summoned from
Britain. The presence of I *Adi.* is made probable by

---

[1] Dess. 2285.   [2] Br. 1416.   [3] Dess. 1025 ; Ag. 26.
[4] Ibid. 9200 (following Ritterling's interpretation).
[5] Front. Strat. i. 3. 10.   [6] Suet. Dom. 6.

the fact that another *tegula* discovered at Mirebeau records the names of four legions known to have been in Upper Germany, but not that of I *Adi.*,[1] while an inscription proves that it was on the Danube in the reign of Nerva.[2]   The withdrawal of II *Adiutrix* from Britain in 86 is not so certain.   It is still in Britain in 83 A. D., because a detachment of it was serving in Germany under C. Velius Rufus in the Lingones territory,[3] along with a detachment of II *Aug.*   Further, on one of the Mirebeau tiles recording the detachments from Britain that were sent to Germany legion II alone is given a *cognomen*, namely *Augusta*.   This must certainly have been added to distinguish its detachment from that of II *Adiutrix*, although in this imperfect *tegula* the name of this latter legion is not inscribed.   On another tile, on the other hand, only one legion numbered II is found and without a *cognomen*.[4]   This probably implies that the detachment of II *Adi.* had been withdrawn because the main body of the legion had left Britain.   Further, a centurion of the same legion was decorated for his services, 'bello Dacico', apparently by Domitian,[5] and a tribune of the legion 'in bello Suebico et Sarmatico'[6] of 92 A. D.   Therefore the legion must have been on

---

[1] Hermes, xix. p. 439, no. 2.   [2] Dess. 2720.   [3] Ibid. 9200.
[4] Ritterling in Jahresh. des Österr. Arch. 1904, Beiblatt, p. 23 sq. Mommsen, Hermes xix. 439, nos. 3 and 4.   *Contra* von Domaszewski in Philologus 66 (1907), p. 165 sq., who thinks that the British *vexillationes* took part in a campaign against the Bructeri in 77 A.D., but Ritterling's case, as represented in P–W. xii., o. c., p. 1442, seems to me the more convincing.
[5] Dess. 9193.   [6] Ibid. 2719.

the Danube some time before this latter war, and may have taken part in the earlier campaign of 86–88 A. D. If so, then the army opposed to the Dacians in 87 consisted of the following legions : I *Adi.*, II *Adi.*, I *Ital.*, IV *F. f.* (moved from Dalmatia),[1] V *Maced.*, V *Alaud.*, VII *Cl.*, XIII *Gem.*, and XV *Apoll.* It was perhaps after this war that Moesia was divided into two provinces, called Moesia Superior and Moesia Inferior, with the camps of the former at Singidunum and Viminacium and of the latter at Novae and Oescus.[2] The legions were now concentrated in these two provinces and Pannonia at the expense of Dalmatia, which was left without a garrison.

An interlude in the fighting on the Danube was occasioned by the revolt of Saturninus, the governor of Upper Germany, who induced the two legions wintering at Moguntiacum in 89 to support his cause, and appropriated for that purpose the deposits of the soldiers in the Savings Bank.[3] The two legions can be identified as XIV *Gem.* and XXI *Rapax.* This mutiny occasioned great alarm at Rome, and Domitian set out for Germany. We know little of the events that followed, but the danger was clearly averted by the loyalty of the legions of Lower Germany, in return for which they received the honorary titles of *pia fidelis Domitiana,*[4] the last epithet being erased when Domitian suffered *damnatio memoriae.* The legions honoured in this way were I *Min.*, VI *Vic.*, X *Gem.*, and XXII *Pg.* One important result of the

[1] Ibid. 2086 and 9110.   [2] Filow, o. c., pp. 66–72.
[3] Suet. Dom. 8.   [4] Dess. 2279.

mutiny was that Domitian issued a regulation forbidding in future more than one legion to occupy the same camp.[1] Further, a redistribution of the legions was rendered necessary. XXI *Rapax* was sent at once into Pannonia, followed by XIV *Gem.* perhaps two years later,[2] for Domitian's projected expedition against the Sarmatae and Suebi. In support of this statement there is the following evidence. 1. There is an absence of *tegulae* belonging to legion XIV *Gem.* on the *limes*. On the other hand, *tegulae* of this legion have been found at Mursella, Vindobona, and Brigetio,[3] which probably represent the camps which the legion temporarily occupied before it superseded XV *Apoll.* at Carnuntum about 114 A.D. 2. Legion XXI *Rapax* has left no records in Germany after the mutiny of Saturninus. In the last chapter we saw that in all probability it disappeared early in Trajan's reign, which must imply its presence on the Danube before his first Dacian War. When to this is added the part the legion played in the German mutiny, the inference that it left Germany for Pannonia about 90 A.D. seems established. For the Sarmatian War, therefore, the following legions were on the Danube:

[1] Suet. Dom. 7.

[2] Probably leg. XIV took part in rebuilding the camp at Moguntiacum before leaving the province (so Ritterling, following G. Wolffs, o.c., P-W. xii, p. 1736).

[3] C. I. L. iii. 8755, 4578, 11365[a]. Perhaps XIV was at Brigetio when XIII was at Vindobona. Then, when XI was posted to Brigetio and XIII was engaged in the Dacian wars, XIV moved to Vindobona, where it completed the buildings started by XIII.

I *Adi.*, II *Adi.*, I *Ital.*, IV *F.f.*, V *Maced.*, V *Alaud.*,
VII *Cl.*, XIII *Gem.*, XIV *Gem.*, XV *Apoll.*, and XXI
Rapax. Despite this unparalleled concentration of
troops, a severe defeat was suffered, and V *Alaudae*
was destroyed. Domitian's campaigns on the Danube
had led to no more than a patched-up peace with
Decebalus, and handed on to his successors a frontier
which was no longer adequate to hold back the incursions of the tribes on the left bank of the river.

Nerva.

Either at the end of Domitian's reign or during
Nerva's brief Principate, legion XXII *Pg.* in Germany
was moved into the Upper Province.[1] The garrison
of Germany thus consisted of six legions (three in
each province), while on the Danube, in the three
provinces of Pannonia, Moesia Superior and Inferior,
there were ten legions. Similarly, Agricola's activities
in Britain had been curtailed by the weakening of his
army to three legions, from one of which a detachment had been taken to Germany. The head-quarters
of the British legions were, at the death of Domitian, as
follows: II *Aug.* at Caerleon, XX *V.v.* at Chester,
and IX *Hisp.* at York, where it had been moved from
its old station at Lincoln.[2]

Trajan.

Trajan seems to have inaugurated his career of conquest by continuing the work which had been begun

[1] Dedication by a centurion of 96 A.D. from the Upper Province
(C. I. L. xiii. 6357).

[2] Ag., *passim*; C. I. L. vii. 248.

in Germany by his predecessors, and to him perhaps may be assigned the building of some forts on the *limes Raeticus*, east of the modern Lorch.[1] Legionary troops were not stationed on the *limes* itself; instead, the scheme was adopted of employing *auxilia* for these advanced posts and of keeping the legions as a second line of defence. Consequently there was no longer the same necessity for a strong legionary army on the Rhine, and the result is seen in the subsequent reduction of the forces to four legions.

The confusion created by Domitian's reverses on the Danube, and the continued threatening unrest of Decebalus, called for a fresh Roman campaign. The danger was great enough to induce the Princeps to increase the army of Rome to thirty legions, and the new legion called XXX *Ulpia* was sent to the Danube district.[2] In addition, XI *Cl.* was summoned from Germany, and traces of it have been discovered at Brigetio in Upper Pannonia.[3] Trajan had consequently a force on the Danube of twelve legions. Unfortunately we cannot trace in detail the part played by the individual legions in the two Dacian wars; in the two campaigns only five can be definitely shown, from distinctions conferred upon them, to have taken part, namely I *Italica*,[4] IV *Flavia felix*,[5] V *Macedonica*,[6] VII *Claudia*,[7] and perhaps XIII *Gemina*.[8] Between the two wars a garrison seems to have been left at Sarmi-

---

[1] Dess. 2002 and 9152.

[2] The actual camp is unknown; later it was in Upper Pannonia (C. I. L. iii. 4663*a*).

[3] Id. iii. 4658*a*.   [4] Dess. 2656.   [5] C. I. L. xi. 5696.

[6] Dess. 2666*b*.   [7] C. I. L. xi. 5992.   [8] Id. iii. 6984.

zegethusa,[1] the capital of Dacia, but it is improbable that a province was formed till after the second campaign. On the other hand the interval of three years may have seen the division of Pannonia into an upper and lower province with the capital of the latter district at Aquincum, which was garrisoned by II *Adiutrix*,[2] while the permanent camps of the Upper Province were at Carnuntum, Vindobona, and Brigetio. Probably in the winter of 101–102 A. D. I *Minervia* was moved from Germany to the Danube,[3] and possibly II *Traiana* arrived to replace the loss of the *Rapax*.[4] After the successful termination of the second campaign Dacia was formed into a consular province. D. Terentius Scaurianus, whose name appears on a *diploma* of Feb. 17, 110 A. D., as provincial governor, is *consularis*,[5] and in addition we know the names of two legionary commanders,[6] which implies a consular province, because in a praetorian the provincial governor and legionary commander are the same. Legion XIII *Gem.* was definitely detailed for service in the new province,[7] and if the right restoration of a *tegula* found at Apulum is ' Leg. XIII Gem. et I Adi.',[8] then the second legion was in all probability I *Adiutrix*. The camp at Vindobona was now garrisoned by X *Gemina* from Germany, perhaps after a short occupation of Aquincum,[9] while

---

[1] The legion forming the garrison was most probably IV. *F. f.* under Avidius Nigrinus (Dess. 2417).   [2] Dess. 9084.

[3] C. I. L. ii. 2424.   [4] See ch. iv, p. 115.

[5] Dess. 2004.   [6] Ibid. 1046 and C. I. L. iii. 1089.

[7] Dess. 2042.

[8] Ibid. 9109 (but see Ritterling, o. c., P–W. xii, p. 1391).

[9] C. I. L. iii. 10479.

XI *Claudia* moved into Lower Moesia. It is certainly found there at the end of Hadrian's reign,[1] and the necessity of holding in check the Rhoxolani, who had taken the side of Dacia, may have been the occasion for its establishment at Durostorum and for changing the head-quarters of V *Maced.* from Oescus to Troesmis.[2] On the other hand I *Minervia* returned to Germany, where with VI *Victrix* it formed the garrison of the Lower,[3] while VIII *Aug.* and XXII *Pg.* remained in the Upper, Province. The army of the Rhine was thus reduced to four legions,[4] and after the second Dacian War the legions were distributed as follows:

Lower Germany	I *Minervia* and VI *Victrix.*
Upper ,,	VIII *Augusta* and XXII *Primigenia.*
Lower Pannonia	II *Adiutrix p. f.*
Upper ,,	X *Gemina*, XIV *Gemina*, and XV *Apollinaris.*
Lower Moesia .	I *Italica*, V *Macedonica*, and XI *Claudia p. f.*
Upper ,, .	IV *Flavia felix*, VII *Claudia p. f.*, XXX *Ulpia victrix*, and (?) II *Traiana.*
Dacia . .	I *Adiutrix p. f.* and XIII *Gemina.*
Syria . .	III *Gallica*, IV *Scythica*, and VI *Ferrata.*
Judaea . .	X *Fretensis.*
Cappadocia .	XII *Fulminata* and XVI *Flavia firma.*
Egypt . .	III *Cyrenaica* and XXII *Deiotariana.*
Africa . .	III *Augusta.*
Spain . .	VII *Gemina.*
Britain . .	II *Augusta*, IX *Hispana*, and XX *Valeria victrix.*

The rest of the reign of Trajan was marked by his

---

[1] Dess. 2288.

[2] See Ritterling on career of Minicius Natalis (o.c., P-W. xii, p. 1697) and Filow, o.c., p. 66. [3] Br. 660. and C.I.L. iii. 6819.

[4] The camps were at Bonna, Vetera, Moguntiacum, and Argentoratum.

great Parthian campaign, which resulted in the formation of three new provinces—Armenia, Mesopotamia,
and Assyria, in addition to Arabia, which was created
in 106 A.D. and garrisoned at first perhaps by one of
the Syrian legions (? III *Gallica*). The actual legions
which took part in the expedition are not known.
Clearly the units which were already stationed in the
East must have formed the nucleus of the army, and
four of these are known from distinctions conferred
upon their officers, namely, IV *Scyth.*,[1] VI *Ferr.*,[2]
X *Fret.*,[3] and XVI *F.f.*[4] In addition, XII *Fulm.* from
Cappadocia, III *Gall.* and II *Traiana* from Arabia and
Syria respectively, with possible detachments from the
two Egyptian legions, may have also been employed.
A passage of Fronto further indicates that some of the
legions which had operated in the Dacian wars took
part in the campaign.[5] For instance, XV *Apoll.* seems
to have moved at this time, as it afterwards superseded XVI *F.f.* in Cappadocia when that legion joined
the Syrian army,[6] and I *Adi.*[7] and VII *C.p.f.*[8] were in
all probability included in the number. Again, the
formation of the new provinces would demand garrisons, and it is difficult to see how troops could have
been spared from Syria and Judaea. Probably, then,

---

[1] Dess. 1062.
[2] Ibid. 2726 and 9471.
[3] Ibid. 2727.
[4] Ibid. 2660.
[5] 'Traianus in bellum profectus est cum cognitis militibus . . .
sagittarum ictus post ingentia Dacorum falcibus inlata vulnera
despicatui habentibus', Fronto, p. 205.
[6] Dio, lv. 23, although the move may not have taken place till
Hadrian's Principate (Dess. 2288).
[7] C. I. L. iii. 6706, from Cyrrhus.
[8] Dess. 9491.

the army of occupation of Armenia at least was drawn from the Danube legions. This redistribution was, however, of short duration. Revolts occurred during Trajan's march to the East, and Fronto [1] talks of a legion being defeated and its commander killed in Mesopotamia, while in Babylon Maximus met with a reverse and died in action.[2] Finally, the death of Trajan himself put an end to all further conquest, and Hadrian withdrew the advanced troops and organized the eastern frontier on the line of the Euphrates.

Hadrian.

The last years of this period were, as a whole, a time of peace. Hadrian put into effect a definite system of frontier defence, and for this purpose the legions were, as far as possible, kept in their own provinces, a plan which was assisted, if not necessitated, by the growing policy of recruiting the army from local sources.[3] This is the period of the construction of the Tyne to Solway wall in Britain, and the policy adopted there of employing the *auxilia* as the first line of defence and keeping the legions in garrisons behind the front, but connected with it by good roads, was probably extended to the other frontiers of the Empire. Some events of importance which involved movements of the legions must, however, be noticed.

Hadrian sent back to the Danube the legions which had been withdrawn from those provinces for Trajan's Parthian invasion, and came himself to Moesia. At-

---

[1] Fronto, p. 217.   [2] Dio, Epit. lxiii. 30. 2.
[3] See ch. vi, pp. 171 and 181.

tacks were threatening from the Rhoxolani and Iazyges, and whereas the former of these was averted by the personal mediation of the Princeps, the latter required a military campaign under Marcius Turbo, who commanded the troops from Dacia and Pannonia.[1] After the war a new organization was put into force. Dacia was made into a praetorian province with one legion (XIII *Gemina*), and I *Adi.*, which had helped to garrison that province under Trajan, was sent to Brigetio in Upper Pannonia.[2] About the same time XXX *Ulpia* was transferred to Lower Germany,[3] so that the garrison of Upper Pannonia consisted now of I *Adi.*, X *Gem.*, and XIV *Gem.* This last movement was occasioned by events in Britain. A serious revolt had broken out in 119 A.D., and reinforcements were required. In consequence, VI *Victrix* was dispatched from the Lower Province of Germany, perhaps in the first year of the rebellion,[4] and XXX *Ulpia* came to fill its place, while in addition a strong detachment drawn from the two legions of the Upper Province and from VII *Gemina* in Spain was sent to Britain.[5] The Roman legions were unable at first to cope successfully with the revolt, and IX *Hispana* was destroyed not later than 122 A.D.[6]

[1] Hist. Aug. Hadr. 6. 6.

[2] Dess. 2288 and Ritterling, o.c., P-W. xii, p. 1288. Probably at the same time the province of Dacia Inferior was formed and governed by a *procurator* with *auxilia*.

[3] C. I. L. xiii. 8197[1]. It was posted to Vetera, I *Min.* being at Bonna.

[4] C. I. L. vi. 1549.   [5] Dess. 2726.

[6] Fronto, p. 217. The legion may perhaps have been destroyed as early as 119 A.D. (the probable date at which VI *Vic.* left Germany) despite two inscriptions of senatorial careers:

Its place was taken by VI *Victrix*, which now formed part of the permanent British garrison.

At the beginning of 123 A.D. war threatened to break out between Rome and Parthia. This, however, appears to have been averted by the strong measures taken by Hadrian, who went to the East himself, and put Claudius Quartinus in command of a combined force drawn from legions II *Traiana* and III *Cyrenaica*.[1] It was probably after this campaign that III *Cyrenaica* left Egypt and garrisoned Arabia, while II *Traiana* moved from Syria into Egypt, where it was shortly to become the only legion in that province. In 132 a great Jewish revolt broke out, the *casus belli* being Hadrian's proposal to make Jerusalem a Roman colony. There is no clear record of the legions employed by Rome to quell this rebellion ; but inscriptions tell of a tribune of III *Cyren.*,[2] a soldier of III *Gall.*,[3] and a centurion of X *Fret.*,[4] and we may believe that most of the legions of the East were employed, with probably some detachments from the Danube army.[5] The revolt, too, was not limited to Palestine, and the magnitude of the danger was not at first realized by Rome. Both Dio[6] and Fronto[7] emphasize the serious losses incurred, and it was almost certainly in this war that

(a) 'L. Aemilius Carus trib. mil. IX Hisp.' is praetorian gov. of Arabia in 142 A.D. ; (b) 'L. Novius Saturninus trib. mil. IX Hisp.' is governor of Numidia in 147 and consul in 150 A.D. (Dess. 1077 and 1070). In both instances the interval between the military tribunate and the later appointments is unusually long.

[1] C.I.L. xiii. 1803 ; Hist. Aug. Hadr. 12. 8.
[2] Dess. 1071.   [3] Ibid. 2313.   [4] Ibid. 2080.
[5] C.I.L. iii. 14155².   [6] Dio. lxix. 13. 1.   [7] Fronto, p. 217.

XXII *Deiotariana* was annihilated or disbanded in disgrace ; for it was still stationed at Alexandria in 119,[1]
but is not found on the army list of the time of
Antoninus Pius.[2] After the revolt Judaea was made
into a consular province by the transfer of VI *Ferrata*
from Syria.[3] Its new camp was at Caparcotna,[4] while
X *Fret.* continued to garrison Jerusalem.

At the end of Hadrian's Principate the legions were
therefore distributed as follows : [4]

Britain	.	II *Aug.*, VI *Vic.*, and XX *V. v.*
Upper Germany	.	VIII *Aug.* and XXX *Ulp. vic.*
Lower „	.	I *Min.* and XXII *Pg.*
Upper Pannonia		I *Adi. p. f.*, X *Gem.*, XIV *Gem. M. v.*
Lower „	.	II *Adi. p. f.*
Upper Moesia	.	IV *F. f.* and VII *C. p. f.*
Lower „	.	I *Ital.*, V *Maced.*, XI *C. p. f.*
Dacia	.	XIII *Gem.*
Cappadocia	.	XII *Fulm.* and XV *Apoll.*
Syria	.	III *Gall.*, IV *Scyth.*, and XVI *F. f.*
Judaea	.	VI *Ferr.* and X *Fret.*
Arabia	.	III *Cyren.*
Egypt	.	II *Tr. fortis.*
Africa	.	III *Aug.*
Spain	.	VII *Gem.*

Antoninus Pius.

The policy, which Hadrian had inaugurated, of keeping the legions in permanent camps in the same provinces was adhered to with only one exception by his
three successors. This was largely a matter of necessity. The danger of barbarian invasions across the

[1] Riccobono, *Leges*, no. 78.
 B. G. U. i. 140.   [2] Dess. 2288.
 [3] The provincial gov. in Diplom. cix, C. I. L. iii, p. 2328[70] of
139 A.D. is *consularis*.   [4] A. E. 1920, no. 78.

frontiers was much greater than it had been during the previous century ; consequently it was expedient to defend the vulnerable points of the frontiers with troops acclimatized to the district and accustomed to the work. At the same time recruiting was now mainly from local sources and the legions were developing into a local militia. Therefore a proposed permanent transfer of a legion from, say, Pannonia to Syria would have met with violent opposition from its soldiers, and might have caused the revolt of the province and the influx of barbarian hordes from beyond the frontier. Despite the permanent garrisoning of the provinces, however, situations still arose when the troops of the threatened province were inadequate to repel the invader. In the first century of the Principate this problem was solved by the moving of whole legions from other provinces to the war zone, but after Hadrian this policy was changed. In place of whole legions, strong *vexillationes* were drawn from a variety of units and placed under officers of rank varying with the strength of the detachments, who had the title of *praepositi*.[1] Such *vexillationes*, as we have seen, were not uncommon in the first century, but now they attained a new significance. Owing to the long duration of the wars of this period these detachments often remained for years away from their own unit, and as a result created for themselves new head-quarters in the war area and became miniature independent legions. This can be illustrated from inscriptions. A certain *legatus* called Pompilius Piso is actually said

[1] E.g. Dess. 1111 and A. E. 1920, no. 45.

to be ' praepositus legionibus I Italicae et IV Flaviae'[1] although he is no more than commander of detach- ments taken from the head-quarters of these two units at Novae and Singidunum. Again, VIII *Augusta* has left in Dalmatia *tegulae* belonging to the period of the Marcomannic War stamped ' Leg. VIII Aug.', but the head-quarters of this legion were still at Argentoratum, and so the *tegulae* must belong merely to a *vexillatio* of the legion.[2] This practice of employing *vexillationes* was prominent in the Marcomannic War ; we must further inquire whether the same policy can be de- tected in the remaining campaigns of the period.

The reign of Antoninus Pius was, as a whole, a time of peace. Such campaigns as took place were carried out by the troops belonging to the province, as, for instance, in Britain, where a new wall was built from Forth to Clyde,[3] and in Dacia, where the Romans ex- tended their area of occupation to the north-west, and the new territory was protected by a wall and formed into a separate province known as Dacia Porolissensis governed by a *procurator*.[4] Only in Mauretania was the danger from the Moors so great that reinforcements were required for III *Augusta*. In this case the same policy was adopted as in the later Marcomannic War. Whole legions were not moved into Africa, but *vexilla- tiones* were formed, chiefly from the armies of Germany and Pannonia.[5]

[1] Dess. 1111.   [2] C. I. L. iii. 10181¹.
[3] Paus. viii. 43. 4.
[4] Hist. Aug. Ant. 5. 4.
[5] Inscriptions mention the following legions : I *Adi.*, I *Min.*, II *Adi.*, IV *F. f.*, X *Gem.*, XIV *Gem.*, XXII *Pg.*, and XXX *Ulp.*

Marcus Aurelius.

In the first year of the Principate of Marcus Aurelius
the Parthian War which Vologeses had for some time
been planning broke out,[1] and early reverses were experienced by the Roman armies under the command of
the governors of Cappadocia and Syria.[2] The traditional
inefficiency of the Eastern army was thus exposed, and
the conclusion forced itself upon the Roman government that a successful end to the war could only be
reached by the dispatch of legions from Europe.   The
position was similar to the situation at the time of
Corbulo's appointment, and it may be that the government was influenced by the events of a hundred years
ago.   In any case the policy adopted in 162 A.D. was
so far parallel to that of Nero that whole legions were
ordered to move from the Rhine–Danube front and
vexillationes were formed from some of the other units.
Epigraphical evidence makes it practically certain that
I *Minervia*, II *Adi.*, and V *Maced.* were present in their
full strength ; for M. Claudius Fronto was in 162 A.D.
appointed 'leg. Aug. legioni primae Minerviae in expeditionem Parthicam deducendae',[3] while II. *Adi.*[4] and
V *Maced.*[5] both served under their own *legati* in this war,
and this most probably means that the whole legions,
and not merely detachments, took part in the campaign.

[1] Hist. Aug. Marc. 8. 6.
[2] See Ritterling in Rhein. Mus. lix, pp. 186–96, and Premerstein in Klio, xi, pp. 355–66.
[3] Dess. 1098.   [4] Ibid. 8977.
[5] Ibid. 2811.   The employment of European legions is further
confirmed by the speech of Marcus Aurelius to the Danube army
after the revolt of Avidius Cassius in 175 A.D. (Dio, lxxi. 25).

In addition there was a variety of *vexillationes* from other legions, of which it will be sufficient to mention contingents from X *Gem.*[1] and XIV *Gem.*[2] and perhaps a detachment of *equites* belonging to Lower Moesia and Dacia under the command of a tribune of XI *C. p. f.*[3] The Parthian War of M. Aurelius thus illustrates a combination of the old and new policies. The danger from Parthia and perhaps the inefficiency of the Eastern army necessitated the use of European legions; the temporary quiet on the Rhine–Danube front made their transfer possible.

But before the Parthian War was over, the Marcomanni, profiting by the weakening of the forces opposed to them, declared war upon Rome. The danger was great and threatened even the safety of Italy, and as the legions sent to the East could not be immediately recalled, the Princeps raised two new legions from Italy, which were later called II *Italica* and III *Italica.* These were used to defend the northern frontier of Italy, and later in the war garrisoned Rhaetia and Noricum.[4]

On the return of the European legions from the East, what I have called the only exception to the Hadrianic policy of keeping the legions in the same provinces took place. Legion V *Maced.* was not sent back to Troesmis in Lower Moesia, but was posted to Dacia. Consular governors can be traced in this province from

---

[1] C. I. L. viii. 7050.   [2] Id. iii. 12091.

[3] Dess. 2723, which more probably refers to this war than Trajan's. (Filow, o.c., p. 75; *contra* Ritterling, o.c., P–W. xii, p. 1281.)   [4] C. I. L. iii. 14369[1] and 5993.

169 A. D.,[1] and the latest records left by the legion at Troesmis belong to the first years of Marcus Aurelius.[2] The province, which for a time had consisted of three divisions, in only one of which a legion was stationed, was now organized as one consular province with leg. XIII *Gem.* at Apulum [3] and V *Maced.* at Potaissa.[4]

In the Marcomannic War, which lasted fifteen years, all the legions on the Rhine–Danube front were engaged, but not as complete units. The permanent camps were not abandoned, but the main body of the legions remained to garrison them, and sent *vexillationes* to the actual scene of the fighting. Apart from epigraphical evidence, this inference is confirmed by the column of Marcus Aurelius.[5] In the reliefs on this column both the legionary *aquila* and the manipular *signa* are missing, and in their place *vexilla*, the standards of detachments, are depicted. This affords a striking contrast with the reliefs on Trajan's column and is a clear indication of the changed policy of the Roman government, which may incidentally account for the long protracted struggle with the Marcomanni.

No changes were made by Commodus in the positions of the legions, and in 193 A. D. they numbered 30, which, with the exception of the transfer of V *Maced.* from Lower Moesia to Dacia and the posting of Marcus' new legions to Rhaetia and Noricum, occupied the same camps as they were garrisoning on the death of Hadrian.

[1] Dess. 1098.   [2] C. I. L. iii. 6189.
[3] Dess. 4006.   [4] C. I. L. iii. 905.
[5] See Premerstein, Klio, xiii, pp. 70-5.

VI

THE RECRUITING AREAS OF THE LEGIONS

APART from the garrison troops of Rome, the imperial Roman army was divided into legions and *auxilia*, and, down to the time of Hadrian, the former were distinguished from the latter by the sources from which their ranks were recruited. Whereas the *auxilia* were drawn from provincials who had not yet received the Roman citizenship, only Roman citizens were eligible for service in the legions. This general condition, which was intended to emphasize the superiority of Italians and favoured provincials from Gaul and Spain over the less Romanized parts of the Empire, was preserved with only slight modifications till the second century. Only three exceptions call for notice. Augustus himself twice departed from the principle he laid down, namely in the revolt of Pannonia in 6 A.D., and after the disaster of Varus in 9 A.D. For the former, freedmen were employed and organized into *cohortes voluntariorum*;[1] after the latter disaster, levies were raised from the *vernacula multitudo*[2] or non-citizen population of Rome to fill up gaps in the army of the Rhine. This extraordinary recruiting did not, however, involve the creation of new legions, and it was not till the year of the Civil War that two new legions of non-citizens were formed by Galba and Vespasian from marines.[3] The very title of these units, *adiutrices*, suggests that they

---

[1] Dio, lv. 31. 1.   [2] T. A. i. 31. 4.
[3] T. H. i. 6 and iii. 55.

were regarded as inferior to the normal legion, and it
may be that the citizenship was only granted to their
soldiers on discharge.[1]

The qualification of Roman citizenship for legionary
recruits carried with it the further qualification of
membership of a Roman town (*municipalis origo*).[2] If a
man had to be a Roman citizen before his enlistment,
he would almost certainly come from a town which had
received some degree of Roman citizenship, i.e. a *colonia*
or a *municipium*. But from the outset both these conditions were interpreted in a liberal sense. This can
be most easily seen in the different policy adopted for
the recruiting of the Eastern army as compared with
the legions of the West. Whereas the latter were
composed of Italians and Roman citizens from the
Roman towns of Gallia Narbonensis and Baetica, the
chief recruiting areas for the former were Galatia and
Cappadocia. Now the Roman franchise had been very
sparingly extended in the East, and the two provinces in
question were singularly devoid, in the Julio-Claudian
period, of Roman towns. Consequently resort was had
to a constitutional fiction, and, in order to secure
soldiers for the legions, the citizenship was given to
individuals. The recruit could therefore honestly describe himself as a Roman citizen, and on his discharge
might enjoy the privileges of Roman town life.[3] The
selection of different recruiting areas for the Eastern

[1] See ch. iv, p. 104.

[2] See Momm. 'Die Conscriptionordnung der röm. Kaiserzeit'
in Gesammelte Schriften, vol. vi, p. 20 sq.

[3] See Homo, 'L'Empire romain', pp. 158-64, and Lesquier,
L'Armée r. d'Égypte', pp. 322-8.

and the Western army is not difficult to understand. The prevalent language of the East was Greek, and the climatic conditions were not suitable for men born in Europe. Consequently the example set by Pompey and Antony was followed by Augustus and his successors, and the principle of a Roman citizen army was maintained by this fiction.

The Augustan policy continued till the reign of Hadrian, when the difference of status between legions and *auxilia* was greatly modified and finally disappeared. After Trajan's unsuccessful attempts at conquest and at further incorporations of provinces in the Roman Empire, Hadrian withdrew the troops inside the old frontiers, which he fortified on a new scheme of frontier defence. The legions were, as far as possible, retained in the same provinces, and to facilitate this plan and to avoid the expense of transport, vacancies in the ranks were filled from local sources instead of by drafts from distant parts. Insistence on membership of a Roman town was no longer rigidly enforced, and soldiers frequently describe themselves as being born *castris*. This implies that their fathers had contracted marriage alliances contrary to Roman law, and the sons born to them during their period of military service were themselves accepted as recruits, even though they had not the citizenship and could not point to any town as their birthplace.[1] At the same time the old prejudice against provincials had greatly diminished with the accession of emperors who were themselves born in the provinces, and by the end of the second century the

---

[1] See further ch. viii, p. 237 sq.

provinces had reached a status of equality with Italy itself. The distinction, therefore, between legions and *auxilia* was no longer important, and Roman citizens are found in similar proportions in either branch of the army. The history of the legions from the point of view of recruiting is thus the gradual change from an army drawn in large proportion from Italians and favoured provincials to a force enlisted from local sources, where obstacles presented by recruits who were not citizens and who could point to no Roman town as their birth-place were easily surmounted.

The evidence for the areas from which the legions were recruited comes almost entirely from inscriptions. The Roman had a great dread of being forgotten, and therefore either composed his own epitaph or left clear instructions in his will, which at first a brother or a fellow soldier, or at a later date [1] a loving wife or son, carried out, being careful to commemorate on the same monument their conjugal or filial piety. These sepul-chral inscriptions frequently give, not merely the legion in which the soldier had served, but also his birthplace and any military distinctions which he may have won. The dating of the records is sometimes difficult, but help is given by the following considerations. We saw in the last chapter that it is usually possible from *tegulae* to assign a definite legion to a camp at some particular period ; the discovery, therefore, of an inscription, which gives the epitaph of a soldier and the name of his legion, near or in the region of a military camp

---

[1] Tombstones erected by wives to their soldier-husbands are not found in the early Principate (Dess. 'Gesch. d. Kaiserz.' i, p. 234).

makes it probable that his service in that legion had
taken place during the latter's encampment in that
district.   Secondly, some legions received honorary
titles for the part they played in certain campaigns.   It
is comparatively safe to argue that on a soldier's epitaph his legion will be given its full title, and consequently the omission of such distinctions in an inscription is a fair but not certain argument that the legion
had not received them when the memorial was erected.
Lastly, the absence of *cognomina* in a soldier's statement of his career usually indicates that his service
was prior to the reign of Claudius, when *cognomina* for
Roman citizens became the customary practice.

I shall first of all deal with such evidence as there is
for the recruiting of the legions of the Rhine.   In the
year 43 A. D. legions II *Aug.*, XIV *Gem.*, and XX *Valeria*
were sent to Britain.   II and XX remained there
throughout the period of this study, and XIV received
the honorary titles of *Maitia victrix* for its services in
Britain before its return to Germany in 70 A. D.   Therefore any records found on the Rhine of soldiers belonging to II *Aug.* and XX *Val.* may be safely assigned to
the period of the Principate before 48 A. D., and inscriptions which describe legion XIV simply as XIV
Gemina, and do not add *Martia victrix*, may be fairly
certainly used for the same years.   About the same
time IV *Macedonica* was moved from Spain to Moguntiacum, where it remained till it was cashiered in 70 A.D.
Consequently records of this legion found on the Rhine
can be used for the period 43–70 A. D.   In either 39
or 42 A. D. XV and XXII *Pg.* were raised, and early in

Claudius' reign the former was posted to Vetera and the latter to Moguntiacum. XV *Pg.* remained at this camp till its disappearance after the revolt of Civilis ; at the same date XXII *Pg.* left the district, and on its return in the reign of Vespasian was detailed for service in the Lower Province. For its loyalty in the revolt of Saturninus it received the honorary titles *pia fidelis Domitiana*, and consequently, when it is later encamped at Moguntiacum towards the end of the Principate of Domitian, the records which it has left may be expected to show at least the two titles *pia fidelis*. Therefore inscriptions from Moguntiacum referring simply to XXII *Pg.* may be ascribed to the period 43–70 A.D. Shortly after 43 A.D. legion XVI moved from Moguntiacum into the Lower Province, and so the records which come from the Upper Province, especially if the soldiers have no *cognomina*, may safely be used for the period prior to 43 A.D. Of the remaining legions I *Germanica* and V *Alaudae* were in the Lower Province till 70 A.D. ; XIII moved to Poetovio about 46, and XXI was at Vetera till about 43 A.D., when *tegulae* prove it to have been moved to Vindonissa. Later, when it was again in Lower Germany, the honorary title *Rapax* is regularly found in addition to the number,[1] and its records can be sitted accordingly. There is, therefore, a sound basis on which the recruiting areas for the Rhine legions can be discovered ; to show modifications, the year 43 A.D. is a suitable dividing line, and the records of six legions, which

---

[1] This title goes back to the time of Augustus (Dess. 6598), but is not found on the earlier inscriptions from Vetera.

were either only in Germany till that date, or which changed camps about that time, may be compared with the inscriptions of three other legions which only came into the province in 43 A. D.[1] The following statistics are a summary of which the details will be found in Appendix B :

(a) Before 43 A. D.

Legion.	Camp.	District from which soldier comes.	
II *Augusta*	Argentoratum	Italy	5
		Gall. Narbo.	1
		Lusitania	1
XIV *Gemina*	Moguntiacum	Italy (including Cottian Alps)	25
		Gall. Narbo.	5
XVI (*Gallica*)	Moguntiacum	Italy	10
		Gall. Narbo.	4
XX *Valeria*	Opp. Ubiorum	Italy	5
XXI	Vetera	Italy	1
		Gall. Narbo.	1
XIII *Gemina*	Vindonissa	Italy	2
		Gall. Narbo.	1

(b) 43–70 A. D.

Legion.	Camp.	District from which soldier comes.	
IV *Macedonica*	Moguntiacum	Italy	7
		Baetica	6
		Gall. Narbo.	15
		Noricum	3
		Tarraconensis	1
XV *Primigenia*	Vetera	Italy	5
		Gall. Narbo.	3
XXII *Primigenia*	Moguntiacum	Italy	14
		Gall. Narbo.	7
		Tarraconensis	1
		Noricum	1

[1] The year 43 A.D. as a dividing line was first suggested to me by some unpublished notes of the late G. L. Cheesman. The figures I have collected mainly from the corpus (cf. Ritterling, o. c., P–W. xii, *passim*).

It would be extremely hazardous to argue for any generalization on the basis of such a small proportion of instances as we possess, but from these details it is clear that, on the Rhine before 43 A.D., out of a total of sixty-one forty-eight soldiers were of Italian origin and twelve were born in the Romanized province of Narbonensis. In other words, about eighty per cent. of the soldiers were Italians, and of the remainder eighteen per cent. were natives of a highly Romanized province. On the other hand, after 43 A.D., out of a total of sixty-three twenty-six come from Italy, twenty-five from Narbonensis, and six from Baetica, i. e. the proportion of Italians has dropped to forty-three per cent., while that of Gallia Narbonensis has increased to about thirty-eight per cent., and Baetica appears on the list for the first time. This last factor is easily explicable on the ground that IV *Maced.* was in Spain before being transferred to the Rhine. Inscriptions, therefore, make it highly probable that up to 69 A.D. the legions of the Rhine were composed largely of Italians and natives of Gallia Narbonensis.

A similar conclusion follows from the records of the two Dalmatian legions—VII and XI. In the last chapter we saw that these two units received the honorary titles of *Claudia pia fidelis* for their loyalty in the revolt of Scribonianus. Legion VII occupied the same camp till it was moved into Moesia, probably in 58 (and certainly not later than 62 A.D.), while legion XI was in the province till the year of the Civil War. On the assumption, then, that honorary titles normally figure in legionary inscriptions after the date of their bestowal, the year 42 A. D. makes a suitable dividing line for studying the areas of recruiting of the two Dalmatian legions, and noting any developments that seem to be taking place. The summarized figures are as follows :

(a) Before 42 A. D.

Legion.	Camp.	District from which soldier comes.	
VII	Delminium	Italy	10
		Macedonia	4
		Asiatic Provs.	18
		Gall. Narbo.	1
XI	Burnum	Italy	10
		Macedonia	2
		Asiatic Provs.	1

(b) From 42–58 A. D.

VII C.p.f.	Delminium	Italy	8
		Asiatic Provs.	2

From 42–69 A. D.

XI C.p.f.	Burnum	Italy	14
		Macedonia	1
		Gall. Narbo.	8
		Spain	8
		Pontus	1

These statistics show that up to 42 A. D. the proportion of Italians was about fifty per cent., and between 42 and 58 or 69 A. D. the proportion had risen to approximately seventy per cent. This seems to be accounted for by the diminution in the number of recruits drawn from the Asiatic provinces, but the curious thing is that Eastern soldiers should be found in a Western province before 42 A. D. Seeck's [1] view that they are the remnants of Antony's army is chrono-

[1] Rhein. Mus. xlviii (1893), p. 602 sq.

logically unsound; more probably legion VII, before its occupation of Delminium, was in Macedonia, and so tended to draw its recruits from Eastern sources, and this may also be the explanation of the unofficial *cognomen Macedonica* which is occasionally given to the legion.[1]   On this interpretation the same principle of recruiting applies to the Dalmatian as to the German legions in the early part of the Principate.

Towards the end of Nero's reign Tacitus states that a *dilectus* was held 'per Galliam Narbonensem, Africamque et Asiam supplendis Illyrici legionibus'.[2]   This levy of soldiers from three Romanized provinces to fill gaps in legions stationed in less Romanized districts continues the practice of the earlier Principate, but the inclusion of Asia and Africa is interesting because, partly from the inferior fighting qualities of their inhabitants and partly on political and sentimental grounds, they had previously provided a very small quota to the legions.   The enforced recruitment of Roman citizens in these provinces may indicate no more than an attempted equalization of the burdens of military service, but possibly the raising of a new legion (I *Italica*) by Nero in the following year, composed entirely of Italians, may account for the exemption of Italy from the earlier levy.[3]

It has been widely claimed [4] that with Vespasian a new policy of recruiting for the legions was inaugurated.

[1] E. g. Dess. 2695: Ritterling, s. v. 'Legio', P–W. xii, p. 1616.
[2] T. A. xvi. 13. 4.   [3] Suet. Nero, 19.
[4] Momm. Ges. Schrift. vi, p. 86; Rostovtzeff, 'Social and Economic History of the Roman Empire', p. 510 n. 8, and p. 523 n. 84.

Italians ceased to be enlisted, with the exception of the Transpadane district,[1] and in their place Roman citizens, notably from the provinces of Spain, were employed. The intention of the new Princeps was to keep up the legionary stock from the propertied classes in preference to the proletariat, and to this end 'Latin rights' were bestowed upon the provincial Spanish towns. Further, the author of the 'History of the Augusti' states that in the reigns of Nerva, Trajan, Hadrian, and Aurelius serious complaints were made by Roman citizens in Spain about the burdens of conscription,[2] while in Trajan's reign certain inhabitants of Bithynia are said by Pliny to have sent *vicarii* to take their place in the levies for the legions.[3] But although it is true that the Flavians and Antonines distributed the franchise widely in the provinces and made a wise and extensive use of the new and perhaps superior material for the legions, the statement that Italians ceased to be recruited is too sweeping a generalization. The supersession of the Italian by the provincial was a gradual and not a sudden process; for in the period from 70–117 A. D. the records,[4] scarce as they unfortunately are, show that in the Rhine army Italian soldiers do continue to figure in much the same proportion as in the Julio-Claudian Principates. For instance, from eleven inscriptions left by XIV *Gem.*

---

[1] Dess. 1068, 1098, and 'Gesch. d. r. Kaiserz.', i, p. 288.

[2] Hist. Aug. Hadr. 12. 4 ; M. Aurel. 11. 7.

[3] Plin. Ep. x. 30.

[4] Similar figures to those which I have here collected are also to be found in Ritterling's article, s. v. ' Legio ', in P–W. xii, *passim.*

M. v. between 70 and 92 A. D. four come from Italy,[1] two from Narbonensis,[2] one from Noricum,[3] and four from Colonia-Agrippinensis;[4] of eight epitaphs of soldiers of X *Gemina*, which was on the Rhine from 70–105 A. D. (*circ.*), three come from Italy,[5] two from Gaul,[6] one from Calagurri and one from Astigi in Spain,[7] and one from Emona in Pannonia,[8] while legion VI *Victrix* has left in Britain[9] records of soldiers describing themselves as 'cives Italici et Norici', and one inscription in its German camp[10] of a soldier of Italian origin. These records, slight as they are, if they do not justify any positive assertions as to the composition of the German legions in the Flavian period, at any rate militate against a view which would exclude Italians from legionary service in these years. In the Danube district, Eastern and local sources were naturally drawn upon earlier than on the Rhine, but the process seems to be analogous; for instance, of eight inscriptions left by legion I *Ital.* in Moesia, two soldiers come from Italy,[11] one from Narbonensis,[12] two from Macedonia,[13] and four from Thrace,[14] while an inscrip-

---

[1] C. I. L. xiii, 6896, 6898, 6920, 6905.

[2] Id. xiii. 6891, 6912.   [3] Id. xiii. 6304, 6894, 6895, 6917.

[4] Id. xiii. 6892.   [5] Id. xiii. 8733, 8734, 8741.

[6] Id. xiii. 8736 and xii. 367.   [7] Id. xiii. 8732 and 8283.

[8] Id. xiii. 8735.   [9] Id. vii. 1095.

[10] Id. vii. 1095 and xiii. 8590.   Cf. too records of leg. I *Minervia*: one from Italy (xiii. 8071), three from Gaul (xiii. 8086, 1844, and IGRR. iii. 80), two from Germany Inf. (xiii. 1844 and 8040), two from Thrace (xiii. 8067 and 1856).

[11] C. I. L. iii. 12352 and v. 7667.

[12] Id. iii. 8198.   [13] Id. iii. 7441, 6144.

[14] Id. vi. 2803, 2601, 2785, xiv. 3631.

tion discovered in the Dobrudja in Lower Moesia 'in memory of the brave men who died in the Dacian wars' shows three men born in Italy, two in Noricum, two in Gallia Narbonensis, eight at Ara Claudia, one in Dalmatia, one in Macedonia, and four in Asia Minor.[1]

The changed system of the second century is seen in an inscription[2] giving the names of soldiers of legion VII *C. p. f.* who were recruited in 169 and discharged in 195 A. D. The summary of their birthplaces is as follows : Thrace 3, Dacia 6, Pannonia 2, Illyricum 3, Moesia 103, *castris* 7. Lastly, an example, in a sense an exception, which further attests this policy of local recruiting is to be found in the two legions raised by Marcus Aurelius. They have the *cognomen Italica* and are numbered II and III, as if to continue the series started by Nero's I *Italica*. This suggests that they were recruited from Italy in contrast to the local pro- vincial areas of the other legions of the period, and the view is confirmed by two pieces of evidence. The only inscriptions giving the birthplaces of soldiers of those legions show that they came from Tereventum and Comum in Italy,[3] and secondly, in 165 A. D., M. Claudius Fronto acts as a recruiting officer 'ad iuventu- tem per Italiam legendam ',[4] which must be for the two new legions of Marcus Aurelius.

The policy of recruiting the Eastern legions from Galatia and Cappadocia is attested by Tacitus when, in describing the preparations for Corbulo's campaign, he

<hr>

[1] Dess. 9107.   [2] C. I. L. iii. 14507.
[3] C. I. L. ix. 2593 and Inscr. Bav. Rom. 1915, no. 420.
[4] Dess. 1098.

says, ' habiti per Galatiam Cappadociamque dilectus '.[1]
The Eastern origin of soldiers of III *Gallica* is further
confirmed by their sun-worship, with Tacitus' explana-
tory comment ' ita in Syria mos est '.[2]   What little
epigraphical evidence there is for the Eastern legions
supports the literary sources.   For instance, two soldiers
transferred from III *Gallica* into III *Augusta* in Africa
come from Syria ;[3] while of three records of X *Fretensis* two mention soldiers of Galatian origin [4] and one
a soldier from Syria.[5]   Fortunately much clearer evidence can be obtained from Egypt, and the recruiting
policy adopted for the legions there may safely be
applied to the other Eastern units.   Lesquier, deriving
his figures from the famous Coptos Inscription,[6] which
gives the names and birthplaces of thirty-six soldiers,
and from other inscriptions relating to legions III *Cyrenaica* and XXII *Deiotariana*, has shown that of sixty-one
soldiers in the first century eight come from Italy,
Gaul, or Africa, and fifty-three from Asia Minor, Syria,
and Egypt, in the proportion of twenty-nine from
Asia Minor, chiefly from Galatia, to twenty-four from
Syria and Egypt.[7]   It is noticeable that there is a great
variety of tribes among compatriots, which suggests a
bestowal of the franchise upon individuals, while as
many as twenty-seven, including already four who give
their birthplace as *castris*, are in the tribe *Pollia*, which
was the tribe usually selected because of its lucky

---

[1] T. A. xiii. 85. 4.   [2] Id. H. iii. 24.
[3] C. I. L. viii. 4310, 2904.   [4] Id. vi. 3614,86 27.
[5] Id. iii. 6697.   [6] Dess. 2483.
[7] Lesquier, ' L'armée r. d'Égypte ', p. 206.

associations for individuals receiving the franchise on their incorporation in a legion.   There is, then, clear evidence for the recruiting fiction to which reference has already been made.   Lastly, the change to local recruiting is attested by an inscription of 194 A. D.[1] referring to legion II *Traiana*.   Of forty-six soldiers thirty come from Egypt, and twenty-two of these give *castris* as their birthplace.

Interesting evidence about legion III *Augusta*, which has a general significance for the whole question of legionary recruiting, has been collected by Cagnat.   In the first century, traces have only been found of fifteen soldiers[2] who give their places of origin; of these, seven come from Italy, two from Aquitania, five from Gallia Lugdunensis, and one from Belgica.   This record exemplifies the normal policy of the Roman government with regard to the recruiting of the Western legions.   In the next century inscriptions from Lambaesis are frequent, being very often dedications by soldiers to the Princeps on leaving their camp. A list of soldiers dated to the Principate of Trajan[3] shows seventeen coming from Africa, one from Cyrene, six from Egypt, sixty from the East, which is chiefly Bithynia and Syria, one from Moesia, and one from Gaul.   Of these only four give their birthplace as *castris*.   The most striking thing about the list is the large percentage of Eastern recruits and the diminution

[1] Dess. 2304.

[2] C. I. L. viii. 2103, 23294, 23295, 23293, 25747, 17334, 23254, 16550, 1876, 27852, 23253, 27850, 16554, 16549 ; xiv. 3472 (Cagnat, 'L'armée r. d'Afrique (1913), p. 287, supplemented by Ritterling, o. c., P-W. xii, p. 1505).   [3] Id. viii. 18084.

of the Western contribution to one soldier. A possible explanation of this factor may be found in the inability of Italy and Gaul to cope with the demands made on them for soldiers for the Western legions, if they had also to maintain the African legion. Consequently Africa is obliged to turn to the East for her recruits, but more probably these Eastern soldiers were *translati* into legion III *Aug.*, while a detachment of it was serving perhaps in Trajan's Parthian War. A second list belonging to the Principate of Hadrian[1] gives a similar result, with a growing tendency to employ local material. Of sixty-one soldiers, thirty-six belong to Africa, and the rest to the Danube provinces and especially Dacia. Lastly, the same process which we have noticed in Egypt and the Danube district comes to light in a list of the year 166 A.D.,[2] which gives the names of thirty soldiers, all of whom are Africans; about one-third of them give *castris* as their birthplace and are included in the tribe *Pollia*.

The evidence that has been given of recruiting returns for the legions shows that both senatorial and imperial provinces provided their quota for the senior branch of the field army. In the choice of particular districts, which should furnish soldiers for the legions and *auxilia* respectively, a complementary system was established. Thus Gallia Narbonensis, an important area for legionary recruiting, provided only two *alae* of auxiliary cavalry, while Rhaetia produced practically no legionaries but as many as eighteen cohorts of auxiliary infantry. Similarly Galatia, a great legionary

---

[1] C. I. L. viii. 18085.   [2] Id. viii. 18067.

area, provided only six auxiliary cohorts, which were raised by Trajan, and, as legionary recruiting became increasingly important in Egypt, so the small contributions which that province had made to the *auxilia* disappeared altogether. Lastly, whereas the soldier of the *auxilia* normally describes himself as belonging to a certain *natio*, the legionary in the first century gives his origin by reference to his native town. The auxiliary is, for instance, *Trever natione*,[1] but the legionary drawn from the same district is described as *domo (Claudia) Ara*, i. e. belonging to the colony of Colonia-Agrippinensis.[2]

Theoretically, conscription was in force throughout the period of the Principate, but there seems to have been a difference in its application in the West and the East. The word *dilectus* is employed by Tacitus for the process of filling up the gaps in the legions of Corbulo's army, and as a special means of bringing the Illyrican legions up to strength in 65 A. D. From this the impression is given that, although strictly the *dilectus* was a *munus* to which all citizens were liable,[3] normally there was little difficulty,[4] in the first century of the Principate, in keeping up the strength of the Western legions by voluntary enlistment in Italy and in those provinces where Roman towns were widely established. On the other hand, the raising of troops from districts which had not yet received the citizenship, or an urgent call for reinforcements, required a

---

[1] Dess. 2523 and Cheesman, 'Auxilia of the Roman Army', pp. 60-2. [2] C. I. L. iii. 4456, 4475.
[3] T. A. iv. 4. 4. [4] Vell. ii. 130. 2.

N

definite levy by commissioners. Such *dilectus* were carried out by the order of the Princeps alone in virtue of his office as commander-in-chief of the army,[1] and although as an act of courtesy the permission of the senate may have been obtained by Augustus and Tiberius for a levy in a senatorial province,[2] this custom was later disregarded; for the *dilectus* held in Gallia Narbonensis, Asia, and Africa is not represented by Tacitus as being *senatus consulto*.[3] Special commissioners with the title of *dilectatores* were employed by the Princeps to carry out the conscription of new recruits, with the additional power of scrutinizing their eligibility and rejecting the medically unfit.[4]   In Italy this duty was entrusted to men of senatorial rank, in the senatorial provinces to the proconsuls, and in imperial provinces to members of the equestrian order.   For instance, Agricola, when of praetorian rank, held a *dilectus* in Italy in the Principate of Vespasian,[5] and in 59 A. D. the proconsul Pedius Blaesus performed the same duty, but with less honesty, in the senatorial province of Cyrene.[6]   Similarly an unnamed *dilectator* enlisted recruits in the *procuratorial* province of Thrace during the reign of Trajan,[7] while an inscription dating from the middle of the second century A. D. describes a certain C. Julius Celsus as ' dilectator per Aquitanicae XI populos'.[8]

---

[1] Dio, liii. 15. 6.

[2] Suet. Tib. 32.

[3] T. A. xvi. 13. 4.

[4] Plin. Ep. x. 30.

[5] Agric. 7.

[6] T. A. xiv. 18. 1.

[7] Bull de Corr. Hellen. 180, p. 507.

[8] C. I. L. xiii. 1808.

VII

THE OFFICERS OF THE LEGION

IN discussing the innovations made by Julius Caesar in the command of the legions, it was shown that *legati* were sometimes used in his army as the officers in charge of the legions when work of special importance had to be carried out. With Augustus this tendency became a rule, and under the Princeps, who was commander-in-chief of the army, *legati* held their commissions as the commanders of the legions. The title of these officers was *legati Augusti legionum*, or more simply *legati legionum*. They were usually senators of praetorian rank and were thus between 30 and 40 years of age. For example, in his account of the career of T. Vinius, Tacitus [1] says that he was 'legioni praepositus post praeturam'. Sometimes even men of quaestorian rank, as, for instance, Cn. Domitius Curvius in Africa,[2] were selected, while in 16 A.D. Asinius Gallus, in advocating the nomination of magistrates to serve for a period of five years, proposed 'ut legionum legati, qui ante praeturam ea militia fungebantur, iam praetores destinarentur'.[3] When the garrison of a province consisted of more than one legion, the provincial governor, who was of consular rank and was called *legatus pro praetore*, held the command of all the troops in his province, and the *legati* of the individual legions served under him. If there was only

[1] T. H. i. 48. [2] Dess. 991. [3] T. A. ii. 36. 1.

one legion in a province, then the *legatus legionis* was also the provincial governor and had the title *legatus pro praetore*. Africa at first formed an exception to this rule. It was a senatorial province, and its solitary legion was under the control of the proconsular governor of the province. In the reign of Caligula,[1] however, the military command was separated from the civil administration, and subsequently legion III *Aug.* was put under the command of a *legatus*, while the proconsul attended to the administration of the province. The remarkable feature of the office of *legatus legionis* is that it was filled by men of comparatively little military experience, who retained their appointment for three or four years. In itself this was necessarily a weakness, and the ill effects of it are seen in the mutiny on the Rhine and in Pannonia in 14 A. D., and in the incompetency of generals like Paetus. To some extent also the selection of senators for the highest command stifled the enterprise of the junior officers, who could never be promoted to the command of their unit. The greatness, therefore, of the Roman army cannot be regarded as lying in the method of appointing the legionary commanders ; it is to be found rather in the perfection of the military organization and, above all, in the efficiency of the centurions and the disciplined obedience of the common soldiers.

Next in order of seniority to the *legatus* came the *tribuni militum*. These officers were young men aspiring either to a senatorial or an equestrian career, and were divided accordingly into *tribuni laticlavii* (with the

[1] T. H. iv. 48.

broad stripe on the tunic) and *tribuni angusticlavii* (with
the narrow stripe). Each class of tribunes had to serve
a period of military service in the legions, but, whereas the *laticlavii* could proceed immediately after the
completion of their year's work to the political *cursus
honorum* of senators, the aspirants to the equestrian *cursus* had, at least from the time of Claudius, to hold two
additional posts as officers in the *auxilia*. The normal
sequence of these *militiae* was *praefectus cohortis* (i. e.
commander of an auxiliary cohort or infantry unit), *tribunus militum* (*angusticlavius*), and *praefectus alae* (i. e.
commander of an auxiliary *ala* or cavalry unit). This
can be illustrated from many inscriptions recording
equestrian careers, and the following shows a man
starting as a municipal magistrate at Libarna
, and then
proceeding to hold the three military posts necessary
as an introduction to the equestrian *cursus*: ' Q. Attio
T. f., Maec. Prisco aed., II-vir. quinquennali (municipal censor), flam. Aug. (official concerned with the
local Emperor-worship) . . . praef. coh. I Hispanorum
et coh. I Montanorum et coh. I Lusitanorum (his service in the auxiliary infantry is unusually prolonged),
trib. mil. leg. I adiut., donis donato ab Imp. Nerva
Caesare Aug. Germ. bello Suebic. (i. e. in 92 A. D.)
corona aurea, hasta pura, vexill. (decorations), praef.
alae I Aug., plebs urbana.' [1] Before the time of Claudius,
on the other hand, centurions of the highest rank,[2] who
were called *primi pili*, were promoted to be *tribuni
militum*, but this practice subsequently died out, and

---

[1] Dess. 2720.   [2] Ibid. 2702 is the latest instance.

with it the purely military character of the office gave
way before its political significance.

The *tribuni* served on the staff of the *legatus*, and that
their work was primarily administrative is shown by
the fact that the staff or *officium* attached to them was
composed of clerks, who were called *cornicularii* and
secutores and had no military duties.[1] Their principal
functions were to keep the lists of the soldiers actually
serving in the legion up to date and to note any casualties that occurred,[2] to give the time-expired soldiers
their official discharge,[3] and to deal with applications
for furlough. They also exercised judicial functions
in the camp, and delinquents in the German mutiny
were arraigned by them before the tribunal of the
legatus.[4] Occasionally they were employed in a purely
military capacity; for instance, the commander of a
vexillatio of cavalry that was sent on Marcus Aurelius'
Parthian expedition was a tribune of legion XI *C. p. f.*,[5]
and Vipstanus Messala was in command of legion VII
C. p. f. in the army of Antonius Primus in 69 A. D.[6]
Lastly, a third class of tribunes, called *tribuni semestres*,
must be noted. As their title shows, they only held
their appointment for six months, when they retired
into private life and subsequently secured posts of civil
importance. Inscriptions [7] relating to this officer have
all been found at the head-quarters of the provincial
governor, and it is therefore probable that he served

[1] Dess. 2395; von Dom. 'Die Rang.', pp. 39–41.
[2] Isid. Orig. i. 24.   [3] T. A. i. 37. 1.   [4] Ibid. i. 44. 4.
[5] Dess. 2723.   [6] T. H. iii. 9.
[7] E. g. Dess. 2381, and even an instance from Lugdunum in
C. I. L. xiii. 1850.

on the 'H.Q. Staff'; after the Flavian period he may
have been in command of the legionary cavalry.[1]

At the start of the Principate a new official called
praefectus castrorum appears in the Roman army. Strictly
speaking he was not an officer of the legion, but was
attached to different camps, and when in the period
before Domitian two or more legions were stationed
together there was only one *praefectus castrorum*. These
praefecti were normally promoted centurions who had
usually reached the rank of *primus pilus*. In the Pannonian revolt the soldiers showed particular animosity
against Aufidienus Rufus, the prefect of their camp, who
had been 'diu manipularis, dein centurio, mox castris
praefectus',[2] and Insteius Capito,[3] a *praefectus castrorum*
in Corbulo's army, had three years previously been sent
as a centurion by Ummidius Quadratus on an embassy
to Vologeses. Occasionally, however, *tribuni militum*,
such as Vespasian's father,[4] or *praefecti cohortium*, such
as Arrius Salanus,[5] were promoted to the rank of *praefectus castrorum*, but in practically every case the post
of *praefectus castrorum* was regarded as the end of a
military career.[6] After Domitian's regulation[7] limiting
a legion to a camp, the *praefectus* sometimes calls himself *praefectus castrorum* of a particular legion. Thus
M. Pompeius Asper,[8] who had been *primus pilus* of III

---

[1] So von Dom. based on Stat. Silvae v. 1. 95 in 'Die Rang.',
p. 47.

[2] T. A. i. 20. 2.   [3] Ibid. xiii. 39. 2 with xiii. 9. 3.

[4] Suet. Vesp. 1.   [5] Dess. 6285.

[6] Alfenus Varus is subsequently *praefectus praetorio*, but this
occurred in 69 A.D. (T. H. iii. 36).

[7] Suet. Dom. 7.   [8] Dess. 2662.

Cyrenaica, became *praefectus castrorum* of XX *Victrix*. Instances of *praefecti castrorum* occur throughout the first two centuries, but after Septimius Severus the title becomes *praefectus legionis*, and this official ultimately under Gallienus takes the place of the *legatus legionis*.[1]

The *praefectus castrorum* was a sort of glorified quartermaster. He was responsible for laying out the camp and keeping it in good order.[2] In time of war he organized the legionary train and supervised the provision of ammunition, and of battering-rams for projected siege operations. In time of peace he was ' O.C. specialists ', who included *mensores* or camp surveyors, *medici*, and even an official called the *horologiarius* who wound the camp clock.[3] Sometimes, in the absence of the *legatus* from camp, the *praefectus castrorum* took command of the legion. Poenius Postumus,[4] *praefectus castrorum secundae legionis* in Britain, on hearing of the successes of legions XIV and XX, committed suicide ' quia pari gloria legionem suam fraudaverat ', and *vexillationes* from legions III *Cyrenaica* and XXII *Deiotariana* were commanded by Liternius Fronto in the Jewish war of Titus.[5] The employment of *praefecti castrorum*, receiving their appointments from the Princeps and taking their orders from the provincial

---

[1] See Wilmann's ' de praefectis legionum ' in E. E. i, p. 95.
[2] T.A. xii. 38. 3.   [3] Veg. ii. 10. 'Die Rang.', pp. 46–7.
[4] T. A. xiv. 37. 6.
[5] Jos. B. J. vi. 4. 3, although probably this *praefectus castrorum* was the commander of the two Egyptian legions, and in this campaign was ' praepositus vexillationibus ' (see below, p. 196, and Lesquier, 'L'armée r. d'Égypte', p. 130).

governors, had both a civil and military significance.
On the political side they kept a watch over the *legati*
who were of senatorial rank and perhaps at the start
of the Principate a possible danger to the welfare of
the Princeps. From the military standpoint their long
experience as soldiers and centurions was a valuable
asset in an army commanded by amateurs.

The province of Egypt was organized differently from
all the other provinces. It was the Princeps' private
possession, and no senators were allowed to cross its
boundaries. ' Ita visum expedire provinciam aditu
difficilem, annonae fecundam, superstitione ac lascivia
discordem et mobilem, insciam legum, ignaram magi-
stratuum, domi retinere.'[1]   Consequently there could
be no *legati* in the province, and, while the provincial
governor was called *praefectus Aegypto*, the commanders
of the legions in the province had the title of *praefecti
legionum*. These *praefecti* were all men of equestrian
rank, but were distinguished from the ordinary *praefecti castrorum* by the fact that they had held the office
of *primus pilus* twice [2] before being gazetted to the command of a legion in Egypt. For instance, L. Cirpinius,
who was *praefectus legionis XXII*[3] not later than the
Principate of Tiberius, had been *primus pilus iterum*, and
'Ti. Cl. Secundinus praefectus leg. II Traianae fortis'
had in the second century A. D. passed through a similar
cursus honorum.[4]

A considerable controversy has taken place on the
identity of these *praefecti*.   Did the *praefectus* in com-

---

[1] T. II. i. 11.
[3] Dess. 2687.
[2] See below, p. 204.
[4] Ibid. 1389.

mand of the legion or legions in Egypt combine the
duties of legionary commander and camp quartermaster, or were there two distinct officials, the *praefectus legionis* or *legionum* and the *praefectus castrorum*?
The paucity of epigraphical evidence, if it does not
admit of a certain answer, lends probability to the
following interpretation.[1]

In the early Principate the Egyptian legions occupied separate camps. Each of them was commanded
by a *praefectus legionis* and to each camp was attached a
praefectus castrorum. There were thus at this date two
distinct posts, and the organization was similar to that
of any other province in which legions were stationed;
for the *praefectus legionis* in Egypt corresponded to the
legatus legionis in other parts of the Empire, while the
praefectus castrorum performed his normal functions.
Early in the Principate of Claudius, however, a change
took place. The two Egyptian legions (III *Cyrenaica*
and XXII *Deiotariana*) were concentrated in one camp
at Nicopolis, which they continued to occupy despite
Domitian's regulation till at least 119 A.D.[2] Consequently there was now only one *praefectus castrorum*,
and, although at first he is subordinate to a *praefectus
legionum*, it is probable that before long his powers were
extended from camp administration till they included
the actual command of the legions stationed in the
camp, while at the same time his title gradually changed

[1] Cf. Lesquier, o. c., pp. 120–32, in answer to von Dom. ' Die
Rang.', pp. 119-21, who regards the *praefectus castrorum* and
praefectus legionum as separate officers throughout.

[2] B. G. U. i. 140 ; Bruns, ' Fontes iuris Romani ', i, p. 421.
Riccobono, *Leges*, no. 78.

from *praefectus castrorum* to *praefectus legionis*. In this way the military organization of Egypt foreshadowed the later developments in the third century of the powers of *praefecti* in other parts of the Empire.[1]

The date at which this change took place cannot be exactly determined, but two pieces of evidence afford some help, the earlier careers of such *praefecti* as are known to us, and their relative seniority to the *praefectus Aegypto*, the commander-in-chief of the province. Before the two legions were concentrated in one camp we saw that their *praefecti* were chosen from men who had been *primus pilus* twice. This particular qualification was introduced to ensure the appointment of experienced soldiers, and if it was thought expedient when the command of only a single legion was involved, still more would it be insisted upon when the two Egyptian legions were put under the control of one man. Now an inscription belonging to the Principate of Claudius refers to a certain P. Anicius Maximus, 'primus pilus leg. XII Fulm...', who was successively 'praefectus castrorum leg. II Aug. in Britannia' and 'praefectus exercitu qui est in Aegypto'.[2] At first sight this looks as if Anicius had been in command of the two Egyptian legions; but he had only been *primus pilus* once. The inscription is thus in all probability abbreviated, and, if written in full, would have read 'praefectus castrorum exercitus qui est in Aegypto'. Anicius was merely promoted from being quartermaster of the camp of legion II *Augusta* in Britain to the much more important post of

[1] See above, p. 192, and E. E. i, p. 95.
[2] Dess. 2696.

quartermaster of the double camp at Nicopolis. It
follows that the identification of the *praefectus legionum*
and the *praefectus castrorum* was not an immediate result
of the concentration of the two legions in one camp.
But by the time of the Jewish war of 66–70 A.D. the
change had in all probability been made. Liternius
Fronto,[1] ' στρατοπεδάρχης ', commanded detachments
from legions III and XXII in Titus' army ; most likely
he was actually the commander of the two legions in
Egypt, and because of the importance of the campaign
had decided to command the *vexillationes* himself and
put the remnant of the legions left behind in the care
of one of his subordinate officers. Similarly Suedius
Clemens, *praefectus castrorum* in 79 A.D., was also in
all probability *praefectus legionum*,[2] while an inscription
of 90 A.D. places Licinius Proculus,[3] *praefectus castrorum*, immediately below the *praefectus Aegypto*, thus
showing that the *praefectus legionum* had ceased to
exist as a separate official from the *praefectus castrorum*. Lastly, in the second century the title *praefectus
castrorum* gives way to *praefectus legionis*, and 'Ti. Cl.
Secundinus praefectus leg. II. Tr.' is both the legionary
commander and the quartermaster of the camp.[4]

After the change in organization from maniples to
cohorts the legion was at first divided into ten cohorts,
each of which was subdivided into six centuries. The
number of centurions was consequently sixty, and that

[1] Jos. B. J. vi. 4. 8.
[2] C. I. L. iii. 88. In this inscription he is the only officer
mentioned, and is called simply '*praefectus castrorum*'. This looks
as if he were the senior officer in the camp.
[3] Id. iii. 13580.   [4] Dess. 1889.

this organization survived into the early Principate is sufficiently indicated by the punishment inflicted by the soldiers upon their centurions in the German revolt, when they administered sixty stripes to each victim 'ut numerum centurionum adaequarent'.[1]   At some date, however, the first cohort was increased in size from *quingenaria* to *miliaria*, and the number of centurions in it was reduced from six to five.   This new formation is definitely established for the period after Hadrian by a dedication put up to the Princeps at Lambaesis by the *optiones* of the first cohort of legion III *Augusta*.[2] These *optiones* were the understudies of the centurions, and in this inscription they numbered only five, and describe themselves as belonging to the five centurions of the first cohort, whose titles are *primus pilus*, *princeps*, *hastatus*, *princeps posterior*, and *hastatus posterior*.   Only one *primus pilus* is mentioned, and there is no *primus pilus posterior*.   At first sight this might seem as if the number of centurions had been reduced from sixty to fifty-nine, but a second inscription [3] from Lambaesis shows that in the legion there were two *primi pili*.   Therefore the number of centurions in the second century was still sixty, but one of the *primi pili* was not in command of a century but served on the 'H. Q. staff' of the *legatus*.   This explains how a man could be *primus pilus* twice over in the same legion.   Although the definite evidence for this change is a second-century document, there is at least a strong probability that it had been effected in the first century A. D.   Inscrip-

[1] T. A. i. 32. 3.   [2] C.I.L. viii. 18072.
[3] Ibid. 18065.

tions of the latter century [1] often mention centurions of the rank of *primus princeps posterior* and *primus hastatus posterior*, but never *primus pilus posterior*; secondly, as we have seen, the expression *primus pilus bis* occurs in all probability as early as the Principate of Tiberius.[2] Von Domaszewski would go even further.[3] He believes that the organization of the first cohort as 1,000 strong divided into five centuries is as old as the change from maniples to cohorts, which he ascribes to Scipio Africanus the younger. Before the time of Marius there were five legionary standards; these because of their religious associations might naturally be in the care of the five senior centurions, and when Marius substituted the *aquila* in place of them he gave it to the *primus pilus*. Therefore the organization of cohort I into five centuries dates from the transformation of maniples into cohorts. This theory is highly plausible and depends for its validity upon the statement that Scipio effected the change in the organization of the legion, or at least that it had taken place some time before Marius' reforms. Now what little evidence there is is strongly in favour of attributing the change to Marius himself,[4] and consequently the question of the care of the five pre-Marian legionary standards can have no bearing on the organization of the first cohort, because it had not yet come into existence in place of the maniple. The five old legionary standards were in all probability protected by the *prima acies*, whose soldiers were called *antesignani*, and when the single *aquila* took their place

[1] E.g. C. I. L. iii. 2883, 9973.
[2] Dess. 2687.
[3] 'Die Rang.', p. 91.
[4] See ch. i, pp. 28-9.

it was natural to entrust it to the care of the leading centurion. Further, it is most improbable that, when a new organization was being exploited, the experiment would be complicated by making one cohort twice the size of any other and thereby increasing the responsibility of its centurions. The change from *quingenaria* to *miliaria* is not a sudden decision, but the result of a long process of testing experiments possibly carried out within the *auxilia*.[1] Its introduction into the legion is to be placed not earlier than the second half of the Principate of Augustus.

The centurions were drawn from five main sources. They might be men promoted from the ranks, who had held some of the minor posts under the centurionate, or they might more rarely gain their promotion after service in an auxiliary unit. Two inscriptions will suffice to illustrate these two modes of approach to the centurionate : (*a*) d. m. L. . . . Proclus mil. leg. V M. (Macedonica), ᴮB lega., (beneficiarius legati, i. e. a clerk on the staff of the *legatus*) optio ad spe(m) ordinis (the understudy of the centurion), ꓨ (centurion) leg. eiusdem . . . . . ꓨ leg. I Ital. ꓨ leg. XI Cl., ꓨ leg. XX V. v., ꓨ leg. IX Hisp., miss. h. m. (missus honesta missione, honourably discharged) vixit an. LXXV h. s. e.[2]

(*b*) An inscription commemorating Trajan's Parthian victory : Victoriae Parthicae Aug. sacr. ex testamento M. Anni . . . . Martialis mil. leg. III Aug., duplic. alae

[1] May the organization of cohort Ibe based on the *cohortes miliariae* of the *auxilia* ?

[2] Dess. 2666ᵇ ; cf. Dess. 9090.

Pann. (i. e. duplicarii, a junior officer in an auxiliary cavalry unit receiving double a private's pay), dec. (decurionis, i. e. a cavalry officer of the *ala*) al. eiusdem, 7 leg. III Aug. et XXX Ulp. Vic. missi h. m. ab imp. Traiano optimo Aug. Ger. Dac. Parth.[1]

The remaining three sources from which the centurions were drawn were, however, the most common. Sometimes they came from a class whose property qualification was below that of the equestrian order, and received their posts in the legions as a reward for merit. These men were often magistrates from a municipal town, who had in this way secured the complete Roman citizenship. Thus they became eligible for legionary service, and were appointed centurions in recognition of their previous careers. An inscription of the time of Hadrian describes a certain Marcius Celer as ' quaest., II-vir. (i. e. municipal magistrate) 7 leg. VII Gem. 7 leg. XVI F. f. ' &c.[2] The fourth and most interesting type of centurion ' ordinem accepit ex equite Romano'.[3] This expression means that before receiving his appointment as centurion he had belonged to the equestrian order, but either through insufficiency of means, or through failure to make any great advance in the equestrian *cursus*, voluntarily resigned his membership of the equestrian order, and accepted a centurion's commission in the legions. In the records of promotions it is this class of centurion that proceeds most quickly to the coveted rank of *primus pilus*. Lastly, mention should be made of *evocati*,[4] or ex-praetorians recalled

---

[1] C. I. L. viii. 2354.　　　　[2] Dess. 2660.
[3] Ibid. 2654.　　　　[4] Ibid. 2665.

to the colours, who in the second century A. D. were often promoted directly to be centurions and, like the *ex equite Romano* centurions, rapidly reached the post of *primus pilus*.

The numerous records left by centurions of their military careers show that they frequently changed their legions, and consequently gained much useful experience. In this way too the possible danger of fraternization between the centurions and their men was effectively diminished.[1] A system of promotion existed similar in many respects to that which we have traced under the Republic, and with the help of inscriptions its machinery can be detected.

In the last century of the Republic we saw that the *primi ordines* were the six centurions of the first cohort, and that centurions were normally promoted from cohort to cohort in the same rank till they were ready to enter the *primi ordines*, where they probably started in the *hastatus* grade and moved up gradually to the final post of *primus pilus*. Under the Principate this system was modified. The *primi ordines* were no longer merely the six centurions of the first cohort, but also included the leading centurions of the other cohorts (i. e. the *pilus prior* of each junior cohort), who in virtue of their command of a cohort had to be soldiers of experience. There were two methods of promotion corresponding to the two main types of centurions, (*a*) those who received their commissions either *ex equite Romano*, or as *evocati*, or less frequently as a reward for service in their municipal towns, and (*b*) those who had risen

[1] Dess. 'Gesch. d. r. Kaiserz.', i, p. 244.

from the ranks. The former class were promoted rapidly, and usually changed their legions in each successive step. The method of promotion was, as under the Republic, from cohort to cohort, but a centurion did not necessarily keep the same rank (i. e. *pilus, princeps,* or *hastatus*) on each promotion. Care was simply taken to ensure that each step in his career was a definite promotion, and, if he was a man of marked ability, he might miss out the usual intermediate stages and quickly enter the *primi ordines,* and so attain the coveted post of *primus pilus.* On the other hand, the ranker moved by slow stages, and did not get very far on the ladder of promotion.[1] Starting as *decimus hastatus posterior* he was promoted successively inside the tenth cohort (i. e. from *decimus hastatus posterior* to *decimus hastatus prior,* &c.) till he became *decimus pilus posterior.* His next move was to *nonus hastatus posterior*; for *decimus pilus prior* being one of the *primi ordines* was reserved for the marked man as a step to the post of *primus pilus.*[2]

The chief duty of the centurions was, of course, the command of their own century, and, if promoted to be *pilus prior,* the command of the cohort in which they held that post. This would imply the same sort of routine as is carried out by the platoon commander and his platoon sergeant to-day. If a century was detailed to find the guards, it was the duty of the centurion to

---

[1] See Diagram on p. 38.

[2] See App. C., p. 277. Despite his slow progress the ranker normally changed his legion on each promotion (e. g. from ' decimus hastatus posterior leg. II Aug.' to 'decimus hastatus prior leg. XX V.v.', Dess. 2658).

name the soldiers for that duty; if camp fatigues were
the order of the day, the centurion had to distribute
his men under his junior officers for the different purposes required.[1] These burdens were probably unpopular with the common soldiers, and Tacitus hints
that it was a common practice to bribe the centurion
to let them off the more unpleasant fatigues.[2] In fact
vacationes munerum seems to have been a recognized
principle; for the soldiers make use of this as one of
their chief grievances in the mutiny of 14 A. D., and
Tacitus says that in 68 A. D. the price of *militare otium*
had become an annual tribute, which was proving such
a source of discontent, that Otho promised to pay the
dues to the centurions from his own private purse.[3]
The centurion of the Roman army thus combined the
military efficiency of the British sergeant-major with
a private avarice which is fortunately rare in our army.

Sometimes the centurions were given special commands of importance. Centurions ' expertae virtutis '
commanded small groups in the guerilla warfare against
Tacfarinas;[4] a *primus pilus* led detachments of eight
legions in the German war of 83 A. D.;[5] while Paccius
Orfitus, another *primus pilus*, was entrusted with the
care of certain garrisons during Corbulo's Parthian
campaign.[6] There was also a definite system of 'second-
ing'. In the inscription [7] from Lambaesis, already cited,
of the time of Marcus Aurelius mention is made of seven

[1] T. A. xv. 30. 1, where the *initia vigiliarum* are announced by
the centurions.
[2] Ibid. i. 17. 6.   [3] Id. H. i. 46.   [4] Id. A. iii. 74. 4.
[5] Dess. 9200.   [6] T. A. xiii. 36. 1.
[7] C. I. L. viii. 18065.

centurions in the first cohort, eight in the sixth, and seven in the eighth. Those centurions who were supernumerary to the legionary establishment were posted to the head-quarters of the provincial governor. The most important officials in this class were the *princeps praetorii*,[1] who kept the military records at 'H.Q.', the *centurio strator*[2] in command of the *pedites singulares*, and the centurion in charge of the *equites singulares*,[3] who formed a special guard of honour for the provincial governor. In a province such as Galatia, where no legionary troops were stationed, these duties at 'H.Q.' were performed by centurions sent from a legion in a neighbouring province.[4]

On leaving his legion the *primus pilus* received the rank of an *eques*, and might continue his career in the equestrian *cursus*, starting with the posts of *praefectus cohortis*, *tribunus legionis*, and *praefectus alae*.[5] More commonly, after holding the office of *primus pilus* for the first time, he served in the garrison troops of Rome as tribune of the *vigiles*, the urban and praetorian cohorts.[6] He then might be appointed *primus pilus* a second time, and was thus qualified for the more important procuratorships and above all for the post of *praefectus legionis in Aegypto*. On the other hand, the *primus pilus* might covet the post of *praefectus castrorum*; and in such cases this was the culmination of his career and he subsequently retired into private life.

---

[1] I. G. R. R. iii. 1280.   [2] Dess. 2418.   [3] C. I. L. iii. 10860.
[4] I. G. R. R. iii. 214.   [5] Dess. 2693.
[6] Ibid. 2726, and see further Stein, 'Der römische Ritterstand', pp. 142–55.

The life of a centurion with the prospect of becoming *primus pilus* thus offered great possibilities to the ambitious man, and with the additional attractions of high pay and a correspondingly good donative on discharge [1] he frequently stayed in the army far beyond his requisite twenty years.

Below the rank of centurion there were in each legion a great number of junior officers, denoted generally by the two terms *principales* and *immunes*. The exact difference between these two classes is a little obscure, but it seems to have been a question of status rather than of function. [2] Both *principales* and *immunes* enjoyed an exemption from the ordinary soldiers' *munera*, but for different reasons. Whereas the *principales* were exempt in virtue of the military rank they held, the *immunes* received this privilege in return for the performance of certain other duties, the nature of which was expressed in the titles they held. For instance the *optio* or centurion's understudy enjoyed *vacatio*, because he was an *optio*; the *custos armorum*, on the other hand, was only exempt because he did in return the minor repairs to the soldiers' arms. There was a further subdivision inside each of these main groups into the 'clerical' staff and the purely 'military' officers, most of whom were attached to the centuries, and inscriptions indicate a definite system of seniority both inside each subdivision and between one subdivision and the other. The *principales* and *immunes* who

---

[1] For details see ch. viii, p. 224.

[2] Pay of an *immunis* = pay of a *miles gregarius*.

   ,, ,, a *principalis* = 1½–2 times   do.   See ch. viii, p. 228

held ' clerical' posts formed the *officium*, or what may be translated the orderly room staff, of the provincial governor, the legionary commander, the *praefectus castrorum*, and the *tribuni*. The number and variety of titles is amazing, and von Domaszewski [1] has drawn up complete lists of the different officials known to us from inscriptions. The increase, however, must have been gradual, and cannot have reached such a high figure as he represents till the legions became more or less permanently stationed in the same provinces. I shall content myself, therefore, with noting the names and functions of those officers found most commonly in the period before Septimius Severus, and with indicating the normal steps in the ladder of promotion.

A. *Orderly Room Staffs.* The most important official who was at the head of the *officia* of the provincial governor, the legionary commander, the *praefectus castrorum*, and the *tribunus laticlavius* was the *cornicularius*.[2] His duties were roughly those of an orderly room sergeant, and consisted especially in keeping the roll of the legion accurate and up to date. At the head-quarters of the provincial governor there were normally three *cornicularii*,[3] and at each of the other *officia* one, and returns were no doubt called for from ' H.Q. ' with the same irritating frequency as in the recent war. Another official common to all the *officia* was the *beneficiarius*.[4] He took his seniority from the official to whom

----

[1] ' Die Rang.', p. 48.   [2] Dess. 2391, 2392, 2395, 2396.
[3] C. I. L. iii. 4452. Only two are found in Spain (C. I. L. ii. 4122), but this is explicable by reason of the distance separating Tarraco from the ' H.Q.' of VII *Gemina* (' Die Rang.', p. 30).
[4] Dess. 2402, 2405, 2406.

he was attached ; thus, while the *beneficiarii* of the *legati*, the *praefectus castrorum*, and the *tribunus laticlavius* were *principales*, the *beneficiarius* of the *tribunus angusticlavius* was only an *immunis*. The title of the rank arose from the fact that it was conferred by the *beneficium* or kindness of the senior officer in question, and the duties of the post were mainly of a personal or clerical nature. The *officium* of the provincial governor was distinguished by the presence of three *commentarienses* and ten *speculatores*.[1] These were judicial officials, and the reason why they are found exclusively at the head-quarters of the province is that the provincial governor alone had the right of capital punishment. The other officers on the *officia* are of less importance and were mostly *immunes*. Mention may be made of the *strator* or *legatus'* groom,[2] the *librarius*[3] and *notarius*,[4] who helped to keep the regimental accounts.

B. *Military Officials.* At the head of the junior officers was the *aquilifer*,[5] who, as his name shows, carried the eagle, and in virtue of the sacredness of his office took precedence under the centurion. Next to him was the *optio ad spem ordinis*.[6] He was a specially qualified *optio*, and is to be distinguished from the ordinary *optio*, because, whereas he was promoted directly to be centurion, the latter normally ranked as inferior to the *signifer*. Perhaps he may in some cases have been ' seconded ' from his century while holding the rank of *optio*, and on his ' restoration to the establishment' have been promoted centurion. The next most important *princi-*

[1] Dess. 2382.   [2] Ibid. 2418.   [3] Ibid. 2424, 2426.
[4] Ibid. 2428.   [5] Ibid. 2389.   [6] Ibid. 2441, 2666[b].

pales were the *signifer*, the *optio*, and the *tesserarius*.[1]
The *signifer* was the manipular standard-bearer, the
optio took command of the century in the centurion's
absence, and the *tesserarius* received the watchword
daily[2] and generally acted as the orderly sergeant.
Beneath these officers came the trumpeters, buglers,
and horn-players,[3] the armourer-sergeant,[4] the doctor,[5]
and the vet.[6] Some idea of the number of *immunes* in
a century may be gathered from a papyrus of 90 A.D.,
which reads as follows :[7]

<u>Present in Century 40 (N.B. well below paper strength).</u>

Custos armorum .	.	1
Conductor . .	.	1 (he supervised the letting of land to the soldiers).
Carrarius . .	.	1 (he was in charge of the baggage train).
Secutor Tribuni .	.	1
Custos Domi .	.	1 (H.Q. Guard).
Scribae . .	.	2
Stationem agens .	.	1 (Picket duty).
Supranumerarius	.	1 (probably on tribune's staff).
Available . .	.	31

Vegetius[8] states that, when a common soldier was
promoted to be a junior officer, he descended to the
tenth cohort and worked upwards from cohort to cohort
till his next promotion, when once again he started in
the lowest cohort. This opinion is confirmed by two
inscriptions from Lambaesis of the third century,
which show that the *optiones* of a cohort were normally

[1] Dess. 2658.　　　　　　　　　　[2] Jos. B. J. iii. 5. 8.
[3] C. I. L. iii. 7449 ; Dess. 2351.　　[4] Dess. 2279.
[5] Ibid. 2482.　　　　　　　　　　[6] Ibid. 2438.
[7] Geneva Papyrus lat. 1-4 ; Lesquier, o.c., p. 140.
[8] Veg. ii. 21.

promoted together to the next cohort above them ; for
five of the six *optiones* who rank from 6–11 in Dess.
2445 become the five *optiones* of cohort I in Dess. 2446.
The sixth *optio* of the second cohort could not be promoted, because there were only five centuries in the
first cohort. Probably he was detailed to some supernumerary job, such as *optio praetorii* [1] under the centurion called *princeps praetorii*, or *optio valetudinarii*.[2] The
promotion of the junior officers was thus from cohort
to cohort, and there was little or no difference in seniority between the *optiones* in the six centuries of the same
cohort. There was also a second important principle in
the promotion of the junior officers. Before an '*immunis*' in either the clerical or military group could
be promoted centurion it was necessary for him to hold
the post of either *tesserarius* or *optio* or *signifer*. Thus,
although it was possible for a *principalis* holding a
' clerical ' post to become centurion, yet, before he obtained the post of *beneficiarius* or *cornicularius*, he must
have held a junior ' military' appointment. An inscription from Burnum illustrates this point. It describes
the previous career of a centurion as ' miles leg. XI,
tesserarius, beneficiarius, cornicularius legati Augusti
pro praetore, centurio '.[3] On the other hand, a ' military'
principalis might become centurion without entering
the group of *beneficiarii*, but probably he would be
retained longer in the junior military posts than the
clerk passing from the lower to the higher subdivision
of his group. This is suggested by an inscription from

[1] Dess. 2439.   [2] Ibid. 2487.
[3] C. I. L. iii. 9908 ; von Dom. ' Die Rang.', p. 48.

Africa, where a centurion's earlier career was ' librarius, tesserarius, optio, signifer (in leg. I Ital.), factus ex suffragio leg. eiusdem militavit centurio leg. I Ital.';[1] and this inscription proves further that, although a soldier started as a clerk and so became *immunis* (i. e. in this example *librarius*), he might on promotion remain a military official till his appointment as centurion. The relative seniority of the junior officers may be summarized as follows. 1. The *cornicularius* of the provincial governor,[2] the *optio ad spem ordinis*, and the *aquilifer*[3] could all be promoted directly to the rank of centurion, and consequently were more or less on an equality. 2. The *cornicularii* attached to the other *officia*, the *beneficiarii*, except those of the *tribunus angusticlavius*, and the *speculatores* rank in one aspect above the 'military' *principales*, represented by the *signifer*, *optio*, and *tesserarius*, because one of the latter posts must be held before the former, but from another point of view as on an equality with them, because the *signifer* was sometimes promoted directly to be centurion.[4] 3. Below the 'military' *principales* are the *immunes* in either group, who were probably more or less on an equal standing, inasmuch as their work was specialized and precluded a systematic scheme of promotion.

Lastly, a word must be said about the legionary cavalry. We saw in an earlier chapter that it disappeared after the Marian reforms, and was not found

---

[1] Dess. 2658 as emended in vol. iii, pars. 2, p. clxxix.
[2] C. I. L. iii. 9908 ; von Dom. 'Die Rang.', p. 48.
[3] Dess. 2842.   [4] Ibid. 2658.

in Caesar's army.   It seems, however, to have been resuscitated by Augustus because, apart from a clear reference to 120 cavalry of the legion in Josephus,[1] inscriptions describe men as *equites* of a legion ; for instance, Aelius Severus is an 'eques leg. III Aug.' in the century commanded by Julius Candidus.[2] From this evidence it may be inferred that each legion had 120 cavalry, and that for administrative purposes the horsemen were divided among the centuries.   Clearly, on the other hand, for tactical work there must have been a cavalry organization of some sort.   Inscriptions speak of an *optio equitum*,[3] who served under a *tribunus legionis*, identified by von Domaszewski as a *semestris tribunus*.[4] The most probable conclusion is that the legionary *equites* drilled under their own cavalry instructors, but for establishment purposes were entered on the roll of the centuries.

[1] Jos. B. J. iii. 6. 2.

[3] C. I. L. ii. 5682.

[2] Dess. 2826 ; cf. Dess. 9090.

[4] 'Die Rang.', p. 47.

VIII

THE CONDITIONS OF SERVICE

(a) *Length of service.* In 18 B.C.[1] Augustus fixed the period of legionary service under the *aquila* at sixteen years, but, before the soldier received his final discharge, he had to serve for another four years as a veteran. These veterans lived apart from the legion, and were organized into cohorts having a special standard of their own called the *vexillum*, and under the command of an officer called *curator veteranorum*.[2] They were nominally exempt from the burdens of camp routine, and were supposed to be called upon only in the event of a hostile attack. The following inscription illustrates these conditions of legionary service in the earlier part of Augustus' Principate : 'princeps II legionis XIV Geminae annorum LXIV stipendiorum XLVI militaria XVI curatoria veteranorum IV evocativa III' (and then promoted and served as centurion for twenty-three more years).[3] In 6 A.D.[4] a change was made, and service under the *aquila* was increased to twenty years, and the veterans were retained for a further period, which was supposed to end after five years. The final discharges of the soldiers were, however, greatly delayed, probably for the perfectly valid reason that there was insufficient money in the new military treasury to pay the recognized donatives, and the soldiers of Germany and

---

[1] Dio, liv. 25. 6.
[2] Dess. 2338.
[3] C. I. L. xiii. 7556.
[4] Dio, lv. 28. 1.

Pannonia profited by the accession of a new Princeps to enforce their demand by a mutiny. They complained that in some cases they had been retained with the colours for thirty or forty years, and that service ' sub vexillo ' was simply ' alio vocabulo eosdem labores perferre '.[1] The danger of the rebellion drove the Princeps to accede for the present to their demands, and the new conditions were a reversion to those existing in the earlier half of Augustus' reign : ' missionem (i.e. final discharge) dari vicena stipendia meritis, exauctorari (i. e. release from service under the *aquila* to service *sub vexillo*) qui sena dena fecissent ac retineri sub vexillo ceterorum immunes nisi propulsandi hostis '.[2] This temporary régime is perhaps illustrated by an inscription of a veteran (*missicius*) called Quartus Iuventius, who cannot have served for more than sixteen years when he left legion XI,[3] and shortly afterwards died. The new conditions, however, remained in force for less than a year, and Tiberius urged as a reason for the change that the *aerarium militare* would not stand such frequent demands for discharge donatives.[4] The reversion, therefore, to the length of legionary service which had been in force in the latter half of Augustus' Principate was largely dictated by the need for economy.

Despite this settlement of 15 A. D. the whole question of discharge from the legions seems to have remained unsolved during the Julio–Claudian period. Tiberius

[1] T. A. i. 17. 4 ; cf. C. I. L. iii. 2014.
[2] Ibid. i. 86. 4.   [3] Dess. 2260.
[4] T. A. i. 78. 8 ; Cf. Dess. 2267.

was apparently anxious to keep to the terms which he had prescribed, but he was still hampered by financial difficulties,[1] while Suetonius shows that the extravagance of Nero made the problem once again acute.[2] This may account for the rapine and plunder which the soldiers indulged in during the year of the Civil Wars, and it was left to Vespasian by a policy of strict national economy to re-establish a definite period of service with an adequate system of discharge. The results are seen in a *diploma* belonging to Domitian's Principate.[3] Discharges from the legions were now made every other year, and soldiers who had completed twenty-five or twenty-six years' service became eligible for their release from further military service. Lastly, in the second century, the corps of *missicii* serving under the *vexillum* disappeared, and legionary service was now entirely under the *aquila* and lasted, as in the *auxilia*, for twenty-five years.[4]

(b) *Pay.* In his account of the organization of the Roman army Polybius states that the legionaries received 2 *obols* a day, which was equivalent to 120 *denarii* a year.[5] From this sum stoppages were made for food and clothing, and it is probable that the soldier actually received considerably less than half this amount. In the third century 10 *asses* were reckoned to the *denarius*, but after the Second Punic War the coinage was depreciated and 16 *asses* became the equivalent of a *denarius*. How this affected the soldiers' pay is

[1] T. A. iv. 4. 4 ; Suet. Tib. 48.   [2] Suet. Nero, 32.
[3] Dess. 9059.   [4] Von Dom. 'Die Rang.', p. 80.
[5] Pol. vi. 39 (S-D., p. 257).

not clear, for the elder Pliny states 'in militari tamen stipendio semper pro decem assibus denarius est datus'.[1] If, as it seems, he is referring to the period after the Second Punic War, the passage may best be interpreted as meaning that the soldier, after the Second Punic War, received the same proportion of the *denarius* as his daily pay as he would have received before the depreciation.[2] Thus, whereas in the earlier period the soldier got 3⅓ *asses per diem*, after the Second Punic War he received 5⅓, both sums being the equivalent of one-third of a *denarius*. When Caesar[3] doubled the pay of the soldiers, the fraction of the *as* seems to have been disregarded, and the soldier received 10 *asses per diem*, which was equivalent to 225 *denarii per annum*, or rather over £8 in our money. This rate of pay is proved for the Augustan period not only by Tacitus' account of the grievances of the Pannonian soldiers,[4] but also by the legacies left by Augustus in his will.[5] The legionaries received 300 *sesterces* or 75 *denarii* each, and this was equal to one-third of their annual pay, which was distributed in three instalments each year. Under Domitian the soldier's pay was raised to 1,200

---

[1] N. H. 33, 45.

[2] Furneaux, note on T. A. i. 17. 8. *Contra* von Dom., in 'Der Truppensold d. Kaiserz.' (Neue Heidelb. Jahrb. x. 1900), who holds that in the late Republic the legionary received 75 *denarii*, which was doubled by Caesar, while Augustus added a further 75. But his arguments presuppose that the soldier got his food free, which seems to me to be against the evidence (see below); nor does Suet. Aug. 49 justify the assumption that Augustus increased the legionary pay.

[3] Suet. Caes. 26.   [4] T. A. i. 17. 6.

[5] Ibid. i. 8. 8.

sesterces or 800 *denarii*, and this was paid in four instead of three instalments.[1]

In order to estimate whether this was a living wage for the soldier, it is necessary to consider what he had to buy out of it. The soldiers in the Pannonian revolt complain that ' denis in diem assibus animam et corpus aestimari; hinc vestem, arma, tentoria, hinc saevitiam centurionum et vacationes munerum redimi '.[2] The absence of the mention of food has led some scholars [3] to the opinion that, although in the Polybian army rations had to be bought by the soldiers themselves, in the early Principate they were distributed free. This is, I think, a mistaken view, and two pieces of evidence seem more or less conclusively to point in the opposite direction.   Tacitus mentions that, after the detection of the conspiracy of Piso in 65 A.D., Nero rewarded the loyalty of the praetorian guard by giving them ' frumentum sine pretio '.[4] This implies that normally the praetorians had to pay for their food, and it would be surprising, if this privileged branch of the army was subject to this condition, that the legionaries should be exempt from it.   It might be argued that the difference in the pay of the branches of the army accounted for this anomaly, but then, surely, the adverse comparison that the mutinous soldiers make between their pay and that of the praetorians might have been effectively countered by the Princeps, by pointing out how much more the praetorians had to expend in order to live? The interpretation of this passage in Tacitus is further confirmed by a papyrus from Egypt,[1] which gives the accounts of two soldiers just before Domitian's increase in the legionary pay. The accounts are similar, except in respect of one expenditure, and I shall give a copy of one and indicate the significance of the difference. The papyrus reads as follows :

. . L. Asin   Cor. (83–84 A.D.)

Q. IVLIVS PROCVLVS DAMASCENVS

Accepit stip. I an. III Do.	dr. 248	stip. II dr. 248	stip. III dr. 248
Ex eis faenaria . .	10	10	10
in victum . .	80	80	80
caligas fascias . .	12	12	12
Saturnalicium K. .	20	—	—
ad signa . . .	—	4	—
in vestimentis (sic) .	60	—	146
Expensas . .	182	106	248
Reliquas deposuit .	66	142	—
Et habuit ex priore .	136	202	344
Fit summa . .	202	344	344

The explanation of this account is as follows. The soldier received 3 *stipendia* or instalments of pay in the third year of Domitian's Principate. This should have amounted to 3 *stipendia* of 75 *denarii* (i. e. 3 gold pieces) and have been equivalent to 3 *stipendia* of 300 silver *drachmae* of Egyptian money, but for some reason it was reckoned in copper *drachmae* of less value, of which 300 were worth 248 silver *drachmae*. Out of these *stipendia* the soldier had to pay for certain necessities, and these were in all probability stopped out of his pay

[1] Pap. Lat. I, Geneva.

before he received it, in the same way as the British soldier has certain compulsory stoppages made against his account.   Some of these stoppages were made out of each instalment, such as bedding (*faenaria*), military boot and strap (*caligas fascias*), and, most important of all, food (*victum*).   Others were annual, and consisted of contributions to the annual camp dinner (*saturnalicium K.*) and to the soldiers' burial club (*ad signa*). With regard to the clothing stoppage there is a difference in the two soldiers' accounts : both have 146 *dr.* stopped out of their third *stipendium*, but, whereas 60 *dr.* is the stoppage for one in the first period, 100 *dr.* is placed against the other's account in the same instalment.   Probably, then, the amount varied with the requirements of the soldiers, but they were compelled to renew their equipment after the receipt of their third instalment of pay in a year.   It seems clear, therefore, that the legionary did have to pay for his food.   The omission of *arma* as a stoppage in the papyrus is perhaps surprising in view of the statement made by the Pannonian soldiers in 14 A.D., but the most probable explanation is that at the start of his military career the soldier had to find his own weapons,[1] but that they served him for a number of years, with certain repairs that the armourer-sergeant could easily

---

[1] Supported by an account of an auxiliary (Fayoum, col. 2, l. 18) where '*arma*' cost 104 *denarii* (Lesquier, o.c., p. 256).   The manufacture of arms, if let out to private firms, was state-controlled. The chief depot was the Castra praetoria at Rome.   An *evocatus* under Vespasian is called 'architectus armamentarii imperatoris'. (C.I.L. vi. 2725, and see ' Die Rang.', p. 25, and Grosse, ' Römische Militärgeschichte, pp. 97–9.)

carry out. Hence *arma* are not mentioned in the soldiers' accounts we have been considering, because they were clearly [1] not in the first year of their military service.

The papyrus shows that a savings-bank system existed to help the soldiers to be economical. Vegetius says that each cohort of the legion had its bank, where the soldiers belonging to the unit could open their accounts. In fact a savings-bank account was compulsory for each soldier, because, if any donative was distributed to the soldiers during their period of service, the state placed half of it in the bank for the soldier 'ne per luxum aut inanium rerum comparationem a contubernalibus posset absumi'.[2] Those entries were called *seposita.* On the other hand, the *deposita*, mentioned in the papyrus, were almost certainly voluntary, because the reverse process of drawing from his current account is indicated by the phrase, found in another papyrus, ' reliquos tulit'.[3] Further, Domitian limited the amount of deposits to 1,000 *H.S.* to each soldier,[4] as a direct result of the revolt of Saturninus in Upper Germany in 89 A.D., who diverted the savings of the soldiers for his own immediate end. As contrasted with the payments into his own account, the soldier paid a contribution *ad signa* for burial purposes into a legionary bank called the *saccus undecimus*, which was under the care of the *signiferi*. This eagerness to en-

---

[1] For they had already made deposits in the Savings Bank.
[2] Veg. ii. 20.
[3] In Berlin Pap., ll. 54–60 ; Lesquier, o.c., pp. 257–9.
[4] Suet. Dom. 7.

sure a decent burial is characteristic of the lower classes
in the Roman Empire. In the *municipia collegia* were
formed expressly for this purpose,[1] and later in the
army of Septimius Severus similar associations were
formed by the *principales* of the legion.[2] The absence
of *collegia* of common soldiers was compensated by this
contribution to the *saccus undecimus*.

The Egyptian papyri indicate that a soldier could live
comfortably on about five-sevenths of his pay. The ordinary diet was simple, consisting of soup, bread, vege-
tables, lard, and vinegar mixed with water, or in later
times a little wine. About sixty *modii* of corn *per annum*
would keep a soldier, and the normal price of a *modius*
was one *denarius*. This simple fare is consistent with
what we know of the dinners held in the *scholae* of the
collegia in the municipal towns, where the entrance and
annual subscriptions only amounted to a few *sesterces*.[3]
Meat was not often found on the menu, and Tacitus
represents the soldiers at the siege of Tigranocerta as
only resorting to the flesh of animals when compelled
by absolute starvation.[4]

Of course the actual wealth of a common soldier depended very largely on his own tastes and character.
In the early years of the Principate there was probably
little opportunity for spending money in the camp itself, but when the garrisons became more permanent,
and *canabae* or civil settlements grew up around them,

[1] Bruns, 'Fontes Iuris Romani', i, p. 888. Dessau 7212 ;
[2] Dess. 2438, 9097–9100.
[3] E.g. the charter of a *collegium* at Lanuvium, Bruns, o.c., i,
p. 888.   [4] T. A. xiv. 24. 1.

the Roman soldier tried his hand at trade. Indeed the condition of the Eastern legions when Corbulo took over command of them [1] suggests that trafficking in luxuries had become a menace to military discipline, and the edict of Nero 'militibus immunitas servaretur nisi in eis quae veno exercerent' was probably designed to correct this abuse.[2] Perhaps the legionary whose account we have been studying was exceptionally thrifty; for one young soldier writes a stiff letter to his parents on the subject of the penurious state to which he has been reduced, because his father gave him no tips, and his allowance was delayed. The following is a free translation of his letter:[3] 'My dear Mother, I hope that this finds you well. On receipt of my letter I shall be much obliged if you will send me £2. I haven't got a farthing left, because I have bought a donkey-cart and spent all my money on it. Do send me a riding-coat, some oil, and above all my monthly allowance. When I was last home you promised not to leave me penniless, and now you treat me like a dog. Father came to see me the other day, and gave me nothing. Everybody laughs at me now, and says "his father is a soldier, his father gave him nothing". Valerius' mother sent him a pair of pants, a measure of oil, a box of food, and £2. Do send me some money and don't leave me like this. Give my love to everybody at home. Your loving Son.'

The annual pay of the Roman soldier was supplemented by a share in the booty of campaigns and by

[1] T. A. xiii. 35. 1. 8.   [2] Ibid. xiii. 51. 1.
[3] B. G. U. iii. 814.

occasional donatives.[1]   These donatives were paid by
the Princeps out of the *fiscus* and were intended to
emphasize his position as commander-in-chief and to
bind the soldiers in closer loyalty to the imperial household.   Augustus himself only made one such distribution after his accession, on the occasion of Gaius' first
commission in 8 B. C.,[2] and this sound precedent was adhered to by Tiberius.[3] With Caligula and his successors,
however, the custom became greatly abused.   Even if
the spread of a mutiny under Lentulus was frustrated,
the distribution of 100 *denarii* to each soldier was
bound to increase the greedy expectation of similar
lavish gifts in the future.[4] This tendency was not
checked by Claudius, who, Suetonius says, was the first
Princeps to make a donative on the occasion of his
accession,[5] and who marked the assumption by Nero
of the *toga virilis* by a similar largesse.[6]   The danger of
the situation is clearly reflected in the murmurings of
the army against Galba ' tamquam usurpatam etiam in
pace donativi *necessitatem* bello perdidissent ',[7] and the
Princeps' reply 'legere se militem non emere consuesse'
merely increased their fury.[8]   Similarly, the disloyalty
of the German legions to Hordeonius Flaccus is largely
the result of unpaid donatives,[9] and it is the greatest
tribute to the character of Vespasian that he was able
in large measure to break this tradition and restore
discipline in the army.

[1] E.g. Suet. Caes. 88.   [2] Dio, lv. 6. 4.   [3] Suet. Tib. 48.
[4] Id. Cal. 46.   [5] Id. Cl. 10.   [6] T. A. xii. 41. 8.
[7] Id. H. i. 18.   [8] Suet. Galb. 16.
[9] T. H. iv. 86 (see further on Donatives Sulser, 'Disciplina',
pp. 66-70).

Besides these donatives, two further sources from which the soldiers' pay was temporarily increased must be noticed. (*a*) In his will Augustus left a sum of 300 *sesterces* to each legionary soldier.[1] The non-payment of this legacy on his death was used by the mutinous soldiers in Pannonia as one of their chief grievances, and Tiberius actually doubled the amount of the bequest to mollify their feelings.[2] (*b*) Tacitus represents the soldiers of the Flavian Expeditionary Force as demanding *clavarium*,[3] or money to buy nails for their boots, and Suetonius seems to be alluding to a similar claim when, referring to *classiarii*, who used to come on foot from Ostia to Rome, he says that they demanded 'constitui aliquid sibi calciarii nomine', and Vespasian 'quasi parum esset sine responso abegisse, iussit posthac excalciatos cursitare ; et ex eo ita cursitant'.[4] The most probable inference to be drawn from a comparison of these two passages is that *clavarium* was an extra donative given to the soldiers because of the long marches entailed by the fighting of 68–69 A.D. and that the concession was subsequently dropped.

Although the common soldier was usually content with what seems to us a small yearly wage, the junior officers of the legions were comparatively well paid. An inscription of a *schola principalium* of the Severan period[5] shows that, while the *immunis* received the same pay as the *miles gregarius*, the *principalis* got from one and a half times to twice the amount. The cen-

---

[1] T. A. i. 8. 3.   [2] Ibid. i. 36. 4.   [3] Id. H. iii. 50.
[4] Suet. Vesp. 8.
[5] Dess. 2354 ; von Dom. 'Die Rang.', p. 71.

turions were even better off, and the following table of their pay at different periods and of the sums received by the *primi ordines, primus pilus,* and *praefectus castrorum* speaks for itself, and shows clearly why the centurions were willing to remain with the colours long after their military service of twenty years was completed.

Officer.	Augustan Period.	Domitian Period.
Centurion . .	8,750 *denarii*	5,000 *denarii*
	(= 5 times a praetorian's pay)	
primi ordines . .	7,500 *denarii*	10,000 *denarii*
primus pilus . .	15,000 *denarii*	20,000 *denarii*
praefectus castrorum .	15,000 *denarii*	20,000 *denarii*
primus pilus bis .	—	80,000 *denarii*

(c) *Employment and exercise.* In the first two centuries of the Principate there were long periods during which no actual campaigning took place, and it was at such times that the conscientious and indolent legionary commanders showed their real characters. The good general was always able to find work for his soldiers, which was useful for future expeditions or strengthened the military camps of the district, and at the same time served to keep the army in efficient training. The achievements of legion III *Aug.* in Africa are very significant in this respect. In addition to the establishment and fortification of the camp at Lambaesis, work of the greatest civilizing importance was carried out. Roads, such as that from Theveste to Carthage, were made, and a military colony composed largely of veterans of the legion was settled at Thamugadi, whose buildings were the direct result of the soldiers' own

labours. The development of the province of Africa
from one of the most backward to one of the most
Romanized districts of the Empire in the third century
A. D. was due to the uninterrupted settlement of legion
III *Aug.* in the country.[1] Similarly Vetus, the governor
of Lower Germany in 58 A. D.,[2] in continuation of a
scheme projected by Drusus some seventy years earlier,
dug a canal connecting the Saône and Moselle, so as to
facilitate future naval expeditions into Germany by way
of the Zuyder Zee.   On the other hand, the effects of
a slack commander are described by Tacitus in his
account of the state of the Eastern legions, when Corbulo
was commissioned to take command of them against
the Parthians.[3] 'The legions moved from Syria', he
says, 'were slothful through a long period of peace,
and grumbled at the different camp fatigues. It is
stated that there were veterans in that army who had
never been on guard, and who looked upon the rampart
and trench as strange novelties. They had no helmets
nor breastplates ; they were sleek and rich ; their military service had been passed in towns.' The soldiers
of the Eastern legions were probably always less highly
trained and disciplined than those in the West. For
this inferiority their origin and the climate to which
they were accustomed were in large measure responsible, and one of the main factors which ensured the
success of Vespasian was the fear which the reported
intention of Vitellius [4] inspired in the Syrian legions of

[1] Cagnat, 'L'armée r. d'Afrique ', *passim.*
[2] T. A. xiii. 53. 3.   [3] Ibid. xiii. 35. 1–3.
[4] Id. H. ii. 80.

transferring them to Germany to take the place of the legions on the Rhine.

The peace routine of the ordinary legion was in many respects parallel to that of the British army. Hadrian visited the army in Africa, and various manœuvres were carried out for his benefit[1] in the same way as generals inspected drafts in this country before they were dispatched to the Expeditionary Force in France. A clear picture of the type of peace-time exercise can be gathered from Vegetius.[2] The infantry were sent out on route marches of 20 miles three times a month, and the rate of marching was varied so as to practise the soldiers in making rapid advances and retirements. Much time was devoted to open order fighting, reinforcing the front line, and adopting formations suitable for repelling ambushes or unexpected attacks. Arms drill was also an important feature of the training. Stakes or sods were set up as targets for the *pila*, and aiming at vital points was particularly encouraged. The words of command seem to have been similar to those employed in bayonet fighting, ' at the left knee— point ', ' at the throat—jab ', and were doubtless carried out with the same ferocious shouts as the British soldier was instructed to utter. Physical training was not neglected, and the soldiers were taught to swim and jump, and were exercised in cutting down trees and carrying heavy packs. Lastly, an interesting papyrus from Egypt[3] gives the work done by thirty-six soldiers in ten days. The duties may be conveniently divided

[1] Dess. 2487.   [2] Veget. i. 26, 27 and ii. 23.
[3] Geneva Pap., Lesquier, o.c., p. 141.

into four classes. 1. Some of the men were detailed for *stationes* or day-time guards over head-quarters and at the orderly room of Serenus, who was probably a tribune; others composed the *vigiliae* or night-guards over the *signa* or at the *strigae* or side-streets, and might serve in other centuries besides their own, as a second centurion called Helius is mentioned. 2. There were various fatigues inside the camp, such as cleaning arms (*armamenta*), perhaps under the orders of the armourer-sergeant, or washing the latrines and generally tidying the camp (*ad stercus*). 3. Other soldiers were detailed as batmen, and one of them cleans Helius' equipment (*ornatus*) and boots (*calceamenta*). 4. Lastly there were duties to be performed out of camp. One soldier goes out ' *cum frumentariis* ' to get food for the camp; another has the more popular duty of bringing in the wine (*exit vino*); a third is sent on detachment to the granary store which provided the food for Rome, and a fourth is on police duty on the ship that guarded the Nile. There were also quarries and mines to be superintended. Perhaps the soldiers were encouraged to do skilled work, as one describes himself as ' στρατιώτης σκληρουργὸς ὑδρευμάτων ;[1] more probably the duties were purely administrative, and the title of a centurion as ὁ ἐπὶ τῆς λατομίας may only signify the supervision of Jewish prisoners ' damnati in metalla '. The peace routine of the Roman soldier was therefore not unlike that of the British soldier to-day. Generally they seem to have been quite contented, and it was only when an opportunist like Curtius Rufus[2] employed his troops

[1] Lesquier, o.c., p. 243.

[2] T. A. xi. 20. 5.

in working an unproductive silver mine in Germany,
in the hope of winning distinction for himself, that
they objected, and sent a secret dispatch to the Princeps with the amusing request ' ut, quibus permissurus
esset exercitus, triumphalia *ante* tribueret.'

(*d*) *Decorations and punishments.* In addition to a
share in the booty and occasional donatives, the Roman
officers and soldiers received various decorations, most
of which were of little value except as *insignia honorum*,[1]
for distinguished service in the field. At first the
bestowal of these honours had some reference to the
actual feats performed, but later the system became
stereotyped and certain decorations were confined to
certain ranks, in much the same way as in the late war
the D.S.O. was regularly given to a colonel or major,
and the M.C. to captains and lieutenants. I shall, therefore, first of all describe the original significance of the
different *insignia*, and then summarize the principle of
distribution.

The imperial army fought under the auspices of the
Princeps as its commander-in-chief, and, strictly speaking, he alone was entitled to a triumph and to the
salutation of *imperator* for a successful campaign. This
privilege was, however, extended to members of the
imperial family and to sharers in the *proconsulare imperium*; for instance, Tiberius triumphed twice before
he succeeded to the Principate,[2] and Germanicus received the title of *imperator* for his work in Germany in
15 A.D.[3] A similar concession to Blaesus,[4] the pro-

[1] Seneca, de Benef. i. 5. 6 ; Sulser, ' Disciplina ', p. 48.
[2] T. A. i. 4. 4.　　　[3] Ibid. i. 58. 9.　　　[4] Ibid. iii. 74. 7.

consul of Africa, for his conduct of a campaign against
Tacfarinas might seem to be an exception to this rule,
but it is only exceptional inasmuch as the position of
the proconsul of Africa down to the reign of Caligula
was exceptional. He was the Senate's nominee and
was therefore fighting *auspiciis suis*, and so legally entitled to be saluted as *imperator*; but Tacitus adds that
he was the last commander, other than a member of
the imperial household, to receive this honour. In
place of the triumph it was customary for the Princeps
to bestow *triumphalia insignia*, which may have included
the honour of a statue, upon the commander-in-chief
of a successful campaign. The *triumphalia insignia*
were thus normally won by the provincial governors
and not by the legionary commanders, upon whom a
similar honour in the shape of *consularia insignia* was
sometimes bestowed.[1]

Next in importance to the *insignia* of a triumph or of
a higher rank in the *cursus honorum* were the *coronae*, of
which there were various types. The *Corona Civica* was
the Victoria Cross of the Roman army, and might be
gained by all ranks for saving the life of a fellow soldier.
This distinction was won, for instance, by the son of
P. Ostorius in Britain and is described by Tacitus as
'servati civis decus ',[2] while Rufus Helvius, a common
soldier, received the same decoration from Tiberius [3]
and appears subsequently to have assumed the *cognomen*
of Civica and attained the rank of *primus pilus*.[4] There
is no certain instance of the conferment of this honour

[1] T. H. i. 79.
[3] Ibid. iii. 21. 4.
[2] Id. A. xii. 81. 7.
[4] Dess. 2687.

after the reign of Claudius, although the speech of
Corbulo to his troops after the defeat of Paetus suggests
that at that date it was not yet obsolete.[1] The *corona
navalis* or *classica* was, as its name implies, awarded for
a naval victory. Pliny says that M. Varro [2] was the
first Roman to receive this honour after Pompey's
victory over the pirates, and Agrippa [3] was similarly
honoured by Augustus after his defeat of Sextus
Pompeius. It appears to have been conferred during
the Principate only upon *legati* of consular rank.[4]
With his curious passion for pompous titles and
decorations, Claudius, after his expedition to Britain,
hung a *navalis corona* beside a *civica corona* above the
door of the Palace 'travecti et quasi domiti Oceani
insigne'.[5] Two *coronae* called *vallaris* and *muralis* [6]
appear commonly in inscriptions, and in origin were
given to the first man over the enemy's *vallum* or over
the wall of a besieged town, while a *corona aurea* was
introduced by Claudius for bravery in the field of battle
and was most commonly won by centurions belonging
to the *primi ordines*.[7] Lastly, the *hasta pura* or silver
spear-head and the *vexillum* or small silver-mounted
standard were conferred upon the most senior officers,
whereas the common soldier might receive *armillae*
(bracelets), *torques* (necklaces), and *phalerae* (embossed

[1] T. A. xv. 12. 5. According to Suetonius (Aug. 25) it was
never conferred by Augustus.

[2] N. H. 7. 115.   [3] Vell. ii. 81. 3.

[4] Sulser, o.c., p. 53.

[5] Suet. Cl. 17.   [6] Id. Aug. 25.

[7] Plin. N. H. 16. 7, and see further von Dom. ' Die Rang.',
p. 110.

disks), which were attached to the corselet by leather straps.

At an early date in the Principate the original significance of the various distinctions was lost sight of, and they were bestowed upon soldiers in virtue of the rank they were holding.[1]   The following summary shows the highest decorations that the different ranks could receive :

Private or junior officer .	*Torques, armillae,* and *phalerae.*[2] Under Augustus and Hadrian only the first two were conferred, but the same decoration could be won a number of times.
Centurion . . .	*Torques, armillae,* and *phalerae,* and either the *corona vallaris* or *muralis.*[3]
Primi ordines . . .	The same as the centurion, with the possible alternative of the *corona aurea.*[4]
Primus pilus . . .	*Corona aurea* and *hasta pura.*[5]
Tribunus legionis . .	*Corona aurea, hasta pura,* and *vexillum.*[6]
Legati (*quaestorii*) . .	2 *coronae,* 2 *hastae purae,* 2 *vexilla.*[7]
„ (*praetorii*) . .	3 „ 3 „ „ 3 „ [8]
„ (*consulares*) . .	4 „ 4 „ „ 4 „ [9]

These decorations, which were worn by the soldiers on dress parades and festivals,[10] were given by the Princeps because the army fought under his auspices. The only exception to this rule is to be found in the

---

[1] Probably this started with Claudius.

[2] Dess. 2272, 2337.   [3] Ibid. 2656, 2658, 2660.

[4] Ibid. 2641, 2648.   [5] Ibid. 2638.   [6] Ibid. 2720.

[7] Ibid. 987.   [8] Ibid. 990.   [9] Ibid. 1005, 989.

[10] E. g. T. H. iv. 46 and T. A. i. 24. 4.

conferment of *torques* and *hasta* (in itself an exceptional combination) by L. Apronius upon Helvius in the war against Tacfarinas.[1]   This, as we have seen, was constitutional because the proconsul was fighting *auspiciis suis*, but it is noteworthy that the additional honour of the *civica corona* comes, as if by way of remonstrance, from the hand of Tiberius.

One of the secrets of Rome's success as a military power was the strictness with which discipline was enforced.   Roman writers on the Republic have recorded numerous examples of austere generals who, like Manlius Torquatus, did not allow affection and sentiment to interfere with their duty as soldiers, and Polybius, writing from the point of view of an outsider, was similarly impressed by the scale of punishments that was in force in his day.   After the period of the Civil War Augustus concentrated upon the re-establishment of the old Republican discipline, and the same system is found in force under the Principate, except that greater latitude was given to individual generals to exercise their discretion in mitigation of penalties. This policy had sometimes bad effects, which Tacitus illustrates in his account of the Eastern legions before Corbulo took over command of them,[2] but except in periods of civil war the impression remains that discipline was maintained at a high level.

Punishments may be divided into two classes, those to which units and those to which individual soldiers were sentenced.   Of the former the most important was the capital penalty, which was meted out to every

---

[1] T. A. iii. 21. 3.   [2] Ibid. xiii. 85. 1–3.

tenth man in a cohort or legion which had deserted
on the field of battle, mutinied, or been guilty of insubordination. This was known as *decimatio*, and the
culprits were beaten or stoned to death by their comrades (*fustuarium*). Under the Principate, examples
of this barbarous severity are rare. In the Dalmatian
War of 34 B.C. Octavian decimated some cohorts which
had run away on the field of battle and condemned the
nine-tenths of survivors to be rationed on barley instead
of on wheat.[1] Apronius, the governor of Africa, ' fusti
necat ' a tenth part of a cohort that had disgraced itself
against Tacfarinas,[2] while Galba [3] inflicted a similar
penalty upon the soldiers of legion I *Adiutrix*, who refused to respect his authority. The reason why this
punishment was so seldom inflicted is not difficult to
explain. In the first place, it was necessary that the
troops who had not incurred disgrace should be in a
majority and be willing to execute the sentence. This
is clearly illustrated by Caligula's failure to carry out
his intention of decimating the legions which had taken
part in the German revolt of 14 A.D. He summoned
the victims unarmed to a meeting and surrounded them
with armed cavalry, but their suspicions were aroused,
and they slipped away to recover their arms. Obviously
this would have been impossible if the surrounding
cavalry had not been favourably disposed to their comrades and hostile to Caligula.[4] Secondly, the inclusion
of innocent men among those singled out for punish-

---

[1] Suet. Aug. 24 ; Dio, xlix. 38. 4.

[2] T. A. iii. 21. 1.   [3] Suet. Galb. 12.

[4] Id. Cal. 48 ; Sulser, o. c., p. 56.

ment was as prejudicial to recruiting as it was inequit-
able. C. Cassius, in a debate in the Senate in the reign
of Nero as to the fate of the slaves belonging to the
murdered prefect of the city, argues, it is true, for the
retention of the old policy of putting the whole household to death on the analogy of *decimatio* in the army :
' nam et ex fuso exercitu cum decimus quisque fusti
feritur, etiam strenui sortiuntur '.[1] But the mere
fact that such a speech was necessary, apart from the
silent protests of the audience, argues a growing sense
among the Romans of the claims of humanity.

A second punishment commonly inflicted under the
Republic for insubordination was revived by Corbulo.
Paccius Orfitus, a *primus pilus*, had been put in command of some garrisons with orders not to engage the
enemy. He disobeyed and was defeated. Corbulo upbraided him for his lack of discipline and sentenced
the auxiliary commanders and their troops to encamp
outside the *vallum*.[2] The point of this punishment was
not so much the disgrace it implied as the danger to
which it exposed the victims of being forced to meet a
sudden attack of the enemy with no other protection
than their own arms. Lastly, we hear occasionally of
the cashiering of whole units for mutiny, which was
known as *missio ignominiosa*. This was the penalty inflicted by Augustus upon a legion X [3] and by Vespasian
upon the remnants of the legions that had espoused
the cause of Civilis, and a similar fate may explain the
disappearance of the *Rapax* at the time of the Dacian

---

[1] T. A. xiv. 44. 6. [2] Ibid. xiii. 86. 5.
[3] Suet. Aug. 24 ; cf. Front. Strat. iv. 1, *passim*.

wars. In such cases the soldiers received no *praemia emeritorum*.

The offences which were punished by death were the same for the individual soldier as for the legion, namely, desertion, mutiny, and insubordination.[1] Two examples will suffice for illustration. In his attempt to re-establish discipline in the Eastern army Corbulo condemned to death any soldier who had deserted the standards.[2] Similarly the leaders of the German mutiny were brought before their commanding officer's tribunal in the presence of the legions themselves, and, if their guilt was attested by their comrades, were led outside the camp to their execution.[3] The sentence was carried out during the Republic by the lictors, but, although these officials may have continued to perform this duty, it is more probable that their place was taken under the Principate by *speculatores*,[4] while Vibulenus actually asserts that Blaesus had handed over his brother to be put to death by his band of gladiators, which as provincial governor he kept for the amusement of the provincials.[5]

Of the minor punishments which were meted out for such offences as stealing, giving false witness, and culpable physical unfitness,[6] the most severe and the most unpopular with the soldiers was flogging. The infliction of this penalty was essentially the prerogative of the centurions, and they used the *vitis*, which was

[1] Jos. B. J. iii. 5. 7.   [2] T. A. xiii. 35. 9.
[3] Ibid. i. 44. 4.
[4] Hence they are found on the *officium* of the provincial governor, who alone had capital jurisdiction.
[5] T. A. i. 22. 1.   [6] Pol. vi. 87 (S-D., p. 253).

the emblem of their office, for the purpose. Tacitus
makes it clear that it is primarily flogging to which the
soldiers were alluding when they said that on ten *asses*
a day they had to buy off the 'saevitia centurionum',[1]
and the same inference may be drawn from his description of the attack of the German soldiers upon their
centurions 'ea vetustissima militaribus odiis materies
et saeviendi principium',[2] and from the nickname given
to the centurion Lucilius 'Cedo alteram'.[3] That the
centurions could inflict this punishment without the
previous authority of the tribunes is rendered probable
both by the absence of any mention of such a command
being issued by the tribunes, and from the consistent
animosity of the soldiers themselves to the centurion
and his *vitis*.

The remaining punishments were primarily marks
of disgrace. A centurion might be deprived of his
rank; an *immunis* might be reduced to a *munifex*; a
common soldier might be cashiered without his discharge emoluments. Frontinus[4] records several particular instances of this type of punishment, and, although
there are fewer details for the Principate, a statement
of Tacitus supported by Suetonius confirms the opinion
that this form of punishment was still in force. Referring to the military reforms of Vitellius in Germany,
he says, 'redditi plerisque ordines, remissa ignominia,
adlevatae notae'.[5] Clearly some centurions and *principales* had been deprived of their rank, and some common

---

[1] T. A. i. 17. 6.   [2] Ibid. i. 32. 2.
[3] Ibid. i. 28. 4.   [4] Front. Strat. iv. 1, 81, 87.
[5] T. H. i. 52 ; Suet. Vit. 8.

soldiers had been branded with marks of disgrace. Of the latter the most common was the Roman equivalent of our ' C.B.' or field punishment. The soldier was ordered to parade for a whole day in front of the orderly room, sometimes only in a tunic, to emphasize the fact that he had failed in his duty as a soldier,[1] sometimes with a pack on his back or a ten-foot measuring rod in his hand, to add a test of physical endurance to the stigma of moral disgrace.[2] Imprisonment was not common and was probably reserved for those soldiers charged with a capital offence or awaiting execution.[3]

All the minor punishments might be inflicted on the authority of the legionary commander. Capital charges were, however, reserved for the provincial governor, a fact which explains the presence of *speculatores* on his *officium* alone, while the cases of senior officers were referred to the Princeps' tribunal at Rome.[4]

(e) *Marriage.* Until 197 A.D.[5] the Roman soldier was not allowed to marry during his period of military service ; but it is clear that the soldiers disregarded this legal barrier. Not infrequently their tombstones were put up by loving wives and dutiful daughters, and in the second century a large proportion of legionaries were drawn, we have seen, from a class which gave their birthplace as *castris.* Further, a *diploma* recently discovered makes mention of an edict of Domitian of the year 93 A.D.,[6] which recognized the marriage contracts

[1] Front. Strat. iv. 1, 26.   [2] Suet. Aug. 24.
[3] T. A. i. 21. 2.   [4] Suet. Tib. 19.
[5] Herodian, iii. 8. 5.   [6] Dess. 9059.

which certain veterans of legion X *Fretensis* had formed
during their period of service, even if their wives were
peregrinae. Similarly a *diploma* of the praetorians grants
conubium to them on their discharge and the citizenship
to their subsequent issue.[1] With this ultimate legal
recognition in view, it is not surprising that soldiers
chose to disregard a technical obstacle and to enjoy
the pleasures of married life. On the other hand, the
legatus and officers above the rank of centurion were
allowed to marry, and to have their wives living with
them, if military exigencies permitted. This is proved
by a passage in Suetonius' life of Augustus,[2] which
authorizes *legati* to have their families with them in
winter quarters, and by epitaphs from the Lambaesis
cemetery, one of which reads:[3] 'Ennia hic sita est
Fructuosa . . . quae, non ut meruit, ita mortis sortem
rettulit: carminibus defixa iacuit per tempora muta ut
eius spiritus vi extorqueretur quam naturae redderetur,'
erected by her husband, Aelius Proculinus, tribune of
legion III *Augusta.*

(*f*) *Discharge.* On the completion of his term of
service the veteran received his discharge. If his service was complete and his conduct satisfactory, he was
said to be *missus honesta missione*; if he was discharged
before his time because of ill-health, his *missio* was
called *causaria*; if he was cashiered, *ignominiosa.*
Soldiers discharged *honesta missione* seem to have
received at first from their *legatus* a *tabula honestae
missionis,*[4] which served as a proof of completed service

---

[1] Dess. 1993.   [2] Suet. Aug. 24.   [3] C. I. L. viii. 2756.
[4] The only extant example is Dess. 9060.

till the *diploma*[1] or official discharge certificate was obtained. This contained (*a*) a copy of the imperial *constitutio* engraved at Rome and set up either on the Capitol or in the temple of Augustus, which conferred privileges upon the unit to which the soldier belonged, with the name and rank of the individual soldier concerned, and (*b*) the seals of witnesses, certifying that the copy was truly and accurately transcribed. It is a curious fact that our knowledge of these *diplomata* comes almost exclusively from those granted to auxiliary units. There are only three legions for which *diplomata* have survived, and two questions call for decision—(*a*) did the legionary soldier always receive such a *diploma*, and (*b*) what can be gathered from the *diplomata* of the three legions in question about the status of the veteran and his children on his discharge?

1. Two of the legions for which *diplomata* survive are legions I and II *Adiutrices*, and the language employed is the same as in the auxiliary *diplomata*. The important words are as follows:[2] 'veteranis qui militaverunt in legione $\left.{I \atop II}\right\}$ Adi., qui vicena stipendia aut plura meruerant, et sunt dimissi honesta missione, quorum nomina subscripta sunt, ipsis, liberis posterisque eorum civitatem dedit (i.e. Galba aut Vespasianus), et conubium cum uxoribus quas tunc habuissent, cum est civitas iis data, aut, si qui caelibes essent, cum iis

---

[1] Bruns, o.c., i. 423. For the use of the word 'diploma' see p. 101 n. 3.
[2] Dess. 1989. Cf. ibid. 1988, where the phraseology is slightly different, viz. 'honestam missionem et civitatem dedit', implying perhaps that the normal period of service had not been completed.

quas postea duxissent, dumtaxat singuli singulas '. The soldiers of these legions were clearly not Roman citizens during their period of service, and we have seen that this fact is explained by their having been recruited from the fleet. The ordinary rule was, on the other hand, that all legionaries must be Roman citizens. Therefore these *diplomata* are exceptional and do not apply to the normal legionary soldier, and so far the evidence does not help.

2. A *diploma* recently discovered [1] is a copy made by a soldier of legion X *Fretensis*, who may be presumed to have lost his diptych, of two edicts of Domitian. One of these edicts is dated 89 A.D. and conferred certain general immunities, such as exemption from *vectigalia* and *portoria*; the other is dated 93 A.D. and is fragmentary, as the beginning is lost. It reads as follows : '. . . veteranorum cum uxoribus et liberis s(ub)-s(criptis) in aere incisis, aut, si qui caelibes sint, cum is quas postea duxissent, dumtaxat singuli singulas, qui militaverunt Hierosolymnis in leg. X Fret., dimissorum honesta missione stipendiis emeritis per Sex. Hermotidium Campanum legatum Aug. pro pr. V Kal. Ian., Sex Pompeio Collega, Q. Peducaeo Priscino cos. (93 A.D.), qui militare coeperunt P. Galerio Trachalo, Ti. Catio et Ti. Flavio, Cn. Aruleno cos. (68 and 69 A. D.),' and at the end, the soldier's oath is inscribed 'in militia sibi . . . omnes tres s. s. natos esse, eosque in aere incisos civitatem Romanam consecutos esse beneficio eiusdem optimi principis '. This latter statement

---

[1] Dess. 9059. I am here much indebted to Lesquier, o.c., pp. 291–332.

is important, because it asserts that the soldier's three children were born *castris* during his service, and that by a special privilege they received the Roman citizenship. The beginning of the inscription therefore, to be consistent with this oath, must have read 'civitatem dedit eis'. If this is right, then these soldiers of X *Fret.* must have been, like the soldiers of I and II *Adiutrices*, non-citizens, and this is rendered probable by the fact that the edict expressly says that only these soldiers of legion X *Fret.* who were recruited in 68 and 69 are to receive the benefits contained in it. May not legion X *Fret.* in the crisis of the Civil War have been reinforced by levies drawn from non-citizens, just as legions I and II *Adi.* were raised from a similar source? If so, then this *diploma* of legion X *Fretensis* is exceptional and will not apply to the ordinary legion. In the absence, therefore, of any regular legionary *diplomata*, it is best to turn to a *diploma* of the praetorian and urban troops,[1] as it is probable that the conditions applying to veterans from these corps will also apply to legionary veterans, because soldiers in each of these two branches of the army had to be Roman citizens on their enlistment.

3. The praetorian *diploma* reads as follows : '. . . quibus fortiter et pie militia functis ius tribuo conubi, dumtaxat cum singulis et primis uxoribus, ut etiam, si peregrini iuris feminas matrimonio suo iunxerunt, proinde liberos tollant ac si ex duobus civibus Romanis natos '. This means that any marriage contract which the praetorian has formed is recognized at his dis-

[1] Dess. 1993.

charge, and his *subsequent* issue is legitimated, and implies further that children born *castris* were not given the citizenship on their parents' discharge. Let us assume that this applied to the legionaries also, and see if there is any confirmation of what seems a strange disability for the senior troops of the campaigning army, when compared with the privileges conferred on the *auxilia*.

(*a*) In a letter addressed by Hadrian [1] on August 4th 119 A.D. to the prefect of legions III *Cyrenaica* and XXII *Deiotariana* at Nicopolis, the Princeps granted the right, withheld by his predecessors, to the children of soldiers born *castris* of inheriting their fathers' property. From this privilege they had been excluded because they were not *heredes legitimi*, as their fathers had married contrary to Roman law. This new concession, then, confirms the hypothesis that the *conubium* granted to veterans on their discharge did not affect the status of children born during their military service, but only legitimated their subsequent issue.

(*b*) An increasing number of legionary recruits describe themselves in the second century as being born *castris*, and they are all in the tribe *Pollia*. To this tribe also there regularly belonged recruits drawn from local sources, who were given the franchise on their incorporation. The conclusion seems clear. Children born *castris* did not receive the franchise till they offered themselves as recruits for the legions.

(*c*) Gaius [2] defines the status of certain veterans as follows: 'veteranis quibusdam concedi solet princi-

[1] B. G. U. i. 140 ; Bruns, o. c., i. 421.   [2] Gaius, i. 57.
Riccobono, *Leges*, no. 78.

palibus constitutionibus conubium cum his Latinis pere-
grinisve quas primas post missionem uxores duxerint :
et qui ex eo matrimonio nascuntur et cives Romani et
in potestatem parentium fiunt '. The important words
to emphasize are ' *post missionem* ', which make clear
that the children mentioned in the second half of the
quotation are born subsequently to the veteran's discharge. Gaius' statement therefore accords with the
praetorian *diploma* and suggests a wider application. It
cannot refer to the *auxilia*; therefore the legionaries
may be included in ' veteranis quibusdam '.

(*d*) In the Principate of Hadrian a change took place
in the sources from which the *auxilia* were drawn.
Previously only non-citizens had been eligible, but in
future Roman citizens might also be recruited. What
seems to be the transition stage is reflected in a papyrus
from Egypt [1] of about 138 A. D., which allows us to de-
tect three classes of veterans as follows :—

1. Those having the citizenship σὺν τέκνοις καὶ ἐγγόνοις.
2. Those having the personal citizenship and *conubium*.
3. Those having the personal citizenship and being
   χωρὶς χαλκῶν.

This third group is unimportant, because it is probably
only a temporary class of veterans who had lost their
diplomata and were deprived of their full privileges
till this mistake had been rectified. But groups 1 and
2 show a difference of treatment for different members
of the *auxilia*. The most probable explanation is that
Class 1 refers to the old type of auxiliary soldier, who
was a non-citizen on his enlistment and received the

[1] B. G. U. i. 265.

franchise for himself and his children on his discharge.
Class 2, on the other hand, refers to those members of
the *auxilia* who were Roman citizens on enlistment,
and whose *conubium* was recognized on their discharge.
This opinion is confirmed by a *diploma* of the *auxilia*
belonging to the Antonine period.[1] 'Imp. Caes . . .
Antoninus Aug. Pius . . . equitibus et peditibus qui
milit. (here follows a list of the auxiliary contingents
concerned) XXV stip. emeritis dimiss. h.m., quorum
nomina subscripta sunt, civitatem Romanam qui eorum
non haberent, dedit et conubium cum uxoribus, quas
tunc habuissent, cum est civitas is data, aut cum is
quas postea duxissent, dumtaxat singulis.' The form
of *diploma* has changed. It no longer grants the
citizenship 'to a soldier, his children, and his de-
scendants', but merely the personal citizenship, if
required, and *conubium* with his wife. Clearly the new
diploma is meant to cover the two sources from which
auxiliary soldiers could be drawn, namely Roman
citizens and non-citizens. If then the legionary *diploma*
had recognized a soldier's children born *castris*, there
would have been no necessity to alter the old auxiliary
diploma any further than by the insertion of the words
'qui eorum non haberent' between 'civitatem' and
'dedit'. It follows that the legionaries only obtained on
their discharge *conubium* and citizenship for their subsequent issue, and that the new type of auxiliary *diploma*
was worded so as to make the same conditions applicable to all veterans of the army on their discharge.

The motive for treating the legionary soldiers less

[1] Dess. 2006.

favourably than the non-citizen auxiliary is a little difficult to understand. Probably it was a mixture of military
expediency and legal argument. If a soldier had been
allowed to marry and had taken to himself a Roman
wife, it would have been an intolerable expense and
encumbrance to have permitted her to follow him into
whatever province he was detailed for service, and, as
the soldier spent most of his twenty-five years of service away from home, what was the good of marrying
if he could not have his wife with him, at least in winter
quarters? If, on the other hand, he chose a wife from
the district where he was stationed, she might well be
a *peregrina*, and it was felt undesirable to contaminate
the Italian stock with foreign blood. When, however,
the soldier, in defiance of military regulations, did
marry during his period of service, the Roman government was forced to make some concession, and so it
salved its legal conscience by acknowledging the *conubium*, but by withholding citizen rights from those
children born before the wedlock was recognized. The
position, therefore, of the children born *castris* was that
to secure citizenship they must offer themselves for
military service, and this admirably suited the Roman
government, because it enabled it to keep the legions
supplied from an old legionary stock, and at the same
time avoided a flagrant violation of Roman law. This
solution of the problem throws light on the decrease of
legionary soldiers in the second century with a citizen
and municipal qualification, and the proportionate increase of recruits born *castris* and drawn from local
sources.

Whether the paucity of extant legionary *diplomata* is accidental cannot definitely be decided. The existence of *diplomata* for the praetorian and urban troops, and a mutilated inscription [1] of 74 A. D. conferring *conubium* on a Moesian legionary suggest that our ignorance of the subject may be simply a misfortune. On the other hand it is possible, I think, that the whole question of the status of legionary veterans was decided by an imperial *constitutio*, and that, as the conditions laid down were of general application to the whole legionary army, *diplomata* were not issued except in extraordinary cases where the *civitas* as well as *conubium* was bestowed, but the *tabula honestae missionis* was accepted as adequate proof of a legionary soldier's *bona fides*.

On his discharge the legionary received a donative of 12,000 *HS*.[2] This figure was fixed by Augustus and was paid out of the *aerarium militare*. If the complaints of the soldiers in the Pannonian revolt are not rhetorically erroneous, it is probable that difficulty was at first found in paying the donative, and that land was substituted in part payment. Augustus himself says [3] that he planted twenty-eight colonies of veterans in Italy. Later, similar attempts were made by Nero to establish colonies at Tarentum and Antium,[4] but Tacitus says that this experiment met with little success, 'dilapsis pluribus in provincias in quibus stipendia expleverant'. On the other hand, colonies in the provinces were a valuable military asset. For instance, 500 veterans

---

[1] C. I. L. iii. 2328⁶⁵.

[2] Dio, lv. 23. 1.

[3] Mon. Anc. 28.

[4] T. A. xiv. 27. 3.

at Thala[1] offered effective resistance to Tacfarinas in
Africa, and inscriptions from the same province show
that veterans whose homes were in the East continued
to live after their discharge in the country of their
military service. Later, *collegia veteranorum*[2] are found,
and this affection of the soldiers for the country where
they had passed their military service is both a proof
of the happiness of the soldier's life and an important
factor in the civilization of the provinces.

[1] T. A. iii. 21. 2. [2] A. E. 1902, no. 147*a*.

IX

ARMS; THE ORDER OF MARCH AND OF FIGHTING

THE strategy and tactics of the imperial army were, like its organization, based on the principles which were laid down by Marius, and developed by Sulla, Caesar, and Pompey. Such changes as were introduced were not so much the creation of new military formations as the modification of those already existing, or even, at a later date, a reversion to the dispositions of the earlier Republic. For the conditions of fighting under the Principate there are two main sources of evidence. 1. Among the historians, Tacitus has some detached references to the armour worn by the legionary soldiers, and to the formations adopted by such generals as Germanicus and Corbulo in their campaigns; but of greater importance and significance is Josephus' narrative of the Jewish War of Vespasian and Titus. Like Polybius, he was of foreign extraction, and in his forced admiration for the success of the Roman armies he was interested to inquire what were the main factors that contributed to this superiority. Consequently he describes in detail the weapons carried by the Roman soldier, the order of march normally employed, and the use made of the legions and the *auxilia* on the field of battle. His evidence is further supplemented by two technical writers. Arrian, the governor of Cappadocia in 136 A.D., had to meet a projected invasion of the Alani into his province, and in a treatise, known as the ἔκταξις κατ' Ἀλανῶν, he has given the orders he issued to the troops under his command, which include the order of march to be adopted and the dispositions to be taken up in the event of attack. In addition he composed a manual on 'field service regulations'. The greater part of this is concerned with the phalanx, and cannot profitably be used for the cohort organization, but the interest shown by the writer in the Macedonian methods of fighting suggests that, at least in the second century A.D., Rome was effecting some modifications in her battle formations, and this, we shall see, is confirmed by other evidence.[1] The second technical writer of importance is Vegetius; the detailed information, however, which he gives about Roman military administration is unfortunately marred by an absence of any indication to which period of Roman history he is referring. Consequently, as the writer lived in the fifth century A.D., his evidence can only safely be employed to supplement or confirm information derived from more reliable sources. 2. The close dependence of tactics upon armour lends great interest to the equipment and weapons of soldiers on monuments of the first two centuries after Christ. The most important of these is Trajan's monument, set up at Rome to commemorate his victories over the Dacians. On this column both legionaries and auxiliaries are depicted in what may be taken as their normal fighting equipment at the start of the second century. This evidence can therefore be safely used for the Trajanic period, and, by a comparison with sepulchral reliefs of

[1] See further von Dom. 'Die Phalangen Alexanders und Caesars Legionen' (Heidelberg, 1926).

R

the first century and the information to be derived from literary sources, such modifications in armour as were introduced during the first century A.D. can be discovered.

In its main characteristics the equipment of the Roman legionary soldier of Imperial times is the same as that worn in the late Republic. The dress consisted of a tunic and military boots (*caligae*), and, on sepulchral reliefs, but not on Trajan's column, *bracae* (trousers); *sagum* (military cloak) and *focale* (military scarf) are also found as a local uniform. The defensive armour[1] included the *lorica* or cuirass (θώραξ of Josephus), the *galea* or helmet (κράνος), and the *scutum* or cylindrical shield (θυρεός), and it is in the cuirass that most modifications seem to have been introduced in the first two centuries of the Principate.[2] On Trajan's column the cuirass is the so-called *lorica segmentata*, which consisted of breast- and back-plates strengthened by iron hoops round the body and arms. On first-century reliefs, on the other hand, only centurions have metal cuirasses; the common soldier has a leather corselet with leather shoulder-pieces and a sort of sporran with strips of metal attached to it. In apparent inconsistency with this latter evidence are several passages of Tacitus, which describe the soldiers as weighed down by the burden of their cuirasses, e.g. 'corpora gravia loricis'[3] and 'non loricam Germano non galeam, ne scuta quidem ferro nervove firmata'.[4] Three conclu-

---

[1] Jos. B. J. iii. 5. 5.
[2] Greaves were at this period worn only by the officers.
[3] T. A. i. 64. 2.
[4] Ibid. ii. 14. 4.

sions seem possible : either Tacitus' statements refer
to the leather *lorica*, and the metal *lorica* was introduced
at the end of the first century ; or Tacitus is describing
the soldiers of the Julio–Claudian period in terms of
the latter half of the first century ; or the common
soldiers wore beneath their leather corselets a coat of
mail. The last alternative is the most probable.[1]

The offensive armour, as described by Josephus, consisted of the *pilum* or throwing-spear (ξυστόν), the *gladius*
or Spanish sword, and the *pugio* or dagger slung on the
left and right sides respectively (μαχαιροφοροῦντες ἀμφοτέ-
ρωθεν). But in the second century, and perhaps as early
as 69 A.D., some of the legionaries appear to have been
armed with the *lancea* instead of the *pilum*. Arrian,[2]
in his order of battle against the Alani, shows that the
legions were drawn up as a phalanx eight deep, and
that the first four ranks were armed with the *pilum*
(κοντοφόροι) and the four rear ranks with the *lancea*
(λογχοφόροι). On this occasion the front ranks were
instructed not to throw their *pila*, but to use them for
stabbing the horses of the attacking cavalry and un-
seating their riders, while the rear ranks were to hurl
their *lanceae* over the heads of their comrades. It
would seem, therefore, that the *lancea* is a lighter kind of
pilum, and this is confirmed by Isidorus, who says that
it was a 'hasta amentum habens in medio' ;[3] for, if
the *amentum* was intended to be used as a sling, it
follows that the *lancea* must have been thrown, and not
employed for thrusting as the *hasta* with which the

[1] See further Couissin, o. c., pp. 439–69.
[2] ἔκταξ. κατ' Ἀλ. §§ 14–16.   [3] Isid. Orig. 18. 7. 5.

auxiliaries were armed. The purpose of the innovation must, then, have been to give the legionaries on certain occasions a lighter throwing-spear, which, by the addition of the *amentum*, would both carry farther and with surer aim. The advantage of such a new weapon is obvious when the phalanx was substituted, as in Arrian's account, for the cohort formation; but a passage in Tacitus [1] suggests that the *lancea* was not unknown in the first century, for he describes the Roman legionaries who fought against the Sarmatians as 'miles facilis lorica et missili pilo aut lanceis adsultans, ubi res posceret, levi gladio inermem Sarmatam comminus fodiebat'. This account may be contrasted with the speech put into the mouth of Suetonius Paulinus, in which he exhorts his troops 'conferti tantum et pilis emissis, post umbonibus et gladiis stragem et caedem continuarent'.[2] Here the *pilum* and *gladius* are the offensive weapons of the legionary infantry soldier, and the normal plan of attack is first to hurl the *pila*, and then rush in and decide the issue at close range with the *gladii*. These are the weapons which distinguish the Roman legionary soldier not only from the Greek hoplite, but also from the Roman auxiliary, whose offensive weapons were the *hasta* or thrusting-spear and the *spatha* or long sword.[3]

The method of advance of the Roman army to the field of battle varied with the chances of attack from the enemy while the troops were on the march. If the country was known to be safe and there was little reason to suspect a sudden attack or ambush, the army

[1] T. H. i. 79.   [2] Id. A. xiv. 86. 4.   [3] Ibid. xii. 85. 6.

proceeded in one long column. In the vanguard was an *ala* of auxiliary cavalry with its baggage; then followed the legions, each with its own baggage in rear; while the rear and flanks of the column were protected by more auxiliary cavalry. This was the normal formation employed by Caesar,[1] and it is analogous to the order of march adopted by Vespasian in his invasion of Judaea, of which Josephus gives the following detailed account.[2] The vanguard was composed of light-armed troops and archers drawn from the *auxilia*, with a view to frustrating any possible enemy attacks. These were followed by a detachment of Roman legionary infantry and cavalry, which preceded a squad of engineers and road-makers. Behind them came Vespasian's own baggage and that of his chief generals, protected by some cavalry, and in rear of it Vespasian himself, with his picked bodyguard of infantry and cavalry, representing the head of the main body, which advanced in the following order. The 120 cavalry, which were attached to each legion, followed by a squad carrying siege apparatus, led the way; then came the legionary general with his cohort commanders and bodyguard immediately in front of the legionary *aquila*, behind which the trumpeters marched. The legion itself came next, drawn up six deep, with a centurion in the rear to keep discipline and prevent men from falling out, and the main body ended with the baggage of the legion carried by servants and beasts of burden. The rear-guard consisted of mercenary troops, which for safety's sake were followed by some *optiones* and a

[1] E. g. D. B. G. ii. 19. 2. [2] Jos. B. J. iii. 6. 2.

picked force of legionary infantry and cavalry. A
similar picture is given by Arrian in his order of march
against the Alani. In this case the vanguard consisted
of scouts (*exploratores*) and two *alae* and six *cohortes
equitatae* of *auxilia*. The main body was headed by
four auxiliary cohorts, followed by the legionary cavalry,
who preceded the *aquila* of legion XV. Then came
the legionary commander with his cohort leaders in
front of legion XV, which was followed in a similar
order by legion XII marching behind its own *aquila*.
On the flank were cavalry, and the rear-guard consisted
of allied troops and baggage animals with an *ala* of
cavalry in the extreme rear. The general purpose,
therefore, of the normal order of march was to place
the legionary troops in the centre of the column and to
protect them with auxiliary infantry and cavalry, to
bear the brunt of any possible attack, and to give the
legion time to deploy.

When the line of advance lay through difficult
country, or when hostile attacks were a probability, it
was necessary to adopt an order of march which could
be easily converted into an order of battle. The disposition most commonly employed in such circumstances was the *agmen quadratum*, or hollow square
formation.[1] The troops were divided into four columns,
which marched parallel to each other, so that, if an
attack threatened from any quarter, the *agmen* could be

---

[1] 'duo genera agminum . . . quadratum, quod immixtis etiam
iumentis incedit, ut ubivis possit considere, pilatum alterum,'
Servius ad Aen. xii. 21 quoting Varro ; and cf. 'intentus paratusque
miles ut ordo agminis in aciem adsisteret' (T. A. ii. 16. 5).

easily transformed into a *triplex acies*. This formation
was adopted by Germanicus against the Bructeri in
14 A. D., and the dispositions are described as follows
by Tacitus:[1] 'Caesar avidas legiones . . . quattuor in
cuneos dispertit. Pars equitum et auxiliariae cohortes
ducebant, mox prima legio, et mediis impedimentis
sinistrum latus unetvicensimani, dextrum quintani
clausere, vicensima legio terga firmavit, post ceteri
sociorum.' By this plan of advance the baggage was
placed in the centre of a rectangle bounded by the four
legions, and, if an attack threatened from either the
front or the flanks, the troops could easily be organized
by a simple manœuvre into three lines of defence. A
similar formation resembling the *agmen quadratum* was
adopted by Corbulo in his advance against Artaxata.[2]
The three legions of his army advanced in parallel
columns, ' recepta inter ordines impedimenta ', while
a thousand cavalry protected the rear. Conversely,
when the Roman army had to retreat under fire, the
hostile attacks were commonly faced by a formation
known as the *orbis*.[3] Naturally this term should mean
' a circle ', but it is clear that the transformation
of a battle array in three lines into a circle is a
manœuvre no less hard to imagine than to execute.
Further, the formation was intended to provide quick
protection for the troops when confused and dismayed
by a sudden attack from a numerically superior enemy.
There would be no time for accurate ' dressing '. Most
probably, then, the *orbis* was not a circle but an

[1] T. A. i. 51. 1.
[2] Ibid. xiii. 40. 2.   [3] E. g. D. B. G. iv. 37. 2.

irregular formation, ' a half square or half circle ' con-
forming to the nature of the ground and the dispositions
of the attacking force.[1] Its strength lay in its solidarity
and compactness, the baggage train being left outside,
or, in exceptionally dangerous circumstances, abandoned to its fate.   Lastly, a word must be said about
the *testudo*, which could be used either in advance or retreat against a violent attack of hostile weapons.   The
soldiers of the front rank, closely linked together, protected themselves by holding up their shields in front
of them as screens, while the rear ranks raised their
shields above their heads, and in this way produced an
artificial roof, against which javelins and spears might
strike with impunity.   The success of this formation
depended upon the men keeping close together, so as
to avoid any gaps in the barrier of shields.   Such a
disposition might be employed instead of the *orbis* in a
retreat under fire, but it was most commonly used by
detachments advancing to the siege of a town or a
camp.[2]

When the Roman army reached the point at which
battle might be offered, a camp was regularly formed,
which varied in its mode of construction with the degree of permanency expected or intended in the district.
This was a peculiarly Roman device, and characterized
Caesar's campaigns in Gaul and Corbulo's expedition
against Parthia.   The motive was the creation of a base
where the baggage and other accessories could be left ;
for the protection of these might be expected to inspire

---

[1] Aul. Gell. Noct. Att. x. 9 ; Rice Holmes, ' Conquest of Gaul ',
p. 712.   [2] E. g. T. A. xii. 35. 5 and xiii. 39. 4.

the troops to a more vigorous offensive, while in the event of defeat a fortified refuge awaited the army in its retreat. From these camps the tactics of the impending battle were decided upon, and dispositions were adopted consistent with the topographical conditions and the size and formations of the enemy's troops. In the Republican period it was normal to draw up the legion in three lines of maniples in the centre with the allied contingents on the flank, and the attack might open by a movement from the centre or from one of the wings.[1] Sometimes, however, the allies formed the main body, and the legions were kept in reserve, or, if two consular armies were operating together, one might act in support of the other. When the cohort organization superseded the manipular, the increased size of the component units of the legion made it possible to draw up the army in one, two, or three lines.[2] Caesar most commonly adopted the *triplex acies*,[3] in which four cohorts were placed in the front rank and three in the second and third, the intervals between the cohorts of each line and the distance of one line from the other in all probability varying with the nature of the ground and the expected manœuvres of the enemy. If, on the other hand, the *duplex acies*[4] was employed, the ten cohorts of the legion were equally divided between the two lines of battle. For the first century of the Principate we possess no order of

[1] Veg. ii. 20.

[2] Or the wings might be strengthened at the expense of the centre as in the battle between Hirtuleius and Metellus at Segovia in 75 B.C. (see Schulten, ' Sertorius ', pp. 108–10).

[3] D. B. G. iv. 14. 1.   [4] Ibid. iii. 24. 1.

battle with a detailed description of the dispositions adopted, but Tacitus' account of Corbulo's campaigns against Parthia suggests that the Caesarian scheme was still adhered to. In one of his battles against Tiridates in 58 A.D.[1] Corbulo placed the allied contingents on the flanks, and the sixth legion, with a detachment of the third organized into one legion to give the impression of strength, in the centre. This looks like the ordinary Republican formation with the legions as the main line of defence and attack. The *auxilia*, on the other hand, Tacitus[2] says, maintained the brunt of the attack at the battle of Mons Graupius, and the legions stood in defence of the rampart, so that the victory was gained ' citra Romanum sanguinem '. The reason given for these tactics is doubtless an invention of the historian, and the probability is that throughout the first century the legions definitely formed the main line of resistance drawn up in a cohort formation, but that sometimes, if the enemy selected a position, as at Mons Graupius, where heavy-armed troops could not operate with success, the lighter-armed *auxilia* were sent first to the attack, while the legions were kept in reserve.

In the second century, however, if not before,[3] a definite change took place in the tactical employment of the Roman troops in battle. Arrian's order of battle[4] against the Alani leaves little doubt that the legions were no longer drawn up in lines of cohorts, but that

---

[1] T. A. xiii. 38. 6.   [2] Id. Agric. 35.
[3] Suggested by Dio, lxii. 8. 3, where the writer says that Paulinus drew up his troops in three phalanges.
[4] ἔκταξ. κατ' Ἀλ. § 15.

recourse was had to the older formation of the phalanx. The reversion to this Greek theory of attack necessarily involved the employment of the *auxilia* for the initial movements of the attack, and the retention of the solid phalanx for the later stages of the battle. Two explanations may be given for this change in Roman tactics. From the time of Hadrian onwards the Roman frontiers were organized on a definite system. In the front line was a series of forts, each occupied by a cohort of auxiliaries, while the legions were kept in reserve in larger camps, connected by roads with the front-line fortresses. If the enemy attacked, then resistance was necessarily first offered by the *auxilia*, till the legions had time to march to the scene of operations; if, on the other hand, the Romans attacked beyond their frontier it was still necessary to safeguard the line of retreat, and this could be best achieved by the more seasoned troops, drawn up in compact masses that prevented the enemy separating the component units of the legion. Secondly, by the second century the *auxilia* had reached a degree of efficiency that they had not previously possessed. They could now be relied upon to offer a disciplined attack and resistance, and there was in consequence no longer the same reason for employing the more heavily armed and more expensively maintained troops for the brunt of the attack and defence. Further, a variety in tactical formation was bound to perplex the enemy, and, even supposing that the cohorts of *auxilia* only attained a moderate success in the early stages of the battle, the advance of fresh troops, organized in disciplined compact units, was likely to have a demoralizing effect on the tired forces of the enemy; while, if the *auxilia* were driven back, the camp was still safe under the protection of the legionary phalanx.

The tactics of the Romans in the second century A.D. represent the evolution of a system of warfare based on the experience of centuries of fighting. If the cohort formation and the military camp were essentially Roman products, the phalanx was the contribution of Macedon, and the *gladius* and *lancea* the discoveries of Spain and Gaul. In this effective combination of inventions and inheritances Rome worked out her military organization and strategy, and the secret of her success lay in her willingness to learn from her enemies, and to assimilate the gifts which they had to offer.

APPENDIX A

(a) The Cognomina.

IN addition to their numbers, most of the Augustan legions were distinguished by particular *cognomina*. These may be divided into five groups : (A) denoting the province in which the legion had fought with distinction; (B) giving the name of the Princeps by whom the legion was formed, or of the general under whom they had served in an important campaign; (C) in honour of some god; (D) describing the successes of the legion ; and (E) suggesting either the origin or method of formation of the legion.

The Augustan legions may be classified on this basis as follows :

Under Group A. I *Germanica* (the *cognomen* only occurs, however, in one inscription,[1] set up after the disappearance of the legion); III *Gallica* ;[2] III *Cyrenaica*; IV *Macedonica*; IV *Scythica*; V *Macedonica*; IX *Hispana*; X *Fretensis* (i. e. denoting the Naval War of Octavian against Sextus Pompeius); and XVI *Gallica* (although the *cognomen* is rare).[3]

Under Group B. II *Augusta*, III *Augusta*, VIII *Augusta*, and XX *Valeria* (i. e. belonging to Valerius Messalinus, who was a general in the Illyrican War of 6 A. D.).

Under Group C. XV *Apollinaris*.

Under Group D. VI *Ferrata*, VI *Victrix*, XII *Fulminata*, XXI *Rapax*.

Under Group E. V *Alaudae*, X *Gemina* (a legion made out of two), XIII *Gemina*, and XIV *Gemina*.

Without cognomina in the Augustan period : VII, XI, XVII, XVIII, XIX, XXII.

(b) The Emblems on the Legionary Standards.[4]

In chapter i we saw that Marius gave each legion one legionary standard called the *aquila*, and the custom arose of

---

[1] C. I. L. xii. 2234.   [2] See further s. v. 'III Gall.', p. 265.

[3] Dess. 2034.   [4] See further von Dom. ' Die Fahn.', *passim*.

decorating both the *aquila* and the manipular *signa* with emblems. These were normally signs of the Zodiac, but sometimes they were drawn from other sources. To understand their significance a tentative classification may be made into (1) emblems standing in some connexion with the founder of the individual legion; (2) emblems referring, perhaps, to the *dies natalis* of the legion ; (3) emblems in honour of the god whose *cognomen* the legion bore ; and (4) emblems denoting some incident in the past history of the legion. Class (3) does not apply to the Augustan legions, but is exemplified by Domitian's I *Minervia*, which had the ram sacred to that goddess as its emblem. On the basis of the three other types, however, the Augustan legions may be grouped as follows:

1. Legions having the bull as their emblem are Caesarian in origin, because the bull is the Zodiac sign for the month starting on 17 April and finishing on 18 May, which was sacred to Venus the goddess-mother of the Julian *gens*. The bull is found on the standards of III *Gallica*, IV *Macedonica*, VII, VIII *Augusta*, X *Gemina*, and X *Fretensis*.

2. Legions having the capricorn as their emblem are Augustan in origin, because the Zodiac sign of the capricorn for the month 17 December to 15 January stands in a definite relation with the birthday of Augustus on 23 September. The capricorn is found on the standards of II *Augusta*, XIV *Gemina*, and XXI *Rapax*, and, in addition to the bull, on the standard of IV *Macedonica*.

3. Legions having emblems suggesting incidents in their earlier history are necessarily older than these episodes. Neptune the emblem of legion IX, and a trireme as an additional emblem to the bull on the standard of X *Fretensis*, imply that these legions took part in the war against Sextus Pompeius, while the elephant on the standard of V *Alaudae* may indicate its share, testified by Caesar himself, in his African campaign.

4. Legions having the lion as their emblem (i.e. XIII *Gemina* and XVI ?) may mean that their *dies natalis* fell between 20 July and 29 August.

Sometimes two or more emblems are found on the standards of the same legion. II *Augusta* has the capricorn and Pegasus. As Pegasus is never found alone on this legion's standards, while capricorn is, it is probable that the latter is the older emblem and the former was added later by Vespasian.[1] The combination of bull and capricorn on the standards of IV *Macedonica* is difficult. May it imply that, although the legion dated back to the army of Caesar, it was reconstituted by Augustus? Lastly, X *Fretensis*, like XX *Val.*, has, in addition to the bull and trireme, the boar as one of its emblems, while V *Maced.* and XIV *Gemina* have the eagle. The explanation of these signs is unknown.

(c) *The Origin and Early History of the Augustan Legions.*[2]

Apart from literary evidence and the help of coins and inscriptions, the numbers, titles, and emblems of the legions may be used for a tentative statement of the sources from which Augustus drew his army. But it is necessary to make an important qualification. The fact that a legion has a number corresponding to one of Caesar's legions, even if it has the bull as its emblem and a *cognomen* such as *Gallica*, does not justify the assumption that the legion, even in the period of the Triumvirate, was identical with the old Caesarian legion of the same number. The veterans of legions VI–XIV were discharged by Caesar himself, and the new units bearing the same numbers were only a continuation of the old Gallic legions in the sense that *evocati* offered themselves for further service and were used to form the kernel of the new legions. With this proviso the most important evidence about the origin and early history of the Augustan legions may be tabulated:

Legion I belonged to the army of Octavian in the triumvirate period, as Appian (B. C. v. 112) shows that it took part in the war against Sextus Pompeius. Whether it dates back further to the time of Caesar, who seems to have raised

[1] See ch.iv, p. 106.

[2] In this Appendix I owe much to Ritterling, s. v. 'Legio', in P–W. xii, *passim*.

legions with the consular numbers in 47–46 B.C., cannot be decided. Later it was in Spain, and after meeting with a heavy defeat was reconstituted by Tiberius in Germany (T. A. i. 42. 6 and see ch. iii, pp. 86–7).

Legion II *Augusta*, from its *cognomen* and emblem, must be one of Octavian's own creations, and was perhaps formed after Philippi. Veterans of the legion were planted at Acci perhaps before the battle of Actium (Cohen, i², p. 152, nos. 632, 633), and its presence in Spain is further indicated by Pliny, who calls Cartenna ' Colonia Augusti legio secunda ' (N. H. v. 20). Probably it remained in this province till 10 A. D., when it moved to Germany (C. I. L. xiii. 7234).

Legion III *Augusta*. Its origin is unknown and no legionary emblems have been found. Probably, as the *cognomen* suggests, it formed part of Octavian's army and may have fought at Philippi (App. B. C. v. 3).

Legion III *Cyrenaica*. Its origin is obscure. The *cognomen* might suggest that it was part of Lepidus' army, but may merely indicate service in Cyrene. However, if III *Aug.* belonged to Octavian and III *Gallica* to Antony, it is almost necessary to suppose that a third legion with the same number must have formed part of the army of the third member of the Triumvirate. The oldest record of the legion in Egypt is 11 A. D. (A. E. 1910, no. 207).

Legion III *Gallica* definitely served in the army of Antony; for Antonius Primus reminds its soldiers in 69 A. D. that the legion had defeated the Parthians when under the command of Antony (T. H. iii. 24). The *cognomen Gallica* and the bull-emblem imply that the legion goes back in origin to Caesar. Ritterling suggests that it is to be identified with legion XV in Caesar's army (P-W. xii, p. 1518). He holds that after Pharsalus Caesar recovered this legion, which he had handed over to Pompey in 50 B. C. and which bore the number III in the latter's army, and that subsequently the legion retained its Pompeian number in Caesar's army. Thus it is identical with a legion III which fought at Munda. This theory is, I think, improbable. 1. The legions formed by Caesar after Pharsalus were clearly composite units, ' legiones

quas ex Pompeianis militibus confecerat' (B. C. iii. 107. 1).
2. Two of these legions had the numbers XXXVI and XXXVII.
Surely it is strange that Caesar neither mentions nor takes
with him to Egypt his old fifteenth legion, if he did recover it
in toto after Pharsalus. 3. Would Caesar have used the
Pompeian number for his old fifteenth ? Ritterling thinks that
it is impossible that no. XV should still have been vacant in
Caesar's army at the time of Pharsalus. But surely Caesar
might still have had hopes of recovering his old legion and
have left the number vacant on purpose ; and, further, when
legions were being raised with great rapidity, it was obviously
much more convenient to continue the series in order rather
than break the enumeration simply to fill a gap at the beginning of the series. It is more probable that Caesar raised
this legion III, which fought at Munda and which is doubtless
identical with III *Gallica,* on his return to Rome from Egypt.
He was consul and therefore employed the consular numbers
for his new legions. The *cognomen Gallica* is then explicable
on the ground that legion III was composed partly perhaps of
veterans of the Gallic legions who had been absent from
Pharsalus through sickness (Bell. Alex. 44. 4) and partly of
soldiers of the old fifteenth who were sent back to Italy after
Pharsalus (see von Dom. ' Die Heere d. Bürgerkr.). The
legion was in Syria as early as 4 B.C. (Jos. B. J. ii. 3. 1),
and an inscription from Cyprus belonging to the early Principate gives its cognomen *Gallica* (C. I. L. iii. 217).

Legion IV *Macedonica.* Dess. 2283 shows that both the
bull and the capricorn were the emblems of this legion. This
suggests that in origin the legion goes back to Caesar, and
probably it is to be identified with a legion raised about the
same time as legion III, which fought at Munda. In 44 B.C.
it formed part of Antony's army in Macedonia, and on being
summoned to Italy deserted with a legion called *Martia* to
the side of Octavian (Cic. Phil. xiv. 27). At Mutina it was
severely defeated by a legion numbered V (Cic. Ad. Fam. x.
33. 4), in which battle the *Martia* was destroyed. Probably
it took part in the Perusian War and at Philippi, and received
its *cognomen* for its share in the latter campaign. Veterans

of the legion were settled by Augustus at Firmum Picenum (Dess. 2340), and later the legion was encamped in Spain (Dess. 2454). The close connexion of the legion with the early career of Octavian will account for its second emblem, the capricorn, signifying that the first Princeps regarded it as one of his own units, even although originally it had been formed by Julius Caesar.

Legion IV *Scythica*. Its origin is unknown. The *cognomen* suggests that it may have fought under Licinius Crassus in the war of 29–27 B.C. against the Bastarnae and Scythians (Dio, li. 23. 3). Perhaps it was raised by Antony to take the place of the 4th legion, which had deserted to the side of Octavian in 44 B.C.

Legion V *Alaudae* is identical with the legion raised by Caesar from the Transalpine Gauls, and which was made a *iusta legio* some time between 51 and 47 B.C. In November 44 B.C. it formed part of Antony's army, in addition to his three Macedonian legions (How., Cic. Epist., no. 89). Later it fought with seven other veteran legions for Antony at Philippi (App. B.C. v. 3), and that it subsequently continued in his army is suggested by the *cognomen Arsaces* belonging to one of its soldiers (C. I. L. ix. 1460).

Legion V *Macedonica*. Its origin is doubtful, and the earliest record of it is the settlement of veterans from the legion at Berytus in Syria by Agrippa in 15 B.C. (Strabo, xiv. 2, 19, p. 756). The *cognomen* may indicate that the legion fought at Philippi, or merely that it garrisoned Macedonia before moving into Moesia. The legion has as emblems the bull and the eagle. This suggests that it goes back to the time of Caesar, and the question arises whether it can be identified with any other legion numbered V. The choice lies between a legion called V *Gallica*, whose veterans were settled at Antioch in Pisidia (Dess. 2237, 2238), and V *Urbana*, whose veterans are found at Ateste (Dess. 2236). But this legion V *Gallica* can only be either the *Alaudae* or a legion numbered V which was lost under Lollius in 16 B.C. (Vell. ii. 97), and neither interpretation makes its identification with V *Macedonica* probable or even possible. It seems, therefore, preferable to suggest that V *Urbana* (unless it is rather to be identified with the legion lost by Lollius) may have formed the nucleus of the later V *Macedonica*. May Julius Caesar have raised this legion as an addition to his consular legions to protect Rome during his projected Parthian campaign in 44 B.C.?

Legions VI *Ferrata* and VI *Victrix*. By their *cognomina* 'iron' and 'victorious' both these legions may date back originally to Caesar's sixth legion. This legion was greatly depleted in numbers in the Alexandrine War, and on its arrival in Italy was only 1,000 strong. It was, however, brought up to strength and fought at Munda. If it is the source of both the later legions numbered VI, then either it must have been divided after Caesar's death, or one of the two later legions is the direct descendant of Caesar's legion, and the other is only Caesarian in the sense that it contained a nucleus of Caesar's *evocati*. The second solution is, I think, the more probable. VI *Ferrata* was probably part of Antony's army (Cohen 1², p. 46, no. 83 ; Ritt., o. c., P–W. xii, p. 1588), and if ἕκτη Μακεδονική mentioned in an inscription from Ephesus (Dess. 8862) is identical with it, then it will have fought at Philippi as one of Antony's eight veteran legions (App. B. C. v. 3). VI *Victrix*, on the other hand, has the bull-emblem and fought for Octavian at Perusia (C. I. L. xi. 6721, nos. 20–3). Possibly, then, VI *Ferrata* is to be identified with legion VI which fought at Munda, and VI *Victrix* was formed by Octavian with a kernel of *evocati*, drawn perhaps from the 1,000 soldiers who composed legion VI on its return to Italy from the East.

Legion VII. Veterans of Caesar's old legion VII were settled at Capua (Dess. 2225). According to Cicero (Phil. xi. 37) and Nic. Damas. (Vita Caesaris, 31) they were recalled to service by Octavian and thus formed the new legion VII, which had the bull-emblem on its standards as an honour to the *evocati*. The legion fought at Mutina (Cic. Phil. l. c.) and possibly at Philippi, if the unofficial *cognomen Macedonica* found on four inscriptions (e. g. Dess. 2695) implies this and not merely the presence of the legion in Macedonia before it was moved to Dalmatia. Veterans were settled at Rusazu

(A. E. 1921, no. 16), Tupusuctu (C. I. L. viii. 8837), and Saldae in Mauretania (ibid. 8931).

Legion VIII *Augusta.* According to Cicero (Phil. xi. 37) and Appian (B. C. iii. 47) this was, like legion VII, a veteran legion of Caesarian origin reconstituted by Octavian, and the *cognomen Mutinensis* on an inscription (Dess. 2239) implies that it distinguished itself at Mutina. Veterans were settled at Forum Julii (C. I. L. xii, p. 38) soon after the battle of Actium and also at Berytus (C. I. L. iii. 14165[6]). In this last inscription the legion has the *cognomen Gallica,* which, in addition to its bull-emblem, indicates that originally it fought with Caesar in Gaul. The position of the legion in 30 B. C. is unknown, but later it was in Pannonia (T. A. i. 23. 6).

Legion IX *Hispana* may in origin go back to Caesar's 9th legion, but it was reconstituted by Octavian. An inscription (Dess. 2240) gives it the *cognomen Triumphalis,* which von Domaszewski interprets as referring to the triumph of the Triumvirs in 43 B. C. (App. B. C. iv. 7). The *cognomen Macedonica* found on another inscription (Dess. 928) may imply its presence at Philippi, and the later title of *Hispana* certainly shows its prolonged garrisoning of Spain, which is further testified by the Spanish origin of some of its soldiers (E. E. viii. 530). It moved to Pannonia before 6 A. D. (gravestones from Aquileia, e. g. C. I. L. v. 911).

Legion X *Fretensis.* The emblem of the bull must imply that some of the veterans of Caesar's old legion served in Octavian's newly constituted unit (How, Cic. Epist., no. 89. 2), and this is further confirmed by the *cognomen Veneria* in an inscription from Brixia, where a colony of veterans was settled (Dess. 2241). A second emblem, the trireme, implies that the legion fought against Sextus Pompeius and so must have been part of Octavian's army. Probably it was in Syria in 6 A. D., although the earliest reference is in T. A. ii. 57. 2 of 17 A. D.

Legion X *Gemina.* Nothing is known of its origin or in which army of the Triumvirs it served, and the earliest records of the legion come from Spain. Veterans are found in the colony of Emerita, founded in 25 B. C. (Dio, liii. 26 and Cohen i[2], 149, no. 594), and its presence in that province is further indicated by inscriptions (e. g. Dess. 2256, 2644). The emblem is the bull and the *cognomen*, according to Caesar's definition, means a legion made out of two. May this imply that Octavian formed a second legion called X partly from legion X *Fretensis* (hence the bull-emblem) and partly from some other unit for his projected campaign in Spain?

Legion XI was in the army of Octavian at Perusia (C. I. L. xi. 6721, nos. 25–7) and may have been constituted by him out of Caesar's XI. The *cognomen Actiacus* found in two inscriptions of soldiers of this legion implies that it fought at Actium (Dess. 2243, 2336), and a similar inference might be drawn from the emblem Neptune (Cohen v², p. 392, nos. 533–6), unless the war against S. Pompeius is indicated. Before moving into Dalmatia it was stationed at Poetovio, as an old gravestone of an equally old veteran testifies : ' A. Postumius Spuri f. Seneca domo Parma veteranus missicius leg. XI annorum XXCV hic situs est ' (quoted by Ritt., o. c., P–W. xii, p. 1691).

Legion XII *Fulminata*. The *cognomen paterna* in Dess. 2242 and *victrix* in C. I. L. xi. 6721, nos. 28–30, suggests a Caesarian origin, and this is confirmed by the fact that Scaeva, the *primus pilus* of the legion, is in all probability Caesar's old centurion (B. C. iii. 53. 5). Probably it was part of Antony's army, as coins struck by him mention a *legio* XII *antiqua* (Dess. 2242 n. 1). Veterans were planted in various colonies, notably at Venusia (C. I. L. ix. 435) and Patrae in Achaea, where an inscription gives the *cognomen Fulminata* (C. I. L. iii. 7261). Later, the legion was perhaps in Egypt when the garrison in that province consisted of three legions, and was subsequently transferred to Syria (see ch. v, p. 128).

Legion XIII *Gem.* fought against Sextus Pompeius (App. B. C. v. 87) and was probably constituted by Octavian from an amalgamation, as the *cognomen* should imply, of two legions. Its emblem, the lion, may conceivably have reference to the month in which the legion was formed. Veterans are found at Hispellum (C. I. L. xi. 1933) and at Uthina in Africa, called on a Hadrianic inscription ' Col. Julia Tertiadecimanorum ' (Dess. 6784). In the early years of the Principate it was probably stationed in Illyricum (Dess. 2638 from Aquileia), and after the Varian disaster moved to Upper Germany.

Legion XIV *Gem.* was another composite legion formed by Octavian, as its emblem, the capricorn, implies. Like leg. XIII, it may have been for a time in Illyricum (C. I. L. v. 8272 from Aquileia), but in all probability was in Gaul or Germany before the Varian disaster. It seems to have been one of the two legions which Asprenas led back to Vetera in 9 A. D. after the Varian disaster (Vell. ii. 120. 1), and may have occupied the territory of the Lingones (see Ritt. on *Hospitium* between the legion and the Lingones in Bonn. Jahrb. cxiv, p. 166), in the period of Drusus' command.

Legion XV *Apollinaris* was probably raised by Octavian before Actium, because veterans of the legion are found at Ateste, where a settlement was established after the end of the Civil War (C. I. L. v. 2516). The *cognomen Apollinaris* further attests its formation by Octavian, as Apollo was his protecting deity. In the early years of the Principate the legion was stationed in Illyricum (C. I. L. v. 891, 917, 928 from Aquileia), and towards the end of Augustus' reign moved perhaps to Emona in Pannonia (Dess. 2264).

Legion XVI. A coin, which is thought to have been struck in Africa before Actium, has on the obverse the head of young Augustus and on the reverse side *Leg.* XVI with the springing lion (Cohen i², p. 89, nos. 186 and 187; Ritt., o. c., P-W. xii, p. 1761). Legion XVI must, then, have been raised by Octavian before 30 B. C. Where it was subsequently stationed is unknown, but all records of it come from Germany (e. g. Dess. 2265, 2266), while the *cognomen Gallica*, found so far only on a few inscriptions (e. g. Dess. 2034), might imply its occupation of Gaul in the time of Drusus.

Legions XVII–XIX must have been formed by Octavian, as two of the Caesarian legions bearing their numbers were lost by Curio in Africa (B. C. ii. 42. 4) and the third perhaps at Curicta (B. C. iii. 10. 5). All three were destroyed in the Varian disaster, and the numbers were never subsequently used. No records exist of XVII; but XVIII is mentioned

THE COGNOMINA 271

in Dess. 2244 and XIX in T. A. i. 60. 4, and Dess. 2268 and 2269.

Legion XX *Valeria* was in all probability an Augustan legion dating to the period of the Triumvirate, and not formed, as von Domaszewski supposes, in 6 A. D. by Tiberius. An inscription referring to a soldier of the legion called C. Axonius, who was a member of the Spanish colony of Emerita (C. I. L. ii. 32) is rightly, I think, shown by Ritterling (o. c., P-W. xii, p. 1769) to be genuine. If so, then legion XX, like legions V and X, must have had some connexion with the planting of veterans at Emerita in 25 B. C. (Dio, liii. 26). Later, the legion was certainly stationed in Illyricum or north Italy, as two inscriptions from Aquileia with *aera* instead of the usual *stipendia* imply (C. I. L. v. 939, 948). For a time it may have garrisoned Burnum (Dess. 2651) and have taken part in a campaign on the lower Danube (Dess. 2270). In 6 A. D. it formed part of Tiberius' army in Illyricum (Vell. ii. 112), and after the revolt was transferred to Germany. The significance of its emblem, the boar, is unknown.

Legion XXI, by its emblem the capricorn, was an Augustan legion. Perhaps it was organized about 15 B. C. to take the place of a legion V lost by Lollius. Some support for this view is lent by inscriptions giving the birthplaces of several soldiers. They come from the villages and towns of the Alpine slopes around Brixia and Tridentum (C. I. L. v. 4858, 5033). Not improbably the legion garrisoned Vindelicia down to 6 A. D., as the governor of that district seems to have the title 'legatus pro praetore in Vindolicis' as opposed to the later procurator (Dess. 847 and see ch. iii, p. 92). After the Pannonian revolt the legion moved to Vetera.

Legion XXII *Deiotariana* was originally one of Deiotarus' legions which fought for Caesar against Pharnaces. Amyntas bequeathed his kingdom to Augustus in 25 B. C. and some time after this a *iusta legio*, subsequently bearing the unofficial *cognomen Deiotariana*, was formed out of his troops. If legion XXI was constituted in 15 B. C., then XXII must have been formed between this date and 8 B. C. when its presence in Alexandria is testified by a papyrus (B. G. U. iv. 1104 and cf.

iv. 1108). Further, an inscription (Dess. 2274), because of the spelling *meiles*, and the absence of a town for the birthplace of a soldier who has no *cognomen*, suggests an early date for the formation of the legion, and not 9 A. D., in consequence of the Varian disaster (Dess. ' Gesch. d. r. Kaiserz.', i. 220 n. 2).

APPENDIX B

THE following details correspond to the summary given on pages 175 and 177.

(N.B.—Gall. Narb. includes Lugdunum.)

A. GERMANY BEFORE 43 A.D.

Legion.	Camp.	Origin of soldier.	Reference.		
II *Aug.*	Argento-ratum	*Italy, 5—*			
		Mediolanum	C. I. L. xiii. 5976		
		Alba Pompeii	,, ,, 5977		
		Luca	,, ,, 5978		
		Bononia	,, ,, 11628		
		Albingaunum	,, ,, 1122		
		Gall. Narb., 1			
		Carcaso	,, ,, 7234	Br. 946	
		Lusitania, 1—			
		Norba	,, ,, 5975		
XIV *Gem.*	Mogun-tiacum	*Italy and Cottian Alps, 25—*			
		Placentia	,, ,, 6885		
		Cremona	,, ,, 6886	,, 1172	
		Aug. Taurinorum	,, ,, 6887	,, 1173	
		Vercellae	,, ,, 6889		
		Hasta	,, ,, 6890	,, 989	
		Histonium	,, ,, 6893	,, 1174	
		Aug. Taurinorum	,, ,, 6899	,, 1181	
		Forum Vibi	,, ,, 6900	,, 1182	
		Veleia (i. e. Parma)	,, ,, 6901	,, 1183	
		Aug. Taurinorum	,, ,, 6902	,, 1184	
		Aquae Statiellae	,, ,, 6903	,, 1185	
		Vardagate	,, ,, 6906	,, 1189	
		Brixia	,, ,, 6907		
		Pollentia	,, ,, 6908	,, 1188	
		Verona	,, ,, 6910	,, 1191	
		Eporedia	,, ,, 6914	,, 1192	
		Aquileia	,, ,, 6916		
		Mutina	,, ,, 7255	,, 923	
		Forum Vibi	,, ,, 7288	,, 1339	
		Placentia	,, ,, 7575	,, 1516	
		Acelum	,, ,, 7236		
		Cremona	,, ,, 1123		
		,,	,, ,, 1383		
		Verona (2 men)	,, v. 3360		

Legion.	Camp.	Origin of soldier.		Reference.	
		Gall. Narb., 5—			
		Tolosa . . .	C. I. L. xiii.	6904	Br. 1196
		Vienna . . .	,,	,, 6909	
		,, . . .	,,	,, 6912	,, 1175
		Reii . . .	,,	,, 6913	
		Forum Iulii . .	,,	,, 1121	
XVI Gall.	. Mogun-	Italy, 10—			
	tiacum	Placentia . .	,,	,, 6936	,, 1197
		Vercellae . .	,,	,, 6939	,, 1079
		Pistoria . . .	,,	,, 6942	,, 1200
		Hispellum . .	,,	,, 6943	
		Placentia . .	,,	,, 6946	,, 1204
		Brixia (2 men) .	,,	vi. 3560	
		Mediolanum . .	,,	v. 5747	
		Venafrum . .	,,	xiii. 11837	
		Mediolanum . .	,,	,, 11858	
		Gall. Narb., 4—			
		Lugdunum . .	,,	,, 6941	,, 1198
		Vienna . . .	,,	,, 6944	,, 1202
		Cabalio . . .	,,	,, 6945	,, 1203
		Vienna . . .	,,	,, 11859	
XX Val.	. Col.	Italy, 5—			
	Agripp.	Parma . . .	,,	,, 8286	
	and No-	Ticinum . . .	,,	,, 8287	,, 377
	vaesium	Patavium . .	,,	,, 8553	,, 268
		Pollentia . .	,,	,, 8554	·
		Mutina . . .	,,	,, 8737	,, 88
XXI .	. Vetera .	Gall. Narb., 1—			
		Nemausus . .	,,	,, 8649	,, 1968 a
		Italy, 1—			
		Fanum Fortunae .	,,	,, 8651	
XIII Gem.	. Vindo-	Italy, 2—			
	nissa	Urvinum . . .	,,	,, 6884	
		Dertona . . .	,,	,, 5206	
		Narbo., 1—			
		Vienna . . .	,,	,, 5239	

B. GERMANY 43-70 A.D.

IV Maced.	. Mogun-	Italy, 7—			
	tiacum	Alba Pompeii . .	,,	,, 6855	
		Ticinum . . .	,,	,, 6859	,, 1155
		Aug. Taurinorum .	,,	,, 6862	,, 1156
		,, ,, .	,,	,, 6870	,, 1163
		Hasta . . .	,,	,, 6875	,, 1166
		Forum Fulvi . .	,,	,, 6877	,, 1170
		,, ,, . .	,,	,, 7235	,, 949
		Baetica, 6—			
		Nertobriga . .	,,	,, 6853	,, 1150
		,, . .	,,	,, 6854	,, 1151
		,, . .	,,	,, 6865	,, 1160
		Tucci . . .	,,	,, 6856	,, 1152
		Corduba . . .	,,	,, 6869	,, 1162
		Nertobriga . .	,,	,, 7506	

Legion.	Camp.	Origin of soldier.	Reference.			
IV *Maced.*	Mogun-tiacum	*Gall. Narb.*, 15—				
		Baeterrae	C.I.L.	xiii.	6857	Br. 1153
		Narbo	„	„	6863	
		Forum Iulii	„	„	6866	„ 1159
		Tolosa	„	„	6867	„ 1158
		Forum Iulii	„	„	6868	„ 1161
		Vienna	„	„	6871	„ 1164
		„	„	„	6872	„ 1165
		„	„	„	6873	„ 1168
		Narbo	„	„	6874	„ 1167
		Lugdunum	„	„	6876	„ 1169
		Baeterrae	„	:;	7009	
		Tolosa	„	„	7237	
		„	„	„	11848	
		„	„	ix.	799	
		Forum Iulii	„	xii.	4368	
		Noricum, 3—				
		Virunum	„	xiii.	860	„ 2058
		„	„	„	6864	„ 1157
		„	„	„	11849	
		Tarraconensis, 1—				
		Auso	„	„	6858	„ 1154
XV *Pg.*	Vetera	*Italy*, 5—				
		Mediolanum	„	„	8079	„ 479
		Aug. Taurinorum	„	„	8080	„ 480
		Mediolanum	„	„	11853	
		Eporedia	„	„	11854	
		Mediolanum	„	„	11855	
		Gall. Narb., 3—				
		Forum Iulii	„	„	8284	
		Antipolis	„	„	8647	
		Ucetia	„	xii.	2928	
XXII *Pg.*	Mogun-tiacum	*Italy*, 14—				
		Vercellae	„	xiii.	6953	„ 1208
		Dertona	„	„	6960	
		Faventia	„	„	6961	„ 1381
		Bononia	„	„	6964	„ 1213
		Albingaunum	„	„	6966	„ 1215
		Mediolanum	„	„	6967	„ 1216
		Mantua	„	„	6973	„ 1218
		Mediolanum	„	„	6975	„ 1222
		Laus Pompeii	„	„	6979	„ 1220
		Eporedia	„	„	6981	„ 1224
		Mediolanum	„	„	6982	„ 1225
		Ateste	„	„	7244	„ 932
		Augusta Praetoria	„	v.	6896	
		Alba Pompeii	„	vi.	2649	
		Gall. Narb., 7—				
		Aquae Sextiae	„	xiii.	6959	„ 1212
		Vienna	„	„	6969	„ 1082
		„	„	„	6972	„ 1382

Legion.	Camp.	Origin of soldier.	Reference.

Narbo .   .   C. I. L. xiii. 6976 Br. 945
    ,, . . .   ,,   ,, 6986
Lucus Aug. .   ,,   ,, 6978 ,, 1223
Apta .   .   ,,   ,, 11860

Tarraconensis, 1—
Forum Aug. . .   ,,   ,, 6958 ,, 1211
  (Tricastinorum)

Noricum, 1—
Virunum. .   .   ,,   ,, 6984

C. DALMATIA BEFORE 42 A.D.

VII . . Delmi-   *Italy, 10—*
        nium   Arretium   .   ,, iii. 2071
             Forum Cornelii .   ,,   ,, 2716
             Ticinum.   .   ,,   ,, 2913
             Florentia   .   ,,   ,, 8723
             Placentia   .   ,,   ,, 8763
             Florentia   .   ,,   ,, 9712
             Aesis .   .   ,,   ,, 9742
             Verona .   .   ,,   ,, 9939
             Forum Cornelii   .   ,,   ,, 14931
             Beneventum .   .   ,,   ,, 14932

             Gall. Narb., 1—
             Vienna .   .   ,,   ,, 14992

             Macedonia, 4 —
             Philippi .   .   ,,   ,, 2717
             Heraclea.   .   ,,   ,, 9734
             Dyrrachium .   ,,   ,, 9741
             Alorus .   .   Bosn. Mitt. xii. 1912, 132 *

             Asiatic Provs., 13—
             Pessinus .   .   C. I. L. iii. 1818
             Sebastopolis .   .   ,,   ,, 2048
             Laranda.   .   ,,   ,, 2709
             Pessinus .   .   ,,   ,, 2710
             Mylias .   .   ,,   ,, 8487
               ,,   .   .   ,,   ,, 8488
             Sebastopolis .   .   ,,   ,, 8493
             Comana .   .   ,,   ,, 9733
             Amblada.   .   ,,   ,, 9737
             Augusta Troas   E. E. iv, No. 349
             Isinda .   Bull Dalm. xxxvi. 14 *
             Ninica .   .   ,,   ,, xxxi. 79 *
             Pasimo .   .   ,,   ,, xxxvii. 66 *

XI   .   . Burnum   *Italy, 10—*
             Ateste .   .   C. I. L. iii. 2835
             Eporedia   .   ,,   ,, 6418
             Cremona   .   ,,   ,, 6416
             Arretium   .   ,,   ,, 6418
             Regium Lepidi   .   ,,   ,, 9885

* I owe these to Ritt., o. c., P–W. xii, p. 1627.

Legion.	Camp.	Origin of soldier.		Reference.
XI	Burnum	Patavium	.	C. I. L. iii. 9892
		Brixellum	. .	„ „ 14321 [13]
		Brixia	. . .	„ „ 14997 [2]
		Cremona	. . .	„ „ 14997 [1]
		„	. . .	„ „ 15001
		Macedonia, 2—		
		Pelagonia	. .	„ „ 2017
		Philippi	. . .	„ „ 2031
		East Provs., 1—		
		Laranda	. .	„ „ 2818

D. DALMATIA 42–58 OR 69 A.D.

VII *C. p. f.*	Delmi- nium	*Italy, 8—*		
		Florentia	. .	„ „ 1814
		Pisaurum	. .	„ „ 2014
		Verona	. .	„ „ 2040
		„	. . .	„ „ 2041
		„	. . .	„ „ 2834
		Arretium	. .	„ „ 8764
		Bononia	. .	„ „ 14244
		Brixia	. .	„ „ 14946
		East Provs., 2—		
		Augusta Troas	.	„ „ 2019
		„ „	.	Bull. Dalm. xxxvii. 65 *
XI *C. p. f.*	Burnum	*Italy, 14—*		
		Aquae Stat.	.	C. I. L. iii. 2833
		Verona (2 men)	.	„ „ 2834 and v. 3374
		Florentia	. .	„ „ 2837
		Tarvisium	. .	„ „ 9903
		Novaria	. .	„ „ 9906
		Aquae Stat.	.	„ „ 9908
		Florentia	. .	„ „ 9909
		Ravenna	. .	„ „ 12815
		Florentia	. .	„ „ 14991
		Placentia	. .	„ „ 14997
		Comum	. .	„ „ 14998
		Feltria	. .	„ „ 15005
		Pollentia	.	Öst. Jahr. vi, p. 85 *
		Macedonia, 1—		
		Heraclea	.	C. I. L. iii. 14999
		Gall. Narb., 3—		
		Forum Iulii	. .	„ „ 2839
		Vienna	. .	„ „ 8740
		Lucus Aug.	.	„ „ 13251
		Spain, 3—		
		Caesar-augusta	.	„ „ 6417
		Segovia	. .	„ „ 6419
		Italica	. .	„ „ 8436
		Pontus, 1—		
		Amasia	. .	„ „ 13263

* I owe these to Ritt., o. c., P–W. xii, pp. 1627 and 1704.

INDEX I. PROPER NAMES

INDEX II. SUBJECT INDEX

CORRIGENDA

P. 24, l. 27 — Delete ' and in all probability for twenty years ' and substitute ' with a maximum liability of twenty years.'

P. 94, l. 24 — Delete ' populi Romani.'

P. 98, l. 21 — For ' Albani ' read ' Alani.' The objective of the campaign was ' the Caspian Gates ' and Tacitus (T.H. I, 6) calls the enemy to be attacked ' Albani.' But it seems clear that by ' the Caspian Gates ' Tacitus' authorities meant not the famous pass south of the Caspian but the pass of Darial, ' the Gate of the Alans,' properly called the Caucasian Gates. It is accordingly best to amend ' Albani ' to ' Alani.'

P. 112, ll. 25-26 — Delete ' because in that case he would have been called *praefectus* ' and substitute ' because legionary commanders in that province were regularly equestrian *praefecti*.'

P. 112, n. 2 — Add ' Riccobono, *Leges*, no. 78.'

P. 120, n. 1 — For ' Mattingly ' read ' Mattingly and Sydenham.'

P. 122, l. 9 — Delete ' the opposition was no longer ' and substitute ' the expected opposition was not.'

P. 131 — Transfer second part of Footnote 3 to Footnote 4.

P. 133, l. 10 — For ' Isca Silurum (Caerleon) ' read ' Glevum (Gloucester).'

P. 133, l. 12 — For ' Caerleon ' read ' Gloucester.'

P. 133, n. 3 — Delete and substitute ' The legion most probably did not move to Caerleon till A.D. 75.'

P. 134, l. 20 — For ' implies ' read ' suggests, although it does not prove, a legionary army.'

P. 138, l. 15 — For ' elected ' read ' appointed.'

P. 139, l. 5 — For ' Bosporus against the Albani ' read ' Caucasus against the Alani.'

P. 143, n. 1 (l. 5) — For ' Mattingly ' read ' Mattingly and Sydenham.'

P. 146, l. 18   For 'Cerealis departed to govern Britain with II *Adi.*' read 'Cerealis departed to govern Britain, taking with him II *Adi.*'

P. 148, l. 16   For 'must' read 'should.'

P. 155, l. 17   Read 'Similarly, the activities of Agricola's successors in Britain had been curtailed by the weakening of his army to three legions.' (Delete the reference to the vexillation which by this time had probably been replaced.)

P. 161, n. 6   *Contra* Eric Birley, *Roman Britain and the Roman Army*, pp. 20-30.

P. 163, n. 1   Add 'Riccobono, *Leges*, no. 78.'

P. 183, n. 1   Compare A. E. 1955, no. 238.

P. 189, ll. 15-16   Delete 'and probably gaining the full citizenship in that way.'

P. 194, n. 2   Add 'Riccobono, *Leges*, no. 78.'

P. 200, ll. 12-13   Delete 'who had in this way secured the complete Roman citizenship' and substitute 'who in some cases had acquired full Roman citizenship by holding local offices.'

P. 200, last l.   For 'veterans recalled to the colours' read 'ex-praetorians.'

P. 208, l. 13   Delete '(he supervised the letting of land to soldiers)' and substitute '(he was in charge of requisitions).'

P. 220, n. 1   Add 'Dessau 7212 ; Arangio-Ruiz, *Negotia*, no. 35.'

P. 227, l. 15   Delete 'to get food for the camp' and substitute 'on duty with the town picket.'

P. 242, n. 1   Add 'Riccobono, *Leges*, no. 78.'

THE ROMAN WORLD

IMPERIAL ROME. *Martin P. Nilsson.*

A completely fresh outlook on Roman history, this book features thorough, yet brief, biographies of all the Roman emperors in the first part. The second part describes the provinces of the empire, their individual circumstances and their histories, as well as a series of essays on politics, finances, religion, customs, etc. Written by the masterful hand of a great scholar, it is one of the most comprehensive works available on the many facets of the life, people, and customs of the Roman Empire. A useful and reliable handbook for both the student of history and the numismatist.
> *ISBN 0-89005-054-6. 376 pp. + 24 pl.* $15

ROMAN PROVINCIAL ADMINISTRATION. *W. T. Arnold.*

A sobering account of the mishandling of the Roman Empire's finances as we watch Roman economic history being paralleled in our own times. Each month Arnold's work takes on dimensions of increasing importance. Particular attention is given to the coinage laws, inflation, price stabilization edicts and their effects on the Roman economy. The politics, administration, causes and effects of economic and other laws are carefully scrutinized to give us insights valuable today. Of special interest to the student of Roman history, the collector of Roman coins, students of economics, and those who wonder where our own economy may be headed.
> *ISBN 0-89005-027-9. 298 pp.* $15

THE PROVINCES OF THE ROMAN EMPIRE.
Theodor Mommsen.

This is a reprint of the 1909 edition of the *complete work*, authorized and translated into English under Mommsen's supervision. One of the greatest ancient historians at his best! No other work on the subject offers such a careful analysis of historical, economic, cultural and religious aspects of the Roman provinces. A well organized presentation which skillfully blends a multitude of diverse historical facts into a logical panorama of the Roman provinces and their place in ancient history.
> *Vol. I, ISBN 0-89005-051-1.*
> *Vol. II, ISBN 0-89005-152-X. 756 pp.* 2 vols. $30

THE ROMANS ON THE RIVIERA AND THE RHONE.
W. H. Hall.

Reprint of the extremely rare edition of 1898 (London). There is no other book in the English Language which describes more vividly or more accurately the history of the long struggle of the Roman Republic for the conquest. of the part of Southern Gaul which later became the "Provincia" and still later the "Gallia Narbonensis." Hall has a first-hand knowledge of the topography of the French Riviera and its coastline as well as a complete knowledge of the Roman ruins, monuments and inscriptions. He gives the best possible history of the area during the Roman period and describes minutely the process of its Romanization.
  ISBN 0-89005-022-8. 208 pp. + 16 pl. + maps   **$10**

THE ELDER PLINY'S CHAPTERS ON THE HISTORY OF ART.
Translated by K. Jex-Blake and E. Sellers.

As delightful and useful today as it was to Roman tourists who took it along while exploring their empire nearly 2,000 years ago. Time has proven Pliny's work to be the keystone reference for the study of ancient Greek Sculpture. Pliny's original Latin text is given with a facing English translation together with commentaries on what ancient sculptures have been identified in the later times on the basis of his descriptions. Updated with a new *Introduction* and *Select Bibliography* (1896-1974) by R. V. Schoder, S.J., of Loyola University. Since many of the sculptures Pliny describes also appear on ancient coins, this work addresses itself to the numismatist as well as the art historian and student of the classics.
  ISBN 0-89005-055-4. 252 pp.   **$10**

TRADE ROUTES AND COMMERCE OF THE ROMAN EMPIRE. M. P. Charlesworth.

The fascinating story of Imperial Rome's struggle to become economic master of its rapidly acquired overseas empire and balance its foreign trade. A valuable and authoritative work for information on the commercial life of the Roman Empire, voyage time from place to place, and both wise and foolish trade policies of the Romans. Many interesting parallels to the trade and economic policies of major world powers in our own times.
  ISBN 0-89005-063-5. 320 pp.   **$10**